EXAMINATION SYSTEM

EXAMINATION SYSTEM

By

Modugula Ravi Krishna

B.Sc., M.A., M.Ed., C.Li. Sc.

Lecturer

R.V.R. College of Education

Guntur–522 006

General Editor

Dr. Digumarti Bhaskara Rao

M.Sc., M.A., M.A., M.Ed., Ph.D.

Reader

R.V.R. College of Education

Srinivasa Nagar Colony

Guntur–522 006

Andhra Pradesh

India

DISCOVERY PUBLISHING HOUSE

NEW DELHI-110002

First Published-2004
Reprint 2005
Reprinted-2006
Reprinted: 2013
ISBN 81-7141-824-4

Published by
DISCOVERY PUBLISHING HOUSE
4831/24, Ansari Road, Prahlad Street,
Darya Ganj, New Delhi-110002 (India)
Phone: 23279245 • Fax: 91-11-23253475
E-mail:dphtemp@indiatimes.com

Printed at:
Dynamic printers, Delhi

Preface

Examination is as old as education itself. The examination process is the last phase of teaching and learning. Traditionally, the examination has been a very tough exercise, fearful enough for students. However, with changing times, the procedure of conventional examination has changed.

Now, the modern concept of examination is quite progressive and scientific. The educationists have introduced new terms like evaluation and measurement. Under evaluation, the level of knowledge and learning is weighed and under measurement, a learner is gauged and allotted score of marks.

The examination, evaluation and measurement processes are undergoing further changes, to make them more scientific, logical, practical and fruitful. The objective type tests are a part of the process.

This book is meant for teacher-students, trainees and student-teachers. It's a comprehensive reference tool for all purposes. Every chapter deals with a separate topic and all efforts have been made to cover all the dimensions of the discipline.

As usual, the author has referred to various kinds of books, while working on this project. He is grateful to all authors and editors, whose works he has benefited from. This book is expected to serve its users as a perfect textbook and a complete guide, as well.

Author

Contents

Foreword

Preface

1. Introduction 1

2. Basic Issues 9
- Meaning and Idea
- Significant Factors
- The Requirements
- Chief Factors
- Constructing Elements
- Chief Features
- Role of Education
- Common Features
- Basis and Relevance
- Assessment in Totality
- Means and Devices
- Measuring the Benefits

3. Fundamental Demands 27
- The Concept
- Various Sciences
- Twin Purposes
- Jobs to be Done
- Rational Evaluation
- Typical Concept
- Various Methods
- Combined Methods
- Particular Test
- Test Defined
- Emperical Angle
- The Categorisation

- Administration System
- Various Items
- Attainment of Marks
- Arranging a Test
- Measurement of Basic Ideas
- Measurement of Common Issues
- Further Measurement

4. Evolution and Growth 67
- Various Types
- Timebound Development
- Development in a Particular Manner
- Great Contributions
- Various Tests Developed
- Typical Inventories
- Indian Scene
- Current Position

5. Formulation of Objectives 95
- Experiences in Teaching
- Behaviours under Change
- Evaluation Techniques
- Evaluation Applied
- Activities in Coordination
- Message of Caution

6. Common Aims and Objectives 105
- Assessment of Jobs
- Assessment of Matter
- Aims Identified
- The Concept
- Various Objectives
- Various Approaches

7. Evaluation of Knowledge 131
- System at Work
- Measurement by Scales
- Significant Features
- Different Tests
- A Particular Item
- Practical Demands
- Treasure of Items

- Methods of Ranking
- Age-old Exercise
- Fault Possibility
- Allotting Division and Position

8. **Procedure of Evaluation** **157**
- Perfect Evaluation
- Two Dimensions
- A Continual Exercise
- Aims of Evaluation
- Practical Work
- Different Types
- Correction Process
- Growth Record
- Scores and Ranks
- Complete Report
- Marks and Scores
- Record on Card
- Record in School
- Roots of Information
- Information Categories

9. **Examination Aims** **187**
- Significant Motives
- Profile of the Teacher
- Applied Angle
- Various Tests
- Counselling a Must
- Career Guidance

10. **Evaluation Approaches** **197**
- The Summatives
- The Formatives
- The Differences
- In House Examination
- Examination under Compulsion

Ascertaining Criteria
- Test Items Invented and Utilised
- Growing Relevance
- Common Factors
- Perfect System

11. **Evaluation Techniques** **225**
- Varied Significance
- The Measurement
- The Importance
- Two Way Classification
- Managing the System
- The Assessment
- Typical Techniques
- Keen Observation
- Sociogram and Sociometric Tests
- A New Technique
- Techniques for Projection
- Current Position
- Teacher's Responsibility

12. **Measurement of Attitude** **251**
- Perfect Method
- Interests Measured
- Specific Inventories
- Personality Profile
- A Typical Method
- Significant and Important

13. **Test for Success** **267**
- Achievement Tests
- Tests of Intellect
- Instruction Marks
- Scheme of Marks
- Test in Objective Manner
- Tests Compared
- Various Problems
- Managing Examinations
- Two Procedures

14. **Aptitude Tests** **295**
- A Particular Type
- Different Types
- Development of Inventories
- Recognised Type
- Cultivation as Growth

- Teacher's Role
- Resources at Disposal

15. **Teaching Motives** 311
- General Objectives
- Aims Fulfilled
- Determining Sources
- Theory of Taxonomy
- Specified Area
- Significance and Utility
- The Precaution
- A Particular Approach
- Different Stages

16. **Identification Process** 325
- The Diagnosis
- Two Type of Tests
- A Warning
- The Utility
- Tests Compared
- Test for Writing

17. **Various Devices** 333
- New Devices
- Scoring Systems
- The Mistakes
- Various Records
- Tests for Intellect
- Academic Achievement
- The Categorisation
- Indian Procedure
- Another Process

18. **Perfect Devices** 349
- Features at Work
- Scientific Features
- Accepted Relevance
- Various Types
- Different Attitudes
- Factors at Work
- The Procedures

• Relevance and Application
• Assessment of Items

19. General Practice 361
• Common Tests
• Age-old System
• Significance of Examinations
• Measures for Improvement
• Syllabus Covered
• Bank for Questions
• Unwritten Examination
• The Practicals

20. Conclusion 383

Additional Reading 389

1

Introduction

Assessment of performance is an integral part of any process of learning and teaching. As part of sound educational strategy, examinations should be employed to bring about qualitative improvement in education.

The objective will be to re-cast the examination system so as to ensure a method of assessment that is a valid and reliable measure of student development and a powerful instrument for improving teaching and learning. In functional terms, this would mean:

(i) The elimination of excessive element of chance and subjectivity;

(ii) The de-emphasis of memorisation;

(iii) Continuous and comprehensive evaluation that incorporates both scholastic and non-scholastic aspect of education, spread over the total span of instructional times;

(iv) Effective use of evaluation process by teachers, students and parents;

(v) Improvement in the conduct of examinations;

(vi) The introduction of concomitant changes in introductional material and methodology;

(vii) The introduction of the semester system from the secondary stage in a phased manner, and

(viii) The use of grades in place of marks.

The above goals are relevant both for external examinations and evaluations within educational institutions. Evaluations at the institutional level will be streamlined and the predominance of external examinations reduced.

After the formulation of the National Policy on Education (1986), Department of Education, Ministry of Human Resource Development, Government of India, prepared a programme of action for the implementation of the NPE.

Chapter XVIII 'Evaluation Process and Examination Reforms' of the Programme of Action contains the following:

Reforms in examinations have been a subject of serious discussion for long. Some changes have been introduced in the system at the initiative of the NCERT in school examinations and the UGC in university examinations. On the whole, however, the impact of these reforms have not been too significant.

The Policy and Strategies for Implementation. The policy visualises integration of the assessment of performance with the process of learning and teaching, and utilising the process of evaluation to bring about qualitative improvement in education. In order to ensure that the method of assessment of students' performance is valid and reliable, the following long-term measures are proposed.

At the School Level

(i) The Boards of Education will lay down the levels of attainment expected at classes VIII, X and XII;

(ii) The Boards will also prescribe the learning objectives corresponding to these levels of attainment in terms of knowledge and comprehension, communication skills in the application of knowledge, and the ability to learn;

(iii) Schemes of evaluation consisting of examinations to test those aspects of learning which can be assessed through formal examinations and the procedure for assessing those aspects which cannot be tested through such an examination, will be developed. Abilities and proficiencies which can and should be assessed through institutional evaluation will be identified and procedures evolved for such evaluation;

(iv) The development of schemes of evaluation is a continuing process. To provide professional support to this process, the Boards of Education will consider setting up a Consortium for initiating research and development in evaluation procedures and in the conduct of examinations;

(v) For performing this task, the Consortium will adapt selected schools as pilot centres and will hold examinations and award certificates for the students of such schools;

(vi) Before question papers are set, a detailed design will be evolved indicating the weightage to be given to various areas of content, types of questions and the objectives of teaching/learning;

(vii) Alongwith external examinations, continuous institutional evaluation of scholastic and non-scholastic aspects of education will be introduced;

(viii) Evaluation of students' performance will move towards cumulative grading system.;

(ix) In the big States, the possibility of establishing more than one Board of Education will be considered, so that the number of students to be examined by one Board does not exceed one lakh; and

(x) Procedures will be developed for the appointment of Chairmen/Secretaries of Boards of Education and Controllers of Examinations to inspire confidence among public.

At the University Level

(i) The possibility of developing alternate system of evaluation in place of external examinations for affiliated colleges will be explored;

(ii) The question of some universities functioning only as examining bodies for a number of colleges will be examined;

(iii) Academic reforms visualised in the policy like flexibility in the combination of course, modular structure, provision for accumulation of credits, redesigning of courses, etc. will lead to considerable decentralisation in the evaluation process. Detailed schemes will be evolved to facilitate transition to new evaluation procedures concurrently with the changes in the content and structure; and

(iv) An agency will be developed either as part of the AIU (Association of Indian Universities) or independently, for continuous research and development in evaluation procedures.

General

(i) Integrity of the examiner is crucial to the credibility of the examination system. This credibility can be established by the openness of the examinations. It has to be recognised that students have the inalienable right to scrutinise their answer scripts and its evaluation and also compare them with those of others:

(ii) The practice of declaring results in terms of over-all divisions and pass/fail may be reviewed and substituted by a system of declaration of results in terms of marks/grades in each subject separately;

(iii) Candidates should have the opportunity to improve upon their grades through subsequent attempts;

(iv) Provisions should be made for clearing examinations in parts, in conformity with the modular pattern of courses;

(v) The practice of scaling marks of different subjects which are not at par may be adopted in determining the grades;

(vi) Intensive training programmes will be organised for paper setters;

(vii) Question banks will be developed to assist paper-setters;

(viii) A detailed marking scheme will be developed to ensure objectivity in scoring answer scripts;

(ix) Innovative ideas like open book examination, diagnostic evaluation etc. may be experimented with;

(x) Separate certificates will be awarded showing the results of institutional evaluation and external examinations;

(xi) The certificate of institutional evaluation may cover academic achievements as well as non-scholastic aspects.

(xii) Attempts will be made to move towards situation in which only those who teach will evaluate their students.

(xiii) Integration of evaluation with the process of teaching and learning will help diagnose the weaknesses and deficiencies in education. This diagnostic aspect will be utilised to develop remedial programme for weaker sections.

(xiv) Facilities will be provided in schools and colleges for maintenance of students' records to facilitate continuous institutional evaluation.

Semesterisation at the school level is relatively a new concept for all those who are going to implement it and they have to participate in the process. Semesterisation is a major deviation from the traditional approach to assessment and it needs a carefully planned and designed strategy, if it is to succeed in a valid, reliable and objective assessment of the competencies achieved by students at various levels. Semester system will include both internal and external assessment.

Following are the important components of the semester system:

(i) Division of academic year into two terms of 16-18 week's duration, i.e. having 90-100 working days (500-600 hours);
(ii) Restructuring the existing courses into units, modules of different credits semester wise;
(iii) Flexibility to choose the semester courses, according to pupils needs, future requirements; satisfying the minimum credit requirements for certification;
(iv) Carrying forward of the credits earned in different semesters;
(v) Reforms in instructional technology;
(vi) 15 hours of instruction in theory per week in a semester may carry one credit and in case of practicals, 21 hours of practicals may carry one credit;
(vii) About 108 credits may qualify a pupil for the award of the certificate, and
(viii) Assessment of each course at the end of a semester which shall include continuous and comprehensive internal evaluation will ensure conduct of periodical tests and organise remedial instructions so that all students attain optimal levels of achievement.

Semester System and Evaluation

(i) Since the public examinations are still occupying a prominent position in the education system, more particularly at the school stage, any consideration of semesterisation has got to be linked with the public examination system.

(ii) Elements of internal and continuous evaluation may be added to this process at a subsequent stage when the semesterisation system has achieved some degree of stabilisation.

(iii) It is presumed that there will be two semesters per year and four semesters in the total duration of the course, i.e. classes XI and XII.

(iv) The end of each semester should mark a definite stage of instruction and evaluation.

(v) The first and third semesters of the two years course should end with final examination to be conducted by the institutions internally, while the second and fourth semesters will end with public examinations to be held by the Board. Consequently, the Board will now be required to conduct two examinations a year and the system of supplementary examinations will then be dispensed with.

NCERT Discussion Document on National Curriculum for School Education (2000) explains the credit system as detailed below:

Semester pattern of education is modeed on Credit System. Each course in a semester carries a number of credits depending upon the quantum of work required to be done at time required to be spent on it. Credits usually connote the number of contact hours in class per week throughout semester in the form of lectures, tutorials and seminars. One credit course normally implies class instructions of 50 to 60 minutes supplemented by 2-3 hours of study at home per week throughout the semester. In a lab-work and field study, one credit course implies 2-3 hours of work per week throughout semester. Usually semester courses carry 2-4 credits each.

A student earns credits in a course after he/she has:

(a) Attended the minimum number of prescribed lectures including tutorials, seminars, etc. delivered or practicals including lab, field work conducted.

(b) Obtained not less than minimum percentage of marks of qualifying grades reserved for internal assessment.

(c) Obtained not less than the minimum percentage of marks/ grades reserved for semester examination in that course.

A student moving with slow pace or studying part time may spread out his/her study over several hours whereas a brilliant student may take more courses and earn additional credits than normal prescribed for a semester.

2

Basic Issues

Meaning and Idea

The teaching learning process is that process which the curriculum (learning experiences) and other elements such as library, laboratory, radio, films, films trips, TV, field trips, subject clubs etc. are organised in such a way as to attain pre-determined objectives. All the various elements of the teaching-learning situation have to be brought into harmonious relationships and built into intelligible whole. In the teaching learning process, both the teacher and the learners are the vital elements. The teacher is the organiser and creator of the learning experiences for the learner. His role is to facilitate learning. Both must actually interact.

Significant Factors

These may be summed up as under:

1. Why to learn or why to teach? This implies formulation of objectives of teaching learning.
2. Who is to learn or whom to teach? The learner (child) is to learn and therefore his abilities, aptitudes and interests must be taken note of. Individual differences must be attended to.

3. From whom to learn or who is to teach? The teacher is to teach. He should, therefore, present a good model.
4. What to learn or what to teach? This denotes acquisition of knowledge, skills and attitudes i.e. development of behaviours.
5. How to learn and how to teach? This includes the active involvement of the learner and the role of the teacher in using strategies of teaching learning. Proper interaction of both the learner and the teacher is needed.
6. What to learn or whom to teach? The teacher has to provide motivational situations so that the learner is at his best in the learning process.
7. Where to learn or where to teach? Classroom is not the only place to learn or to teach. There are various other sources of learning such as workshop, laboratory, etc.
8. To what extent has the learner learnt or the teacher taught? This is to evaluate the learning outcomes or to find out the extent to which the objectives have been achieved.

The eight steps in the teaching learning process include 3-way communication which is the principal function in effective teaching learning i.e. communications from the teacher to the learner (steps 1 and 2), from learner to teacher (steps 3 and 5; step 4 is concerned with the learner) and again from teacher to learner (steps 6 to 8).

The formative evaluation in step 7 and KR (knowledge of Response) is equally important to conduct the teaching learning process. K.R. is a kind of feedback information and is of several types. For example, in responding to the behaviour of the learner, the teacher says 'good', 'wrong', 'no', 'well', 'hu', 'wonderful' etc. Evaluation of appraisal helps to provide a solution to the following issues:

(i) Should the objectives be modified or eliminated?
(ii) Are the objectives realistic for the particular groups of learners?
(iii) Are the necessary references available for achieving the objectives?

The above mentioned description seems theoretically very sound. In fact this should be the broad objective of evaluation. But in actual practice, such a situation does not exist. By and large, the main objective remains to get good grades in the examination, (though this term is gradually being replaced by a broader term, namely evaluation).

Evaluation has four major aspects namely (i) Objectives, (ii) Learning experiences, (iii) Learning appraisal and (iv) Relationship among the three.

The Requirements

The word evaluation is now being increasingly used in current educational literature in place of the word 'examination'. However, there is a great difference in the views of scholars as regards its meaning. Following definitions are intended to throw light on its various dimensions.

H.H. Remmers and N.L. Gage point out, "It is the felt need that has caused the shift from the term 'measurement' – implying mathematically precise mensuration of knowledge to the term 'evaluation' which widens the areas to be studied to include subjective opinions and qualitative changes as well as objective and quantitative changes to include changes in attitudes, appreciations, and understandings as well as acquisitions of knowledge and skills."

Wiles defines evaluation as, "Evaluation is a process of making judgments that are to be used as a basis for planning. It consists of establishing goals, collecting evidence concerning growth or lack of growth toward goals, making judgments about the evidence, and revising procedures and goals in the light of the judgments. It is a procedure for improving the product, the process, and even the goals themselves."

Chester F. McNernly observes, "The purpose of any programme of evaluation is to discover the needs of the individuals being evaluated and then to design learning experiences that will solve these needs ... Evaluation is an important and delicate process not only from the standpoint of determining the needs and growth of programmes and individuals but also from the standpoint of what it does to the individuals being evaluated ... An evaluation cannot adequately be made by using a single check list, an isolated anecdotal record, or a battery of examinations; a complete evaluation will require the use of many techniques."

Shane and McSwam conceive evaluation, "as a process or inquiry based upon criteria cooperatively prepared and concerned with the study, interpretation, and guidance of socially desirable changes in the developmental behaviour of children ... It is a process within the child as a result of which he responds to the psychological interpretations he makes of his school-community environment."

According to Good, "Evaluation is a process of ascertaining or judging the value or amount of something by careful appraisal. 'Values' imply the outcome of the learning activity whereas 'amount' signifies the acquisition of knowledge of skill. It means that evaluation concerns itself with scholastic achievement as well as with behaviour changes."

Thomas M. Briggs and Joseph Justman write that evaluation is "a process by which the values of an enterprise are ascertained." Further they write, "Evaluation should be conceived primarily in terms of educational purposes which the programme of supervision is intended to serve."

(i) If the purpose is to stimulate teachers to improve their techniques of class-room instruction, evaluation must concern itself with ascertaining the extent to which such improvement is being effected.

(ii) If the purpose is to enrich and vitalize the course of study, evaluation must seek to determine whether the pupils are really deriving greater educational value from the "enriched" and "vitalized" programme than they did formerly.

(iii) If the purpose is to re-establish faculty *'esprit de corps'* and school morale, the objective of evaluation will be to assess in various ways the degree of improvement in personal and professional attitudes in human relations, and ultimately, therefore, in efficiency of teaching and learning.

(iv) If an important purpose of the supervisory programme is to promote greater educational attention to individual needs of pupils, evaluation will necessarily concern itself with estimating the success with which guidance procedures, differentiated programmes of study, courses and units of learning experience, individualised teaching and learning procedures, and other educational measures designed to achieve greater satisfaction of individual needs are operating.

C.E. Beeby describes evaluation as, "The systematic collection and interpretation of evidence leading as a part of process to a judgement of value with a view to action."

In simple language evaluation may be described as a process by means of which changes in behaviour of children are studied and guided towards pre-determined objectives.

Need and Significance of Evaluation. Evaluation fulfills various purposes in the educational field. It is needed for several objectives. Of course the primary concern of evaluation is to bring about improvement in the teaching-learning process so that the learner develops his potentials to the optimum level.

Evaluation is useful in the following ways.

To Evaluate the Achievement of the Students. The abilities and the achievements of the students must be evaluated. Evaluations are conducted to discover whether or not the learner has been able to acquire the required knowledge, skill and attitude.

To Measure Personality. Evaluations are used to test the power of clear thinking, quickness of mind, calmness and perseverance.

To Find out the Efficiency of Teachers and of the School. Evaluations provide a suitable occasion for the authorities to judge the efficiency of the teachers. The efficiency of the institution is also judged. They provide a proper occasion to the teachers to know whether or not their methods of teaching-learning are appropriate.

To Help in Diagnosis. They help to discover the specific weak points of an individual or class and thus give an opportunity to the teachers as well as to the taught to remove these defects.

To Act as Incentives. Stimulation to work hard is provided to the students through the system of evaluation. Some objectives are placed before the students and for the realisation of those objectives, the students develop in them the habits of constant hard work.

To Help in Prognosis. Evaluations have a prognostic value also. With this device, the aptitudes of the students are determined.

To Give Uniformity of Standard. The external evaluations facilitate the problem of uniformity of standards attained by the students of the different institutions.

To Help in Grouping. They facilitate the work of grouping individuals for the purposes of teaching by bringing those together who have more or less the same attainment.

To Measure Fitness for Admission to Higher Courses. They are designed to determine the capacity and fitness of the candidates to pursue higher courses of general or professional study or training. Evaluations which serve this purpose are called Entrance or Qualifying Examinations.

To Help in Selection by Competition. Evaluations are also conducted to select the best candidates for appointment to public services or for awarding prizes and scholarships.

Thus evaluations serve various purposes. They are an instrument of quality control in education, selection/entrance to a higher grade or tertiary level. In fact effective decision-making process in various tasks in education involves evaluation. It is intrinsic to the teaching learning situation

Chief Factors

The definition of evaluation given by C.E. Beeby highlights the following aspects of evaluation:

(1) Evaluation as systematic collection of evidence – Data, facts and figures concerning the outcome of teaching learning.

(2) Interpretation of the evidence.

(3) Arriving at some value judgement i.e. result of the interpretation.

(4) Taking further action on the basis of judgement (feedback).
Importance of each element in the definition of evaluation is given below:

Systematic Collection. This implies the following:

(1) Information must be gathered in a systematic way and not in a haphazard way.

(2) Information must be up-to-date.

(3) Information must be reliable and accurate.

(4) Information must be gathered through different sources and methods.

Interpretation of evidence. Interpretation must be done in a logical way. All reliable facts must be scrutinised very carefully.

Value judgement. This involves the issue about how well a programme is helping to meet larger educational goals.

Action. The entire exercise has a definite purpose and is a deliberate one. Action implies taking remedial measures as to formulate and implement better teaching learning policies and strategies. (See also definitions in the previous answer)

Summing up. Whatever be the definition of evaluation, it must serve the following objectives:

(1) Assist learners in their learning.

(2) Diagnose learning difficulties of learners.

(3) Determine readiness for new learning experiences.

(4) Assist learners in their problems of adjustment.

(5) Prepare reports of learner's achievement.

(6) Assist teachers in adopting proper strategies of teaching learning.

(7) Fulfil classroom objectives of instruction.

Constructing Elements

Following are the five components of evaluation:

1. Specifying learning outcomes.
2. Collection of evidence about pupil's growth through reliable data gathering devices.
3. Analysis and interpretation of performance or pupil's growth.

4. Diagnostic appraisal i.e. indicating the level of performance rather than the judgement on the performance.
5. Redefining and readjusting the instructional objectives on the basis of feedback.

Chief Features

A publication of the NCERT entitled Reforming Examinations: Some Emerging Concepts (1978) lists the following generalisations:

1. Evaluation is a function of the learner and instruction and, therefore, good evaluation is one which is done by the teacher, of the taught as an individual.
2. Evaluation provides quality control at every stage of the teaching-learning process and therefore, evaluation would be treated as an integral part of the teaching-learning process.
3. Since evaluation provides feed-back about the rate of pupil's learning and the effectiveness of instruction, evaluation should be done unit-wise after teaching every unit.
4. As the purpose of teaching is learning by students, focus of teachers' evaluation should be on improvement of pupils' achievement and not on judging their achievement. Therefore, diagnostic testing and remedial teaching should go side by side.
5. Pupils' achievement is the outcome of the integrated process of learning within a given set of conditions. Evaluation of pupils' learning should, therefore, be also integrated with regard to both the process and product of learning.
6. Keeping in view explosion of knowledge, the new curriculum stresses the learnability aspect more than the knowledge aspect. Emphasis in evaluation should, therefore, shift from testing of rote memory to that of problem solving abilities and attitude development.
7. For appraisal of the total development of the learner, it is essential that evaluation should not be limited to

scholastic achievement alone, but it should encompass all aspects of pupils' development. As such evaluation techniques will have to be extended beyond written and practical examinations to include oral testing, observations, checklists, rating scales and interviews.

8. Since independent learning by students is considered an important method of learning in the new curriculum, self-assessment by pupils of their own learning should be practised in the evaluation system of an institution, so that cooperative assessment of the teacher and the learner is encouraged.
9. Since it is impossible to achieve 100 percent or even near to 100 percent reliability of the various tools used for evaluating pupils, it is desirable that students should be classified broadly into 5 to 7 grades rather than using 101 point scale as at present.
10. As every pupil learns at his own rate, he should be judged in terms of his own capacities and goals and not in terms of the standards of his class, institution or the board of secondary education. As such passing of a student in all the subjects at a time cannot be considered essential.
11. The grades of every pupil indicate only his level of performance which may be satisfactory or unsatisfactory in terms of his own standard. Thus, a grade howsoever low it may be, cannot be taken as failure but as an indicator of his present level of achievement.
12. Given more time and proper remedial teaching a student can improve his achievement. Therefore, a student should get the opportunity of improving his grade in one or more subjects, if he so desires.
13. The more accurately and meaningfully the evidence about pupils' growth in different aspects of his development is reported to students, teachers, parents,

employers and institutes of higher learning, the more appropriate and reliable would be the decision taken for classification, certification and selection of students for different purposes. Therefore, regular recording of pupil performance in various areas of development is a prerequisite to every evaluation programme.

Role of Education

Evaluation cannot be done in a vacuum. It is always with reference to the objectives of a particular system of education. The traditional system of examination in India owes its origin to the objectives as laid down by Macaulay and as the objective of education was to produce a class of clerks, the examination system was also meant to serve that end. Our traditional type of examination, thus, is one-sided and concerned with the academic subjects only and entirely ignores the non-academic aspects. Here, too, it fails to measure scientifically and objectively the achievements of the students.

Common Features

The characteristics of good evaluation may be classified as under:

Characteristics of Good Evaluation

	Practical		*Technical*
	This includes		This comprises.
(i)	Acceptability	(i)	Discrimination
(ii)	Cost effectiveness	(ii)	Items
(iii)	Ease of administration	(iii)	Norms
(iv)	Ease of scoring	(iv)	Objectivity
(v)	Ease of interpretation	(v)	Reliability
(vi)	Face validity	(vi)	Standardisation
(vii)	Fairness	(vii)	Validity
(viii)	Meaning of test scores		
(ix)	Purposefulness		
(x)	Time element		
(xi)	Usefulness		

The inter-relationship of these four aspects of evaluation clearly indicate that the process of evaluation is a continuous one and involves continual appraisal of objectives of the teaching-learning process and of the testing procedures used by the classroom teacher.

The inter-relationships of these four aspects of evaluation clearly indicate that the process of evaluation is a continuous one and involves continual appraisal of objectives of the teaching-learning process and of the testing procedures used by the classroom teacher.

Validity of Evaluation. In the words of Thorndike, "A measurement procedure is valid in so far as it correlates with some measurement of success in the job for which it is being used as a predictor."

Leo J. Cronback states that "validity is the extent to which a test measures what it purports to measure."

Gulliksen has defined validity as, "the correlation of the test with some criterion."

According to Freeman, "The first necessary condition of a valid test is that it has an adequate degree of reliability. If the reliability coefficient of a test is 'zero', it cannot correlate with anything. A test that correlates poorly even with itself cannot correlate well with a measure of another variable." As Anastasi puts it "the question of test validity concerns what the test measures and how well it does so."

A test is said to be valid if it succeeds in measuring what it aims at measuring. The validity of a test can be judged in more than one way. (1) A test is said to be valid if its results correspond to the judgment of competent judges. The scores of an individual on the test may be compared with a list prepared by the class teacher and the correlation can be found. (2) By comparing the scores obtained through new test with the scores compared through the Simon-Binet Test. (3) By correlating the results of a group test with those of an individual test given to the same group of students.

Reliability of Evaluation. The reliability of a test is defined by different authors in different ways. Some of these definitions are given here:

In the words of Anne Anastasi, "Reliability refers to the consistency of scores obtained by the same individuals when re-examined with the same test on different occasions or with different sets of equivalent items or under other variable examining conditions."

This definition of reliability underestimates the error of measurement.

In the words of Garrett, "The reliability of a test or of any measuring instrument depends upon the consistency with which it gauges the ability to whom it is applied."

Stodola and Stordahl defined reliability as "the correlation between two or more sets of scores on equivalent tests from the group of individuals."

A test is said to be reliable if it gives the same results whenever it is repeated. If there is no variation in a pupil's score obtained in a test today and obtained after a sufficient long time, the test is said to be reliable. The test should also give the same result, if it is applied by different persons who follow the set instructions. There are two methods which are usually employed to determine the validity of test: (1) The test-retest method (2) The split-half method. According to the first method, the same test is applied after some months to the individuals and the scores of two administrations of the test are compared and correlation of co-efficient is calculated. The test is said to be fairly reliable if the correlation is 90. In the second method, test is arbitrarily split up into two equal halves, the scores on odd and even items are counted separately and correlation co-efficient is calculated.

Objectivity. Objectivity has two aspects – objectivity of items and objectivity of scoring. Objectivity of item construction implies that the items should be as simple as possible. Student should be able to interpret the item correctly. If the examiner puts a particular item in the test which means to him something, but the student takes it in some other sense and replies the item, naturally the objectivity of the item would be considerably reduced. Words like 'perhaps', 'always', 'never', 'should' be avoided.

Objectivity of scoring means that personal judgment of the examiner should not affect scores. Variations, in the mood and feelings of the examiner, his attitudes and prejudices, his predetermined standards should not affect scoring. Essay-type examinations are very defective from this viewpoint.

Standardization. A standardized test is one in which the procedure, apparatus and scoring have been fixed-so that precisely the same test can be given at different times and places, i.e., 'Uniformity of testing conditions'.

If scores obtained by different individuals are to be comparable, testing conditions must obviously be the same for all. In a test situation, the single independent variable is usually the individual being tested.

Every condition which affects performance must be specified if the test is to be regarded as truly standardized, The formulation of directions is a major part of the standardization of a new test, e.g., oral instructions to testee, preliminary demonstrations, handling queries from testee, surroundings, etc.

Establishing norms is another essential part of standardization. Norms are those scores which are usually earned by representative subjects. The best type of norms are the local norms based upon individual in our own school system. They permit the tester to compare the subject with his prospective comparisons and competitors. Norms should always refer to defined and clearly prescribed population. If appreciable differences between group exist, e.g., literacy, then separate norm tables should be provided.

Discrimination. A test must discriminate, i.e., it should be able to measure differences in achievement, intelligence or some other measured dimension. In an achievement test it is possible when every item is discriminating between poor and good students. If an item is answered by an equal number of good and poor students it has no discriminative value. But if only good students are able to do it and a large number of poor students miss it, it has high discriminating value. If items in a test are discriminating, reliability and validity of the test would be enhanced.

Basis and Relevance

Garrett has given the example of a watch to distinguish between reliability and validity. Suppose, the watch of my neighbour strikes 10 at particular time, today my watch has stopped. But seeing my neighbour's watch, I also set my watch at 10. Next day if I compare my watch again with that of my neighbour and if it strikes the same as his watch, it is reliable. This is neither fast nor slow. But if it strikes 10-20 when the neighbour's 10.0 it is not reliable. Now suppose my watch strikes 10 as that of my neighbour, but the radio time is 10.5, the time in my watch is not valid or truthful. The reliability is measured by repeated measurements, but validity by comparing with some standard.

Ross has given another example. A man returns from a vacation with picturesque story of the fish he claims to have caught. He relates the same glowing account to each of his friends he meets. The story is reliable in statistical sense. But it is not valid necessarily, because we do not know whether it is true or not.

Reliability is self-correlation. But validity is correlation with some outside criterion. To be valid, however, a test has to be reliable. But every reliable test is not necessarily valid a test having high correlation with itself may not have equally high correlation with a criterion.

Assessment in Totality

Evaluation has to be very comprehensive in a system of education which aims at the many-sided development of the personality of the learner. In the words of the Secondary Education Commission, "The school of today concerns itself not only with the intellectual pursuits but also with the emotional and social development of the child, physical and mental health, his social adjustment and other equally important aspects of his life; in a word, with an all-round development of his personality".

Means and Devices

The tools and techniques of evaluation can be categorized into four categories:

(i) Testing Procedures.
(ii) Self-report Techniques.
(iii) Observational Techniques.
(iv) Projective Techniques.

Testing Procedures. Generally following methods are used for evaluation:

(i) Written Tests
(ii) Verbal Tests
(iii) Experiments

Self-Reporting Tests:

(i) Autobiography
(ii) Direct Questions
(iii) Discussion
(iv) Interview
(v) Personal Diary
(vi) Questionnaire

Observational Tests:

(i) Check List
(ii) Guest who Technique
(iii) Rating Scale
(iv) Sociometric Technique

Projective Techniques:

(i) Doll Play
(ii) Rorschach Test
(iii) Sentence Completion.
(iv) TAT.

Any one of the above tools can be used according to the needs and aims of evaluation.

Measuring the Benefits

According to Wrightstone, "Evaluation is a relatively new technical term introduced to design a more comprehensive concept of measurement that is implied in conventional tests and examinations." In examination and measurement the emphasis is upon the academic subjects only whereas evaluation includes all the changes that take place in the development of a balanced personality and measures the qualities of head, hand, health and heart of an individual.

In the words of Clara M. Brown, "Evaluation is essential in the never ending cycle of formulating goals, measuring progress towards them and determining the new goals which emerge as a result of new warning. Evaluation involves measurement which means objective quantitative evidence. But it is broader than measurement and implies that considerations have been given to certain values, standards, and that interpretation of the evidence has been made in the light of the particular situation."

Panton, M.Q. (1985) in an article 'Evaluation, Assessment and Measurement' published in 'The International Encyclopaedia of Education' (Husen and Posthethwatle (Editors-in-chief) states that in the minds of many educational practitioners the words evaluation, testing and measurement appear to be used 'interchangeably'. In the United States during the 1970's and now increasingly in other parts of the English speaking world, evaluation is being used with less and less regard to its original meaning. Panton further observes, "What evaluation, assessment and measurement have in common is testing. Each frequently (but not always) makes use of tests, but none of them is synonymous with testing, and the type of tests required for each of the three processes may be different." The author defines these terms as given below.

Measurement. The regulatory definition of "assigning a numerical quantity to..." will serve in most educational applications. While instruments such as rulers and stop watches can be used to determine height, speed, and so on, many intellectual capacities or other quantities of educational interest must be measured indirectly. Thus tests are typically used to measure such dimensions as level of intelligence, the ability to apply a given principle in a variety of situations, the proportion of material learned or forgotten. Measurement is rarely carried out for its own sake. It may be included in an assessment or evaluation, but is more to be regarded as a basic research procedure."

Assessment. "As far as possible the term assessment should be reserved for application to people. It covers activities included in grading (formal and non-formal), examining, certifying, and so on. Student's achievement on a particular course may be assessed. An applicant's attitude for a particular job may be assessed. A teacher's competence may be assessed. Throughout the world, most educational systems find it appropriate to record student's achievement in some way, whether with a number, a letter code, or a comment such as 'satisfactory' or 'needs improvement.' Such assessments are based on the internal synthesis of a wide variety of evidence, and although they often include test results, they rarely have much in common with scientific measurement. These procedures are increasingly being labelled 'Student Evaluation' in the United States."

Evaluation. "In general, it would seem preferable to reserve the term educational evaluation for application to abstract entities such as programmes, curricula and organisational variables. Just as assessment may be characterised as a routine activity in which most educators will be involved, evaluation is an activity primarily for those engaged in research and development."

The Dictionary of Education (1982) explains the concept evaluation and assessment as, "Evaluation is often used interchangeably with assessment. This is because there is a considerable overlap in their meanings. Both involve measurements designed to describe the amount of certain attributes. Both involve procedures for obtaining these measurements which can involve tests as well as less objective instruments such as rating scales. There is a tendency, however, for evaluation to be used in a more general way, involving a wide range of measures with a great acceptance of subjective judgements. There is also a tendency for evaluation to be used more when the subject of the evaluation is not a person (or group of persons) but the success of a course of teaching or method of teaching. Assessment is therefore used more usually in situations where the procedures involve more objective instruments and when these instruments are measuring personal attributes."

"Measurements is the process of assigning symbols to dimensions of phenomena in order to characterise the status of a phenomenon as precisely as possible. Evaluation is the assignment of symbols to phenomenon in order to characterise the worth or value of a phenomenon usually with reference to some social, cultural or scientific standard" (Bradfield and Murdock). For example, if we take a type learner, he is examined for typing. The result indicates that he typed 40 words per minute with 5 errors. This is measurement. The main phenomenon here is typing. Speed and accuracy is the result of typing, which are measured. 40 words and 5 errors are symbols, through which his typing ability is measured. Now if the results of this boy is compared with other boys and he is given 'B' grade, then this process is evaluation.

This example clarifies the difference between measurement and evaluation. But in several situations it is not so easy to identify measurement and evaluation separately. This happens in situations when evaluation becomes a natural process after measurement without giving much thought.

As a matter of fact evaluation is a process of qualitative judgment. Thus it is also a kind of measurement. The only difference is that measurement is objective while evaluation is mostly subjective.

To conclude, has a narrow meaning than evaluation but broader meaning than measurement. Evaluation involves assessment and measurement. It is a wider term and includes assessment and measurement also.

3

Fundamental Demands

Measurement came to natural sciences so naturally that no need of thinking about it ever arise. Some scientists believe that the procedures which are known measurement in psychology is not truly measurement. It is true to some extent, because, the term some times is so defined that number of dimensions are not included in it, but even then it is called measurement in psychology.

Measurement became essential to study of science. Mathematics is not a science which is not based on observation and experience. It does not collect the facts on the basis of nature's observation. Science is collection of informations and observation about the natural or physical phenomenon. Mathematics is a universal language which be easily and powerfully utilized by any science ; its terminology is unlimited yet well defined. It is easily possible to communicate, correctly and objectively through measurement, which can also be easily manipulated in thoughts. Objectivity is one of the main aim of science. The objective description is called measurement, is a useful mean to obtain these goals.

J. P. Guilford has defined the term Measurement

"Measurement means the description of data in terms of numbers and this, in turn, means taking advantage of the many benefits that operate with numbers and mathematical thinking Provide".

Campbell defines measurement as the "Assignment of numerals to objects or events according to certain rules is called measurement."

There are many problems and difficulties in measurement. Charles Spearman have stated "The path of science is paved with achievements of the allegedly unachievable. The mathematical treatment is psychology, has made a surprising progress in this area. Psychology is unable to attain those functions of measurement, the way for which is paved by physical sciences. Such type essentials of measurement have been discussed in this chapter.

The Concept

The term "measurement" and "evaluation" are often used interchangeably. However, in psychological, sociological and educational researches these two terms are used separately because they connote two different meanings. "Measurement" refers to the process of assigning numerals to events, objects, etc. according to certain rules. Tyler defines measurement "as assignment of numerals, according to rules." A still more elaborate and wider definition has been given by Nunnally "Measurement consists of rules for assigning numbers to objects in such a way as to represent quantities of attributes". An analysis of the definition of measurement given by Nunnally reveals the following main properties of measurement.

1. In the process of measurement numbers are assigned according to some rules. A number is a kind of numeral which is assigned some quantitative meaning. In the process of measurement the investigator does not assign numbers of his own choice, but according to certain fixed and explicit rules. Usually, such rules are of two types. One type is where the procedure is obvious and explicit. For example; when one measuring the length of cloth in feet and inches, rules for assigning numerals are very explicit and clear. But suppose one wants to measure the extroversion trait of personality or the intelligence of a

child. Obviously, in such a situation the rules would not be as clear as in the first example. For measuring psychological, sociological and educational attributes the rules are generally vague and less explicit.

2. Measurement is always concerned with certain attributes or variables or features of an object. It is these attributes or features of the object which are measured and not the object itself. For example, one would measure the aptitude, intelligence, attitude etc. of a person and not the person himself. When an investigator is measuring the attribute of a person, he is faced with two difficulties. First, he may be asked to measure an attribute the existence of which is doubtful. Extra sensory perception is one such example. Most investigators have failed to show such perception in many individuals. In such a case, measurement is not difficult but rather an impossible task. Second, the investigator may be asked to measure attributes which are not unitary but rather a mixture of several sub-attributes. Usually, this happens when one is asked to measure "personality adjustment". Adjustment may relate to home, school, emotion, etc. each of which requires a separate measurement and any attempt to measure them together may create difficulty. In such a situation the investigator can, however, measure the attributes with more sophisticated instruments specially designed for the purpose.

3. In the process of measurement, numerals are used to represent quantities of the attribute. In other words, measurement involves the process of quantification. Quantification indicates how much or to what extent that particular attribute is present in a particular object. For example, when the investigator is measuring the achievement of a child in arithmetic, he quantifies it by saying that the child has an 80 percent mark in his class. This percentage indicates how much of arithmetical knowledge he has gained in the class.

Measurement is different from its so-called synonym "evaluation". By evaluation is meant appraisal or assessment with respect to some standard. Tuckman (1975) defines evaluation as, "a process where in the parts, processes, or outcomes of a programme are examined to see whether they are satisfactory, particularly with reference to the programmes stated objectives, our own expectations, or our own standards of excellence. Thus evaluation involves a process of appraisal of an object or event with reference to some standard. The standard may be social, cultural or scientific. The standard may also be true or arbitrary. An investigator may measure the height of a child (which say, is 30") and type him as short. A typist typing 80 mores per minute may be described as a 'Grade A' typist. Description of the height of the child (which is 30") and the typing speed of the typist (which is 80 words per minute) are examples of measurement. However, when the child is said to be short or the typist is classified as a 'Grade A' typist, it means the performance of the typist and the height of a child are being compared with reference to some standard. A child is short because he is shorter than the general mean height of children of his age group and the typist is a 'Grade A' typist because his speed is faster than the average speed of most the typists. Thus, the height of the child and the typing behaviour of the typist are being evaluated and not being measured.

Measurement and evaluation are the very old processes which are not only used in behavioural science- psychology and education but it is an origin of physical sciences and arithmetic. The development measurement goes side by side the human development. The advancement of any nation and country is based on its precise devices and technique of measurement. The precision of measurement is most important criterion of the development of human civilization. The evaluation is an informal and continuous process. It takes place every time in every walk of life. The objects, facts, events and behaviours are continuously evaluated, Measurement is the formal process which is used in planned and objective way. The measurement in psychology and education is the origin of twentieth century. The measurement is the process of quantification of a trait or characteristics or assigning numerals. The direct measurement is used in physical and bio-sciences while measurement is indirect in psychology and education. The traits and attributes are abstract. We can not percieve them through our senses such as intelligence, attitude aptitude, achievement and personality. These variables are measured through the behaviours Thus, measurement can be categorized into two-

(1) Measurement in Physical Sciences and

(2) Measurement in Behavioural Sciences.

Various Sciences

It is simple and precise process of quantification of physical traits of the objects are percievable and measured directly. The measuring instrument is placed along the trait such height is measured by placing the meter along the height of a person and similarly his weight is also measured. The body temperature is measured by placing thermometer in his month.

In physical measurement the units are fixed or definite. The height or length is measured in meters and centimeters The weight is measured in kilograms and quintals. The liter is the Unit of liquid.

The zero is the reference point in physical measurement. It is also known as absolute measurement. The obtained units are easily interperatable. The zero has its value in physical measurement.

The another characteristic of physical measurement is that every trait has its own unit of qualification. The meter is used to measure height, length and width. The liter is used to measure the volume of a liquid. It employs the ratio scale for the process of quantification of the physical trait.

Measurement in Behavioural Sciences

The process of measurement in behavioural science is difficult as well as complex, because it employs the indirect process of measurement. The trait is not directly measured by the scale but the trait is measured indirectly by the behaviours. The basis of measurement is the behaviour of a subject. All the behavioural traits are measured with help of behaviours. The overt behaviours and covert-behaviours are employed in the process of measurement.

The behavioural observation is the means of measurement which can be classified broadly into two.

(1) The observation of actual behaviour or overt-behaviour and

(2) The observation of remembered behaviour or emission of covert behaviour.

The actual behaviour is observed, that is, the persons or objects engaged in producing the behaviour remain physically present and interact with each other. A group of the college students solving a problem and the teacher-pupil interactions are examples of the actual behaviour and its observation is known as the observation of the actual behaviour. In remembered or emitted behaviour, the persons or objects engaged in producing the behaviour do not remain physically present. However, they are symbolically represented. For example, a person maybe asked to recall the scene of a classroom in which the teacher is extremely dominating. Such observation is called observation of remembered behaviour. The observation of actual behaviour is easier than the observation of remembered behaviour because in the former things are ready-made and the observer has simply to make a decision on the basis of what is around him, whereas in the later, the observer has to take a decision on the basis of his previous experiences and/ or on the basis of his ability to perceive what an object looks like because it is not present physically. This is why remembered behaviour is also known as perceived behaviour. Rating scale and observation are techniques to assess both actual behaviour.

The remembered behaviour or emission of responses are measured by employing tests, inventories and questionnaire etc. The behaviour is the main basis in psychology, education and sociology. A person can evoke limited number of behaviours which are used for measuring several traits and characteristics.

One of the crucial problem in behavioural science is that there is no single behaviour which can measure only one characteristic. A behaviour measures more than one characteristic simultaneously at a time. The fact can be illustrated by an example which is used in intelligence as well as an achievement tests.

1. Sky : Blue : : Milk : ? (white)
2. Sky : Gas : : Milk: ? (liquid)

An examinee has to percieve the relationship between sky and blue i.e. colour. The same relationship has to establish with milk i.e. white, but he must acquire the vocabulary of colour white. Therefore, perceiving relationship is a mental ability (perceptual) and acquiring the vocabulary of colours is an achievement. The both items measure partially mental ability (intelligence) and partially achievement in responding correctly. In both the situation responses white and liquid but measure the two different characteristics i.e. intelligence and achievement. This may be the item of intelligence test and also of an achievement test of language.

There is no fixed unit of measuring any trait and characteristic. The raw scores obtained by administering a test are meaningless. The scores are to be transformed into standard score to interpret.

The behavioural sciences measurement is relative while physical measurement is absolute. The zero has no meaning in this. The group performance is the reference point to understand meaning of a score. A boy has scored 60 in maths and 29 in English. If we apply arithmetic to convert into percentage. It would mean that 60 percent marks in maths and 29 percent marks in English. Thus, the performance is good in maths and poor in English. If the statistical technique is used to convert into percentile ranks, it may yield that the percentile in maths is zero, means that all other students have scored higher than him but the percentile rank in English is 100, means that non has scored higher than him. This interpretation has been done with reference to group performance which is most accurate than the earlier one's. Therefore in behavioural science measurement is relative to other examinees.

The zero-score has no meaning in this area. A student has scored zero, it does not mean that he does not know any thing but could not attempt correctly the items given in the test, therefore, zero mark has been assigned to him.

Measurement has two broad dimensions – psychological or qualitative measurement and physical or quantitative measurement. Psychological measurement comprises the measurement of mental processess, traits, habits, tendencies, and the likings of an individual whereas physical measurement comprises the measurement of objects, things, etc., which are often physically present in the world. Usually, physical measurement is concerned with the measurement of height, weight, length, size, volume etc. Given below is a clearcut distinction between psychological and physical measurement.

1. In physical sciences measurement the unit of measurement is fixed and constant throughout the measurement whereas in psychological measurement the unit of measurement is not fixed and varies during the process of measurement. For example, a kilogram or an inch has the same meaning at whatever place the measurement is being taken and it conveys the same physical significance or meaning throughout the measurement. But suppose one is measuring intelligence. There is no fixed unit of measurement in this case because some may measure intelligence on the basis of verbal questions or items answered in a specified time; others may prefer to measure intelligence on the basis of some manipulative tasks done in a specified period; still another group may prefer to measure intelligence on the basis of both time and error in the completion of a task, and so on. Moreover, these units tend to vary themselves during the process of measurement because there is no standard method of presenting uniform set of difficulties to all examinees. For example, a particular item to measure intelligence may seem very easy to one examinee but may seem very difficult end challenging to another.
2. In physical sciences measurement there is a true zero point whereas in psychological measurement there is an arbitrary zero point. By a true zero point is meant a point which actually represents the underlying absence of the trait being measured whereas by an arbitrary zero point is meant a point which does not represent the underlying absence of the trait being measured. For example, when a

person gets a score of zero in a numerical ability test, it does not mean that he has no knowledge of numerical operations at all. But an object having zero length will be said to have no length at all.

3. Physical sciences measurement is more accurate and predictable than psychological measurement. This is because in physical measurement there is a true zero point. For example, a stick of 20" length means the stick is definitely 20″ above the zero inch, and similarly, a stick of length 60" means that it is thrice as long as the first stick. But a person scoring point 15 in an intelligence test cannot be said to have scored 15 points above the zero point because here zero point is itself not known. Like-wise, another person securing score 30 cannot be said to be twice as intelligent as the first person. Therefore, no prediction can be made with definite accuracy.
4. Physical measurement is direct whereas psychological measurement is indirect. When we want to measure the length of a cloth, we place it before us and directly measure its length in inches or feet. However, it is not possible to measure the "extroversion" trait of personality of intelligence in a like manner as they cannot be placed physically before us. Extroversion can only be measured indirectly through some response given by the person concerned and for measuring intelligence we will have to depend upon some responses—verbal or manipulative.
5. In physical sciences measurement the entire quantity can be measured whereas in psychological measurement the entire quantity cannot be measured but only a sample representing that quantity or trait. Say for instance one is to measure the length and weight or all tables and chairs in one's home. The entire length and weight of all the tables and chairs can be measured and expressed in terms of inches and kilograms respectively. But suppose one is measuring the mechanical aptitude of class X students of U.P. State, then ordinarily, it is not possible to measure

the mechanical aptitude (through an appropriate test) of each boy of class X belonging to the State of U.P. Naturally, one would randomly draw a sample of students who are taken to be representative of class X and measure their mechanical aptitude.

In behavioural science a trait or variable is defined in several ways and there are several theories available to explain the nature of variable which also varies significantly. For example, intelligence is an ability of abstract thinking. Intelligence is an ability to adjust in the naval situation. These definition will require different type tests of measuring intelligence. Thus, there is no final definition and final theory of any psychological and educational trait or variable. Thus, a test does not measure whole trait but its one or more aspects. Therefore, no final test has been developed to measuring a trait, comprehensively.

The Comparison

Physical Sciences Measurement	*Behavioural Sciences Measurement*
1. It is a absolute measurement.	1. It is a relative measurement.
2. The reference point is zero.	2. The reference point is group performance.
3. It has the fixed units for measuring a trait.	3. There is no fixed unit for measuring any trait-or variable.
4. The data are interpreted directly.	4. The raw data are meaningless but these have to be trasnformed into standard scores.
5. The trait is directly measured.	5. The trait is indirectly measured with help of behaviours.
6. It is perfectly objective and valid.	6. It is an subjective measurement but tries to make it objective and valid.
7. There are fixed tools for measuring the separate traits.	7. There is no fixed or final measuring instrument for a one trait or variable.
8. It is almost at ratio-scale.	8. It is at nominal, ordinal and internal scales.
9. It has a great precision.	9. It has less precision.
10. It is mainly the prognostic and diagnostic purpose.	10. It is prognostic, diagnostics as well as predictive functions.

Twin Purposes

The psychologists and educators have been interested in measuring in two general areas, (1) what is person can do and (2) what he will do. Measures of the first sort are measures of ability. In our discussion we will divide ability measures and measures of aptitude; measures of achievement. Again, roughly speaking, an aptitude test undertakes to measure what a person could learn to do, whereas an achievement test measures what he has learned to do.

The functions of psychological and educational measurement can be used to answer the following questions :

1. What a person can do?—Achievement test (Prognosis) why a person can not do ?—Diagnostic test (Diagnosis).
2. What a person will do ?—Aptitude test (Prediction).

The distinction between aptitude tests and achievement test is far from a clear one, because we often use what a person has learned as a cue to what he can learn. Thus, a measure of the amount of knowledge of mechanical devices a person has gained in the past may be one of the most accurate indicators of the amount of further knowledge of things mechanical will acquire in the future. The clearest distinction between aptitude and achievement tests lies in the direction of our interest. In an aptitude test, our interest is to predict what the individual can learn or develop into in the future; in the achievement test our interest is in what he has learned in the past.

Measures of the second major category of what the person will do correspond to the area we may roughly label personality measurement. "What the person-will do" is a somewhat broad and loose definition of personality. It is also a somewhat external one. That is, we have indicated a concern for what a person does rather than for how he feels or what his inner urges and conflicts are. We may be interested in those to a degree. But, so far as a testing or observational procedure is concerned, it is always based on what a person, does how he acts, what answers he marks, or what he says. His actions are the basic material that we study.

In the long run, we study his actions in the present so as to be able to predict something about him in the future. We want to predict whether he will graduate from college, whether he will be happy and persist in a sales job, whether he will behave in a more socially acceptable fashion after a particular type of therapy. For such prediction and understanding we are likely to find it helpful to group our observations of specific actions into clusters that seem to belong together. And these "constructs" that we use to tie together the observations that we make may often imply something "inside" the individual-an interest, an attitude, a need, a conflict. But these terms referring to the inner life of the individual represent inferences that we make as a way of structuring and organizing our observations of behaviour. We cannot see a strong need for approval. What we observe is that a child often brings things into class attempts to monopolize discussions, buys candy for other children, and tries to worm his way into social groups in the playground. He may infer a need for approval as a common underlying factor giving unity to the various behaviours, but what we observe is a series of actions.

Jobs to be Done

We cannot describe everything about a person, so we must choose for description those attributes that are relevant to our present concerns. We may be content to describe him roughly and qualitatively, or we may try to describe him more precisely and in quantitative terms. The more we try to make our description precise and quantitative, the more we got involved in measurement. A person can not be measured, we can measure his characteristics.

Measurement in any field always involves three common steps:

(1) Identifying and defining the quality or attribute that is to be measured,

(2) Determining a set of operations by which the attribute may be made manifest and perceivable, and

(3) Establishing a set of procedures or definitions for translating observations into quantitative statements of degree or amount.

An understanding of each of these steps and of the difficulties that it presents provides a sound foundation for understanding the procedures and problems of measurement in psychology and education.

Identifying and Defining the Attribute

We never measure a thing or a person. Measurement is always of a quality or attribute of the thing or person. We undertake to measure the length of the table, the temperature of the blast furnace, the durability of the auto tire, the flavor of the tophy, the intelligence of the school child, the emotional maturity of the adolescent when we deal with the simplest physical attributes, such as length, it rarely occurs to us to wonder about the meaning or definition of the attribute. A clear meaning for length was established long ago in the history of both the race and the individual. Though mastery of concepts of "long" and "short" may represent significant accomplishments in the life of the preschool child, the concepts are automatic and axiomatic in adult society. We all know what we mean by length. However, this is not true of all physical attributes. What do we mean by durability in an auto tire ? Do we mean resistance to wear and abrasion from contact with the Toad ? Do we mean resistance to puncture by pointed objects ? Do we mean resistance to deterioration and decay with the passage of time ? Or do we mean some combination of these three and possibly other elements ? Until we can reach some agreement as to what we mean by durability, we can make no progress toward measuring it. To the extent that we disagree on what durability means, we will disagree on what procedures are appropriate for measuring it, and if we use different procedures, we will disagree in the value that we get as representing the durability of a particular brand of tire.

The problem of reaching agreement as to what a given concept means is even more acute when we start to consider those attributes with which the psychologist or educator is concerned. What do we mean by intelligence ? What kinds of behaviour shall we characterize as intelligent ? Shall the concept refer primarily to dealing with ideas and abstract concepts, or shall it include dealing with things-with concrete objects ? Shall it refer primarily to behaviour in novel situations, or shall it include response in familiar and habitual settings ? Shall it refer to speed and fluency of response, or to level of complexity of reaction without regard to time ? We all have a general idea as to what we mean when we characterize behaviour as intelligent, but you can see that there are many specific points on which we may disagree as we try to make our definition precise. This is true of almost all psychological concepts-some more than others and the first problem that the psychologist or educator faces as he tries to measure the attributes that he is interested in that of arriving at a clear, precise, and generally accepted definition of the attribute that he proposes to measure.

We must decide which attributes it is relevant and important to measure if our description is to be useful for our present needs. A description may fail to be useful for the need at hand because we choose irrelevant features to describe. Thus, in describing a painting we might report its height, its breadth, and its weight. We might report these with great precision. If our concern were to create the picture for shipment, these might be just the items of information we would need. On the other hand, if our purpose was that of characterizing the painting as a work of art, our description would be worthless. The attributes of the picture we had described would be essentially irrelevant to its quality as a work of art.

Similarly, a description of a person may be of little value for our purpose if we choose the wrong things to describe. Thus, a company selecting employees to become truck drivers might test their verbal comprehension and ability to solve quantitative problems, getting very accurate measures of these functions. It is likely, however, that information on these factors would help little in identifying men who would have low accident records and be steady and dependable on the job. Other factors, such as eye-hand coordination, depth perception, and freedom from uncontrolled aggressive impulses might prove much more relevant to the tasks and pressures that a truck driver faces.

Again, we have known a high school music teacher who tested very thoroughly his pupils' knowledge of such facts as who wrote the Emperor Concerto and whether andante is faster than allegro, getting a very dependable appraisal of their information about music and musicians, without presenting them with a single note of actual music, a single theme or melody, a single interpretation or appraisal of living music. As an appraisal of musical appreciation his test seemed to us almost worthless because it was using bits of factual knowledge about music and composers in place of any indication of progress in the appreciation of music itself.

Behaviours to Expose the Attribute to View

The second aspect of measurement is finding or inventing a set of operations or behaviours that will isolate the attribute in which we are interested and display it to us. Once again, the operations for measuring the length of an object such as a table were laid down in the early history of mankind. We convey them to the child early in elementary school. The ruler, the yardstick, the tape measure are uniformly accepted as appropriate instruments, and laying them along the object as an appropriate procedure for displaying to our eye the length of the table, desk, or other object we are studying. But the operations for measuring length or distance are not always so simple. By what operations do we measure the distance from New York to Chicago? From the earth to the sun? From the solar system to the giant spiral nebulain Andromeda? How shall we measure the length of a tuberculosis bacillus or the diameter of a neuron? Physical science has progressed by developing instruments that extend the capabilities of our senses and indirect procedures that make accessible to us amounts too great or too small for the simple direct approach of laying a measuring stick along the object. The operations for measuring length or distance have become indirect, elaborate, and increasingly precise. And they are accepted because they give results that are consistent, verifiable, and useful.

We can see that the operations for eliciting or displaying that attribute will depend upon and interact with the definition that we have accepted for it. If our definition is in terms of resistance to abrasion, we need to develop some standard and uniform procedure for applying an abrasive force to the specimen and gauging the rate at which the rubber wears away-some standardized simulated road test. If we have indicated puncture resistance as the central concept, we need a way of applying graduated puncturing forces. If our definition has been in terms of deterioration from sun, oil, and other destructive agents, our procedure must expose the specimens to these agents and must provide some index of the loss of strength or resilience that results. If our definition incorporates more than one aspect, then each must be incorporated, with appropriate weight, in our assessment.

The definition of an attribute and the operations for eliciting it interact. On the other hand, the definition we have set up determines what we will accept as relevant and reasonable operations. Conversely, the operations we are able to devise to elicit or display the attribute constitute in a very practical sense the definition of the attribute. We speak of an "operational definition." What we are saying is that the set of procedures we are willing to accept as showing the durability of an auto tire become the effective definition of durability so far as we are concerned.

The history of psychological and educational measurement during this century has been in large part the history of invention of instruments and procedures for eliciting, in a standard way and under uniform conditions, the behaviours that serve as indicators of the relevant attributes of persons. Thus, the series of tasks devised by Binet and his successors constitute operations for eliciting behaviour that is indicative of intelligence, and the Stanford-Binet and other tests have come to provide operational definitions of intelligence. The fact that there is no single universally accepted test, and that different tests vary somewhat in the tasks they include ,and in the order in which they rank people is evidence that we do not have complete consensus as to what intelligence is on the one hand, or what the appropriate procedures are for eliciting it on the other. And this lack of consensus is generally characteristic of the "state of the art" so far as psychological and educational measurement are concerned. There is enough ambiguity in our definitions on the one hand, and enough variety in the instruments we have devised to elicit the relevant behaviours on the other, so that different measures of what alleges to be the same trait may rank persons quite differently. Consider, for example, the rubric "citizenship", which appears as a trait to be rated on a number of school report cards. What does good citizenship mean in a schoolchild? How well can we agree in defining it? And once we have had a try at defining it, what operations can we devise to asses its presence or absence?

Quantifying the Attribute

The third step, once we have accepted a set of operations for eliciting an attribute, is to express the result of those operations in quantitative terms. We ask the question, How many or how much? In the case of the length of a table the question becomes How many inches ? The inch represents a basic unit, and we can demonstrate that any inch equals any other by laying them side by side and seeing their equality. This is the direct and straight forward proof of equality for some of the simplest physical measures. For other measuring devices such as the thermometer, equality of units rests upon a definition. Thus, we define equal increases in temperature as corresponding to equal amounts of expansion of a volume of Mercury. Long experience with this definition has shown it to be a useful one because it gives results that relate in an orderly and meaningful way to many other physical measures.

None of our pshychological attributes have units whose equality can be demonstrated by direct comparison, in the way that the equality of inches or kilograms can. How shall we demonstrate that arithmetic problem X is equal, in amount of arithmetical ability that it represents to arithmetic problem Y ? How can we show that one symptom of anxiety is equal to another anxiety indicator ? Thus, for the qualities with which the psychologist or educator is concerned, we always have to fall back upon some definition to provide units and quantification. Most frequently, we call one task successfully completed – a word defined, an arithmetic problem solved, or an analogy made-equal to any other task in the series successfully completed, and count the total number of successes for an individual. The raw score of tasks done correctly is converted into some statement about the age or grade group that a person matches, or about his standing within such a group by procedures discussed. This type of a count of tasks successfully completed or of choices of a certain type provides a plausible and manageable definition of amount, but we have no really adequate evidence of the equivalence of different test tasks, or different questionnaire responses.

Thus, the definition of equivalent tasks, and consequently of units for psychological tests is rather shaky at best. When we have to deal with, a teacher's rating of a child's cooperativeness or a supervisor's evaluation of an employee's initiative, for example, where some set of categories such as —"superior," "very good," "good," "satisfactory," and "unsatisfactory" is used, the meaningfulness of the units in which these ratings are expressed is even more suspect.

In psychological and educational measurement, we encounter problems in relation to all three of the steps that have just been set forth. First, we have problem in selecting the attributes with which to be concerned and in defining them clearly, unequivocally, and in terms upon which all can agree. Even for something as straightforward as "reading ability" we can get a Tango of interpretation.

Second, we encounter problems in devising procedures to elicit the relevant attributes. For some psychological attributes, we have been fairly successful in setting up operations that call upon the individual to display the attribute, and permit us to observe it under uniform and standardized conditions. This holds true primarily for the domain of abilities, where standardized tests have been assembled through which the examinee is called upon, for instance, to read with understanding, to perceive quantitative relationships, or to identify correct forms a English expression. But there are many attributes with which we have been clearly less successful. By what standard operations can be elicit, in a form in which we can assess it, a potential employee's initiative, a school pupil's anxiety, or a soldier's suitability for combat duty ? With continued research and with improved ingenuity we may hope to devise improved operations for making certain of these qualities manifest. But one suspects that there are many psychological qualities for which the identification of suitable measurement operations will always remain a problem.

Finally, even our best psychological units of measure leave something to be desired. Units are set equal by definition. The definition may have a certain amount of plausibility, but the equality of units cannot be established in any fundamental sense. So the addition, subtraction, and comparison of sources will always be somewhat suspect. Furthermore, the precision with which the attribute is assessed – the reliability from one occasion to another or from one appraiser to another is often discouragingly low.

Rational Evaluation

We can not measure a man or an object but we measure its characteristics or attributes even in physical sciences. A table can not be measured but its height, length and width can be measured. Similarly in education and psychology we can not measure a child or person but his characteristics are measured. Measurement is used for quantifying achievement, intelligence, aptitude etc.

Generally the educational and psychological measurement and evaluation techniques have been developed for the following variables.

Abilities : Evidence of what the individual can do if he tries e.g. intelligence.

(A) Aptitudes, performances serving as an indicator of what he can learn to do or will do.

(B) Achievements, performances used to show what he has already learned to do.

Trait or Personality Variables : Indication of what an individual will do, of how he will respond to the events and pressures of life. These are social traits.

Typical Concept

A person as "cheerful," as "sociable," or as "introvert" implies that his behaviour shows a consistency over time and place, and that we recognize certain behaviour as belonging together as a unified aspect of this person. For this cluster of related behaviours we often use the term "trait."

Evidence for a trait is often largely intuitive. That is, the term "sociable" has come to signify to us a range of behaviours that we have sensed as belonging together which involve seeking out the companionship of others, indicating satisfaction with the companionship of others, participating in activities involving others, choosing free-time activities that bring one into a group, and so forth. We sense that some persons tend to show this behaviour with a consistently high frequency, whereas others are consistently more often solitary in their pursuits. Evidence for a trait may also be statistical using the methods of correlation and of factor analysis. We verify, through analysis of the data on groups that certain behaviours do tend to "hang together," so that if the person exhibits one he is likely to exhibit the other.

(a) Character, certain qualities defined by society as estimable or the reverse.
(b) Adjustment, the degree of ability to fit into and live happily in the culture in which one is placed.
(c) Temperament, qualities relating to energy level, mood and style of life.
(d) Interest, activities that are sought and avoided.
(e) Attitudes, reactions for or against the people, the phenomenon and the concepts that make up society.

Various Methods

The measurement of the individual characteristic has a great diversity both of methods and of content area. The variation of method may be due nature of variable and purpose of measurement. The following are the methods of measurement.

Test Methods : It involves a defined task and testing period in which the situations are such it may be right or wrong. One score is assigned to the correct answer and zero to wrong answer. It involves covert behaviours of a subject.

A. Permanent record or product available for scoring or analysis.
B. Process must be observed and evaluated as it occurs.

Use : These methods are applicable for quantifying abilities and aptitude.

Observational Methods, in which behaviour is observed in the natural situations of life. There are various techniques of observation. It involves overt behaviours a subject.

Self- observation in which the individual reports on his own reactions as far as he is aware of them.

(a) Planned observations-planned in advance to cover a specified period.

(b) Retrospective observation, based on present memory and evaluations of past reactions.

Observations by an Outsider, in which relative employer, teacher, etc. reports on the individuals reactions.

1. Planned observations
2. Retrospective observation

Use : This method is used to measure abilities, aptitudes and traits.

Combined Methods

Inventories characterized by some of the aspects of test but also relying upon observations and evaluation of observed behaviour.

1. Inventories,
2. Situational tests,
3. Ratings and projective techniques are used.

Use : These methods are used to measure the traits : Personality, interest, attitude, adjustment.

(a) Appraisal by tests versus appraisal by observation in natural situations.

(b) External observes versus self-observation.

(c) Planned versus Retrospective observation.

(d) Observation and test combined. The situational test.

The techniques of appraising the individual have been developed in great variety, and they have been applied to many aspects of his abilities and personality.

The usual tests are that-

(1) It occurs at a specified time and place.

(2) It consists of a set of taskes uniform for each person tested.

(3) It is seen as a test situation by person being appraised.

(4) to extend over an definite period.

(5) to be based upon situations that vary from person to person and

(6) not be perceived as test by the person being appraised.

A test situation and yet for the naturalness of real-life events, may be called situational test. They represent a compromise between the objectivity and standardization of the testing approach and naturalness of real-life situation. It is very difficult to prepare the situational tests.

Particular Test

A dictionary definition of the verb "to test" states that it means the subjection to conditions that show the real character of a person or thing in a certain particular. It has also been stated that a test is a series of questions or exercises or other means of measuring the skill, knowledge, intelligence, or aptitude of an individual or a group.

These definitions apply to all psychological tests; but psychological tests are more than these definitions indicate. A dictionary of psychological terms defines a psychological test thus:

"A set of standardized or controlled occasions for response presented to an individual with design to elicit a representative sample of his behaviour when meeting a given kind of environmental demand ... it is now common usage to include as a test any set of situations or occasions that elicit a characteristic way of acting, whether or not a task, and whether or not characteristic of the individual's best performance. That even a self-inventory or an attitude survey is called a test".

A concise definition then, is thus,

"A psychological test is a standardized instrument designed to measure objectively one or more aspects of a total personality by means of samples of verbal or non-verbal responses, or means of other behaviours".

The key words in this definition are standardized, objectively, and samples.

A psychological test has the following main characteristics –

1. It ensures the objectively or eliminates the personal error which concerns with the subject and score.
2. It is standardized situations on testing, it means that the obtained data from a test are transformed to standard scores or norms have been developed and can be easily

interpreted. The feature involves the reliability and validity of a test.

3. A test has standardization sample for which the derived scores have been developed. It means that a test is designed to use for a specific population of subjects.
4. A test is used as speeded test, the duration is fixed empirically and instruments of administration and scoring are also standardized or uniform. Tests yield data or extent of the trait or variable.
5. A test is organized succession of stimuli which means to provide situations for emission of responses on his remembered observations.

Test Defined

A psychological and educational test are a standardized procedure to measure quantitatively or qualitatively one or more than one aspect or trait by means of a sample of verbal or non-verbal behaviours. The purpose of a psychological test is two-fold. Firstly it attempts to compare the same individual on two or more than two aspects of trait; and second, two or more than two persons may be compared on the same trait. A psychological test has two main functions :

1. That a person can do-ability,
2. Why a person can not do—weaknesss or diagnosis,
3. What a person will do—prediction.

Such a measurement may be either quantitative or qualitative. In the words of Bean (1953) a test is:

"An organised succession of stimuli designed to measure quantitatively or to evaluate qualitatively some mental process, trait or characteristic".

This definition reveals two important characteristics of a psychological and educational test. First, test is an organised succession of stimuli, which means that the stimuli (popularly known as items) in the test are organised in a certain sequence and are based upon some principles of test constructions. Usually, the items of a test are placed in increasing order of difficulty and its procedure of administration is standardised to ensure maximum objectivity. Second, both quantitative measurements are possible through psychological and educational tests. The reading ability of a child may be measured with the help of a test specialty designed for the purpose, His reading ability score may be evaluated (or qualitatively measured) with respect to the average performance of the reading ability of the other children of his age or class. Thus, a test provides both quantitative as well as qualitative measurement of a trait.

Although tests of general intelligence, specific aptitudes, educational achievement, and personality are designed for their own particular purposes, all them have certain basic principles in common and have been constructed by certain common procedures, they are mutually exclusive, for any combination of tests might be used in studying a specific individual or in attempting to solve a particular psychological problem, either practical or theoretical. But probably the most important use of tests has been their contribution to the analysis and description of an individual's characteristics; to the evaluation, prediction, and guidance of his education and behaviour; and to sounder determination of his vocational preparation and selection.

Emperical Angle

A test must have the characteristic of objectivity i e., it must be free from the subjective element so that there is complete interpersonal agreement among experts regarding the meaning of the items and scoring of the test. Obviously, objectivity, here, relates to two aspects of the test-objectivity of the items and objectivity of the scoring system. By objectivity of items is meant that the items should be phrased in such a manner that they are interpreted in exactly the same way by all those who are taking the test. For ensuring objectivity of terms items must have uniformity of order of presentation (that is, either ascending or descending order). By objectivity of scoring is meant that the scoring method of the test should be a standard one so that complete uniformity can be maintained when the test is scored by different experts at different times.

Test Objectivity

"The basic definition holds that a test is objective only in so far as testing operations or activities prevent distorting or obscuring processes from intervening between the tester and the events to be measured".

More precisely, we meant that on an objective test a subject can not misrepresent himself on whatever behaviours or characteristics are being measured by the test.

In physical measurement of bodily dimension rule, as height and weight are objective because subject can not change his score value easily, from what it actually is.

The testing operations or activities and test taking behaviour are such that the relation between subject and score is, determinate in the sense that conscious conation or failure of memory can not affect it.

The purpose of standardizing a test is to give it objectivity, that is, to device an instrument that, so far as possible, will be free from subjective (personal) judgments regarding the ability, skill, knowledge, trait, or potentiality to be measured and evaluated. There are several elements, or aspects, that make a test objective. These are the six elements-

(1) Everyone who administers the test does so according to a uniform and specified set of instructions.

(2) The responses to test items are uniformly scored according to specific answers, or specimen answers, provided in a manual.

(3) Norms of performance are based upon a population sample that has been scientifically selected for the purposes of the particular test.

(4) The mental activities or the personality traits to be tested are defined and specified, and the psychological rationale is given.

(5) The activities or traits to be tested have been selected on the basis of analyses of the operations or behaviours to be evaluated, upon the views of a number of experts, and upon information available from previous research.

(6) The content of the test under construction is subjected to analysis by means of established techniques of test standardization.

Objectivity in Administering and Scoring. Each psychological test is administered under a prescribed set of procedures. These instructions prepare the respondent by means of introductory and explanatory remarks. The phrasing of instructions for presentation of each part (or at times, each item) is prescribed and time limits, if any, are set. Instructions are provided as to when directions should or should not be repeated, when encouragement should be offered by the examiner or silence maintained, and when questions from the examinee should not be answered.

A key provided with the test, is used to score the responses; or as in the case of the Stanford Binet and the Wechsler scales, the scoring criteria are defined, specified, and illustrated so the subjective judgements of individual examiners do not influence or are reduced to minimum. An objective test provides uniformity in the scoring of responses and results found by one competent examiner are comparable with those obtained by others.

The most objective kind of scoring is that of group tests, graded by hands with a stencil or by an electronic machine. The hand stencil can be used by a clerk who knows nothing about psychological testing, but he must be able to count correctly. The scoring electronic machine requires a skilled operator, but he also knows nothing about testing. Recently the scoring is done by the computer, by feeding the examinee responses and then the answer key of correct responses.

Test-objectivity and Test-validity

Test-objectivity referers to a relation between subject and score, while validity is an empirical relation between test scores criterion test scores.

Though the two concepts – objectivity and validity are easily confused, while there is no relation between them. The validity is the characteristics related to the constant error and indicate the truthfulness or purposiveness of test scores. The objectivity is the characteristics related to the personal error and indicate the relation between administring, scoring activities and scores. The measurement can still be invalid if uncorrelated with a validating criterion. Similarly, a test can be valid though the test subjective. The subjective test can be a valid test. Both these characteristics of a test are independent to each other.

Test-objectivity and Test-reliability

The objectivity of a test concerns with relation with the subject operations and test scores. It is a measure of personal error. The reliability of a test is the consistence of test scores or true score. The reliability indicates the extent of variable error. The error may be due to the subjects operations of administration and scoring. Thus, objectivity is related to personal error.

Advantages : The following are the main advantages of test-objectivity.

(1) The objectivity and validity are not necessarily related, but test objectivity may often increase the probability of test validity.

(2) The objectivity of test minimises the personal errors or subject operational errors in administering and scoring.

(3) The objectivity contributes to the consistency of scores or reliability of the test. These characteristics are inter related to each other.

(4) Test objectivity also adds precision to interpretations of whatever relationships to do emerge with test validity. The interpretation is more rigorous operation which is done by the user of the test, interpretative operation which is done by the user of the test. Interpretative error is reduced by developing norms of the test. The procedure of scoring and instruction of administration are also standardized or uniform to maintain the objectivity.

(5) The objectivity depends on the type measuring instruments. The observation technique is relatively less objective, but the efforts are being made to raise its objectivity. The class room teaching or classroom interaction is being measured by observation-technique of Flanders and others are highly objective.

(6) The objective test aims at the elimination of distorting or obscuring processes between the final observer and the events he intends to study.

(7) The objective tests require agreement among observers on the numerical value assigned as score. An arrangement which naturally would be expected in accurate perception of a real event.

(8) At present, perfectly objective test are required in the area of personality measurement, as we could develop objective tests in measuring intelligence, achievement and aptitude.

The Categorisation

The educational and psychological test can be classified into different sub-categories. Ordinarily, such classification has been done keep in view the different purposes. The following are the main classifications of psychological and educational tests

Administration System

Given here is a broad classification of the psychological and educational tests done on the basis of the modes of their administration.

Speed Tests. A speed test is a test where is a time limit within which examinees must answer all the items. In these tests the test constructor evaluates the examinees on the basis of who can answer the items accurately in the quickest time. In a perfect speed test, all the items are of the same degree of difficulty. Clerical speed and accuracy test of the Differential Aptitude Test is good example of this type of test.

Power Tests. In this type of tests there is sufficient time to answer all the items. The purpose of this test is to assess the underlying ability (or power) of the examinees by allowing them sufficient time. In a perfect power test, the items are generally arranged in an order of increasing difficulty. Intelligence tests and achievement tests generally belong to this category.

Speeded Tests. In practice, there is no power test, but all the power-tests are used as speeded tests because the time limit is imposed for administering a power test. Every examinee can not reach to the last item. During the time limit (duration of administration) majority the examinees (75 percent) are able to reach the last item. The items are arranged in the difficulty order. These are known as speeded tests.

Individual Tests. These are tests which can be administered to only one person at a time. Performance tests generally belong to this category. The Kohs Block Design test, Pass Along test, and cube Construction test are some good examples.

Group Tests. These can be administered to one or more than one individual at a time. Tests requiring verbal comprehension and symbolic responses usually belong to this category are The Lorge Throndike Intelligence test, Differential Aptitude test. Mohsin General intelligence test, and the differential Aptitude test. Mohsin General Intelligence test, and the Differential Personality Scale are good examples of this category of tests.

Besides the above mentioned tests, oral tests and written tests also belong to this classification. In an oral test, the items and instruction may be orally presented to the examinees who are also required to answer them orally. In a written test, the items and instruction may be given in written form to the examinees who are required to answer them in writing. Essay type examinations belong to this sub-category.

Various Items

Psychological tests utilise different types of items. Depending upon the nature of these items tests may be divided into two categories. Essay or Free-answer tests and objective or New type tests. Both these types are formal teacher-made tests.

Essay or Free-answer Tests. Essay tests (or essay type examinations) are tests that are composed of items or questions which are intended to test an examinee's ability to organise a comprehensive answer, to recall and select important information, and to present the same logically and effectively. Since in these tests an examinee is free to write and organise the answer, they are also known as free-answer tests. The following items may be included in an essay test :

1. Discuss the role of past experience in perception.
2. What are the major goals of education ? To what extent have these goals been achieved in India ?

When an examinee is answering these questions or same other similar questions, he usually selects, recalls and organises his experiences in the manner he likes.

Objective Tests. These are tests whose items contain both the problem as well as its answer along with the distractors. The problem is known as the stem of the item. A distractor answer is the answer which is similar to the correct answer but is not actually the correct answer. The examinee is required only to indicate the correct answer. Such tests are also known as new-type tests or limited answer tests.

Attainment of Marks

Psychological and educational tests are classified on the basis of the methods of scoring. Based upon this criterion, all psychological and educational tests can be divided into two broad categories – machine-scored tests and hand-scored tests. In machine scored tests, as the name implies, items are scored mechanically by a machine. In hand-scored testes scoring is done by tallying the correct answers with the scoring key and subsequently adding the total number of correct answers one gets the raw score. In some tests, especially in aptitude tests and intelligence tests, the test constructor develops some formulae on the basis of which the raw score is further transformed into the total score. For example, the Numerical Ability test of the Differential Aptitude test developed by Bennett, Seashore and Wesman (1951) uses a formula (Right – 1/4 wrong) to convert the raw score into the total score if it is hand scored.

Besides these two general types of tests, there are some tests which have neither a hand scoring key nor a machine scoring key but need some qualitative evaluation by a subject expert. Essay tests, which are still popular today for measuring the classroom achievement of pupils, are good examples.

Arranging a Test

Tests falling under this category are of two types – standardised tests and teacher-made informal tests like oral tests, short time interviews, etc. The standardised tests are tests which have been subjected to the procedure of standardisation. The meaning of the term "standardisation" is controversial. However, it at least includes the following four basic conditions. The first condition essential for standardisation is that there must be a standard manner of giving instructions so that uniformity can be maintained in the evaluation of all those who take the test. The second condition essential for the procedure of standardisation is that there must be uniformity of scoring, and an index of fairness of correct answers through the procedure of item analysis should be available. The third condition is that reliability, validity and individuals for whom the test is intended should be explicitly mentioned. The fourth condition, which is controversial one, is that a standardised test should have norms. However, according to Cronbach (1970), a test even without norms may be called a standardised test. But a majority of psychologists favour the idea that a standardised test should have norms also. If the above four criteria are met, a test may legitimately be called a standardised test. Another category of tests is one where no explicit principles of construction are laid down but such tests are used because it has become a convention to use them. Such tests are often made by teachers for assessing classroom achievement. Oral tests and short-time interviews are examples of such tests. These are called Teacher-made informal tests.

Measurement of Basic Ideas

Tests may also be divided into several categories on the basis of the theme to be measured, such as intelligence or general intelligence test, aptitude scale, achievement test, interest test, adjustment inventory, attitude scale value test, etc.

Culture-free and Culture-fair Tests (Non-verbal test)

R. B. Cattle developed (1961) the Cattle Culture Fair Intelligence Test. The Cattle test is based on the premise that general intelligence is matter of seeing relationship in things with which we have to deal, that the ability to see the relationship can be tested with simple diagrams or pictorial material and for a test to be usable in different cultures. It is fairly universal.

The Raven's Progressive Matrices (1938-66) developed in England and used widely in the British Armed Forces during the second World War. It is no-verbal scale designed to evaluate the ability of a subject to apprehend relationship between geometric figures and designs to percieve the structure of the design in order to select the appropriate part the given alternatives for the completion of each pattern or system of relationships. This test is used in different culture. It has no influence of culture, therefore, it is known culture free test.

Resemblance of Test Items to Actual Behaviour or Experience

Achievement Test. Reviewing the types of test items, shows that the degree of resemblance between the tasks presented by the items and actual behaviour or traits to be discerned or predicted varies with the several kinds of instruments. Tests of educational achievement utilize items that are samples of acquired or developed skills. These tests seek to answer such question as : How much information has the testee acquired in Indian history of a given period ? How well can he perform arithmetical processes of a certain level of difficulty ? How much does he know about punctuation or grammatical usage ? In other words, educational achievement tests measure directly that which they are intended to represent.

Aptitude Test. This is true, also, of some aptitude tests as, for example, those in music that measure the several forms of sensory acuity, those in comprehension of mechanical principles and those in law that present cases and problems of the sort studied in law schools. On the other hand, tests of spatial perception, speed and accuracy of eye-hand movements are indirect measures of some aspects of mechanical aptitude, since they are intended to provide signs or symptoms of a general type of functioning, rather than direct measures of an activity for which persons are being selected by means of the test.

Tests of General Intelligence. Tests of general intelligence, with a few exceptions, are concerned with the forms, complexity, level of difficulty, quality, and at times, rate of mental activity, rather than with the specific content. When, for example, an author of an intelligence test uses problems in similarities and differences, or synonyms-antonyms, he is not concerned primarily with the particular objects or words being compared. What he wishes to test are the mental processes involved in teaching a correct answer. When an author decides to include rote or logical memory in his test, the particular series of digits or words (whether in a disconnected series or in a meaningful sentence) are unimportant as long as they meet certain elementary conditions, such as length and familiarity. What he wants to measure is "memory span", or "immediate recall", since this form of mental functioning is regarded as significant in the more general aspects of intelligence.

The items in a sub-test of general information, when included in tests of intelligence, are not selected because they are most worth knowing or deserving of more attention than others are. They are chosen in order to provide a measure of an individual's range of intellectual curiosity and activity and of his assimilation and retention of experiences for these aspects are among those symptomatic of intellectual level and quality. Items in arithmetical reasoning are included to obtain evidence of complex reasoning ability with the use of abstractions, rather than to find out specifically and primarily the testee's proficiency in arithmetic.

All the types of sub-tests incorporated in tests of general intelligence should be similarly viewed. The fact that specificity of content is not of primary significance can be readily determined by comparing and noting the differences among the items of several different instruments, each of which is intended to measure the same mental functions and to serve the same purposes.

Personality Inventories. Personality inventories projective tests present still different forms of content, so far as correspondence with actuality is concerned. Inventories consist of verbalizations of a variety of behavioural situations or of conditions experienced. Thus, they are representations of actual behaviours; but they are as close to actual behaviour and experience as can be approached without observing a person in the behavioural situations themselves. In projective tests, the closeness or remoteness of content materials varies with each instrument.

Thematic Apperception Test. The pictures presented in this test are intentionally ambiguous. They are not designed to represent situations that might have been experienced by many persons taking the test. For example, one picture shows a young boy resting his head on his hands, looking at a violin lying on the table. Many of the T.A.T. pictures present situations which, if taken literally, are remote from actual experiences of most persons; others are thoroughly ambiguous, or even products of fantasy. The purpose of these pictures is not to offer situations representative of those actually experienced by testes but, rather, to present a variety of situations wherein each individual can impose his own interpretations. As a matter of fact, some of the projective tests portray animals rather than persons, the assumption being that the testee will more readily respond to animal pictures than to those of humans in these situations. Then, by contrast, the Michigan Picture Test, for children, and the Symonds Picture-Study Test, for adolescents, represent a number of situations common to these age groups, the Michigan being more specific in its representation than the Symonds. The purpose of both is to elicit such responses to each situation as will reveal attitudes toward, feelings about, and values concerning persons, groups, and institutions in the environment.

Rorschach Inkblot Test. By contrast with all others thus far mentioned, utilizes content materials that are completely unrepresentational. Inkblots are ordinarily not encountered in learning situations. They provide unfamiliar visual percepts upon which the respondent exercises his imagination ; and the products of his imagination are analyzed for evidence of his personality characteristics.

In discussing and briefly illustrating the degree of similarity of test content to the actualities of learning, behaviour and personality traits, the purpose is to demonstrate the several methods of obtaining psychological information, each depending upon the traits or functions to be assessed and upon the objectives to be served by each instrument.

Measurement of Common Issues

Science is a kind of social institution. Its scientific value lies in meaningfully communicating the observations of events or individuals to other persons. It is towards this end the measurement, which is a sort of quantitative description of events or individuals, makes a significant contribution. As a matter of fact, the progress of any discipline is today judged by the extent to which it has been able to make a quantitative description (i.e. measurement) of its subject matter. The reason why we attach such importance to measurement is that it allows extremely accurate and objective quantitative description of events. In fact, accuracy and objectivity, are its two principal advantages.

Despite the fact that measurement is the heart of the social sciences. It has certain basic problems, which social scientists need to look into. Measurement would not be of much importance till these difficulties have been moved. Some of these problems are enumerated below.

Overlapping of Behaviours in Measurement. Measurement in psychology and education is indirect; the traits or characteristics are measured with help of behaviours. The human behaviours are limited, but all the human traits and characteristics are measured with these limited set of behaviours. A set of behaviours of homogeneous nature is used to measure a specific trait or variable. No single behaviour is related to one trait, it relates to more than one trait at a time. It means that same items are used in different tests, to measure different traits. The items of a test partially measures the trait for which the test has been designed and partially measures some other traits. Therefore no psychological test is perfectly valid.

Final Definition of a Trait. There is no final test for measuring any trait. There are several tests have been constructed for measuring the same trait, because psychological traits can not be defined comprehensively or universally. There are several definitions and theories of intelligence and personality traits. The test is designed in the light of its definition stated or adopted by the designer. All definitions can not be considered simultaneously in designing, test for measuring a psychological trait. It is said that intelligence means, what intelligence means ?, what intelligence tests measure ?

Indirectness of Measurement. Most psychological and educational measurements are indirect. This is because most psychological and educational variable cannot be observed and studied directly. For example, suppose a teacher wants to measure the intelligence of students of a particular class. As intelligence cannot be directly seen, touched, or experienced, the teacher has to depend upon measures which include a sample of behaviours representative of an intelligent act. Such a sample however may itself suffer from a number of limitations. For example, these measures may not be objective and truly representative of the actual behaviour being measured. In such a situation, measurement of any trait or variable itself becomes a source of perpetual difficulty.

Incompleteness of Measurement. Psychological and educational measures are generally incomplete, and, therefore, the measurement of any psychological or educational variable is also incomplete. For example, when an investigator is assessing the attitude towards co-education, he is required to construct a scale in which a number of samples of behaviour expressing such an attitude need to be incorporated. This number has no limit. Any attempt, therefore, to measure such an attitude would be partial and incomplete. In such a situation measurement will be dubious and tend to create a misleading index of attitude.

Relativity of Measurement. Psychological and educational measurements are relative. This is also true of sociological measurement. The concept of relativity in measurement can be explained through an example. Suppose Mohan, a student of class X was given two tests-a test of arithmetical knowledge and a test of the English language. Let us further suppose that he answered correctly 60% of the items in the English language test but could not answer even a single item on the arithmetic test. On the basis of such a measurement can we say that Mohan's performance in the English language test was good. The answer obviously can not be given with all certainty. 60% of the items answered by Mohan may be the percentage for even those students of the class who were much below the average. On the other hand, the test of English language may have been a very difficult test and only Mohan and nobody else might have answered 60% of the items correctly. Thus the measurement is not absolute but relative and we cannot draw any inference from the measurement of Mohan's performance unless it is compared with the reference group, that is, with other members of the class. Likewise, can we say, on the basis of his performance on the arithmetical knowledge test, that Mohan has no knowledge of arithmetical operation. We cannot say so because the obtained zero in arithmetical knowledge test does not reflect the absence of arithmetical knowledge. Nothing can be definitely said until a comparison with other members of the class is done. All these measurements are, therefore, relative and must be carefully dealt with if measurement is to be meaningful and objective.

Errors in Measurement. Measurement in the physical sciences, as well as in the behavioural sciences, is never pure. It contains some uncontrolled factors, which produce gross errors. Suppose a weighing machine determines a woman's weight to be 50 kg. This weight might not be her pure weight. There may be some minor mechanical troubles in the machine itself so that her weight is inflated; it may be that she has just taken her meal; it may be that she is pregnant; there may be other factors present in the physical environment. All these sources of error might inflate or reduce her actual weight. Similar sources of error run into psychological, educational and sociological measurement. When we are measuring the intelligence of a child with the help of an intelligence test, there can be several such factors which tend either to decrease or increase his actual score. For example, the child might be nervous; he might have been distracted by the sound of an aeroplane; he might not have understood the meaning of the items clearly; and so on. All these sources of errors in measurement create problems which adversely affect the scientific value of measurement.

Further Measurement

Certainly, our present ability truly to measure many of the attributes of persons that appear to be relevant and important for making decisions about them and planning actions with respect to them leaves much to be desired. However, while recognizing this fact we must also appreciate that enormous strides have been made since 1900 toward more objective and more accurate appraisals of human beings. The fact that we are limited in some directions does not lessen the value of increased precision wherever such increased precision has been achieved. While keeping a critical eye upon the limitations of measurement procedures, we should still use them for all they are worth in increasing the accuracy of our information about students, employees, or clients.

Though instruments for psychological and educational measurement have proliferated, and their use has become widespread through the United States, and to a somewhat lesser extent in many other countries, the enterprise of measuring the abilities and attributes of man has come in for a good deal of criticism from a variety of sources. Educational philosophers, humanists, scholars in certain disciplines, and even politicians have voiced hostility and concern. In part, the criticisms have been directed at the basic logic of measurement of man. These criticisms have focused on the limitations that we have just been discussing as well as other problems concerning the equivalence of units and scores. In part, however, the criticisms have been directed at the effects that the measurement procedures have had upon our society, and especially upon our schools. The following types of criticisms have been made

1. Standardized measurement procedures have fostered undemocratic attitudes and methods. An early focus of this criticism was on the use of tests of intelligence or achievement to form homogeneous classroom groups. More recently, concern has centered on the appropriateness of the tests and norms for use with socially deprived and minority groups.
2. It has been contended that standardized tests have tended to freeze school curricula and to prevent experiment and change, in that the standardized educational tests have typically lagged behind the progress of educational thought and practice.
3. The limited scope of many standardized tests has been pointed out, and it has been indicated that they appraise only a part of the changes in children that schools should be interested in producing.
4. Achievement tests have been alleged to reward the person who has partial or superficial knowledge and to penalize the person who is really expert in the subject, since the ablest student is said to see qualifications and exceptions to the formulation of the item that make him question the generally accepted answer.

5. Psychological tests (especially those that delve into personality and temperament) have been viewed as an unwarranted invasion of individual privacy. They are used to delve into personal matters that may be of no legitimate concern to the inquirer, especially if he uses the information for selfish and personal ends.

There has been at least a germ of truth in each of these criticisms. Some of them we shall consider in more detail in later chapters. The criticisms make it clear that there are hazards and pitfalls in an attempt to measure man. The hazards lie partly in poor technique and partly in misuse of the information that the techniques provide. Any new tool presents problems. We have to know how to sharpen it and how to use it.

It cannot be too much emphasized that measurement at best provides only information, not judgment. A test will yield only a score, not the conclusion to be drawn from that score. The information provided in a test score is not a substitute for insight. The information is the raw material with which insight must work in the clinic, in the classroom, and in the research laboratory. Experience, training, and basic sagacity must provide the insight that will take the available data about an individual or group, know how much faith to place in them and what meaning to give them, and draw from them a sound conclusion or plan for action.

Furthermore, it should be emphasized that the information that any measurement procedure gives is limited. It is limited by the nature of the measurement instrument itself. An intelligence test given to an emotionally disturbed and resistant child may give a very inadequate picture of what that same child could do if the disturbing influences were removed and the resistance overcome.

QUESTIONS

1. "Measurement became essential to study of science. Mathematics is a universal language which is utilized by any science to communicate objectivity through measurement". Discuss this statement.

2. "The path of science is paved with achievements of the allegedly Unachievable"- Charles Spearman. Elaborate this statement with reference to psychology.
3. Define the term Measurement and differentiate with evaluation. Enumerate its main characteristics.
4. Differentiate between physical science measurement and behavioural sciences measurement. Illustrate your answer with examples.
5. Explain the term 'Tasks of Measurement'. Enumerate the tests of measurement and describe them in detail.
6. Explain the 'Concept of Trait' and differentiate with abilities. Enumerate the methods of measurement.
7. Define 'Psychological Test'. Explain objectivity as characteristic of a test. Differentiate it with validity and reliability of a test. Indicate the advantages of objectivity.
8. Give a classification of tests, with reference to different purposes.
9. Indicate the resemblance of test items to actual behaviour or experience with reference to different type of tests—achievement, aptitude, intelligence and personality inventories.
10. Write short notes on the following—
    (a) General problems of measurement.
    (b) An appraisal of psychological and educational measurement.
    (c) Speeded test and power test.
    (d) Culture fair and culture free tests.
    (e) Overlapping of behaviours in measurement.

4

Evolution and Growth

It has been the curiosity of man since the very beginning of human history to know about objects and persons around him. To 'know' an object or a person really means to be able to describe him accurately and comprehensively. But any description of an object or phenomenon or person is selective. We can not describe everything about a phenomenon of a person, because every phenomenon is multi-dimensional or has several attributes which are relevant to understand and describe the phenomenon or a person. A phenomenon of a person can not be measured as such it is the major limitation of measurement but we can measure the characteristics of a person or a phenomenon.

Various Types

The evaluation process is both formal and informal and continuous to 'know' the objects and persons. On the basis of evaluation we can describe roughly and qualitatively. The evaluation process does not satisfy the curiosity of man. He wants to make the description more precise and quantitative which involves the process of measurement. It is the later development of human history. In the present chapter "Development of Measurement' has been summarized in the following manner.

Periodical Development

A_1-The Beginning of Psychological Measurement.
A_2-Development in the Nineteenth Century.
A_3-Development in the Twentieth Century.

Topical Development

B_1-Beginning of Experimental Psychology.
B_2-Early Study of Individual Differences.
B_3-Clinical Study of Deviates.
B_4-Early Educational Measurement.

Contributions of Great Psychometricians

C_1-Francis Galton's Contribution.
C_2-Alfred Binet's Contribution.

Development of Various Type Tests

D_1-Individual test,
D_2-Group test,
D_3-Performance test,
D_4-Aptitude test,
D_5-Interest inventories,
D_6-Test Batteries,
D_7-Multifactor tests,
D_8-Personality tests,
D_9-Rating scales,
D_{10}-Projective tests,

Development of Psychological Tests in India

Main Land Marks of Measurement: The review of the literature reveals the following land marks on the way of development of Measurement. In 1850 psychology was considered as independent Science.

Timebound Development

The periodical development has been classified into the three periods-The beginning, nineteenth and twentieth century.

Beginnings of Psychological Measurement : Psychology in 1850 was still in large measure a part of philosophy. Courses dealing with man and his actions presented under the title "Moral Philosophy," and discussed in an armchair fashion the nature of the Mind and the Soul. Psychology was almost entirely non-experimental, and the idea that one could measure in quantitative terms the speed of responding, the amount of forgetting, or the level of intelligence would have been received in most quartets with hostility or more probably, ignored as not worthy of rebuttal. The nearest approaches to psychological measurement were a few scattered experiments by physicists and physiologists on the measurement of the ability to make sensory discriminations and the speed of simple elementary responses.

By 1900 psychology had felt the impact of the physical and biological sciences and was striving mightily to become a science itself. It was shaking off the ties that bound it to philosophy and forming new alliances with the biological sciences. It had adopted the experimental method and was measurement-conscious. The basic tool of experimentation is measurement, and psychology was expanding its measurement techniques in all directions. The record since 1900 is the record of the attempt to expand and adapt measurement techniques to cover all aspects of human behaviour.

Three main streams combined to yield the vigorous measurement movement in psychology and its spread through education. Some of the flavour and some of the emphasis have come from each stream. These were-

(1) The physiological and experimental psychology that had its main growth in Germany in the nineteenth century.
(2) Darwinian biology, and
(3) The clinical concern for the maladjusted and underdeveloped individual.

Measurement has its root in both biological and behavioural sciences. In biological sciences, measurement has a long history but the history of psychological and educational measurement dates back to only 1850. Prior to 1850, psychology was not considered to be an independent science but only a branch of philosophy. Any attempt to measure human behaviour through experiments was ridiculed by philosophers. According to Kant, measuring human behaviour was useless because human reactions were such that could not be observed and measured directly. But beginning with 1850, psychology began to shake off this old relation with philosophy and started forming a new alliance with the biological sciences. The concepts that were discovered in the fields of physics, chemistry, and biology were proving to be of immense help in measuring human characteristics such as forgetfulness, intelligence, speed of responding, sensation, perception, etc. Biologists and physicists were pioneers in conducting experiments for measuring human behaviour. Influenced by their experiments, psychology started getting measurement-conscious and the movement of measurement was being spread through experimentation and demonstrations. As a matter of fact, the history of psychological and educational measurement during the period 1850 to 1900 was nourished by three major influences, namely, psychophysics, Darwinian biology and clinical practices.

Development in the Nineteenth Century : Although the fact that persons differ in intellectual and other psychological characteristics had been apparent to observers for many centuries, it was only about a hundred years ago that these differences were first studied scientifically and subjected to measurement and objective evaluation.

Francis Galton (1822-1911) was the first scientist to undertake systematic and statistical investigations of individual difference. He was preceded, before the middle of the nineteenth century, by other men who are important in the history of psychology; but these men, who belonged to one of two groups, were not concerned with devising means of measuring individual differences. Some were non-experimental, speculative psychologists who were concerned largely with problems of the dualism of mind and matter, the nature of ideas, intellectual "faculties," and classical associationism. Others, through experimentally oriented, directed their attention to general problems and theories rather than to variations and differences in human abilities.

Among these was Ernst Heinrich Weber (1795-1878), educated as an anatomist and physiologist, who experimented on weight discrimination, vision, hearing, and the "two-point threshold" of the skin. He is best remembered for his quantitative experimental approach to psychological problems and for what we know as Weber's law. Gustav Theodor Fechner (1801-87), who started his career in physics and chemistry, was basically concerned with the application of the exact methods of the natural sciences to the study of man's "inner world," that is, the relations of mental processes to physical phenomena. Johannes Miller (1801-58), a professor of physiology, was especially interested in the physiology of the senses and in reflex action. In his significant experiments in space perception, he attempted to reconcile the opposed theories of " nativism" versus "empiricism." William Hamilton (1788-1856) and James Mill (1773-1836) were concerned with reformulating more completely and rigorously the classical association theory.

One of the most significant writers in psychology at mid-nineteenth century was Alexander Bain (1818-1903), who was professor of Logic, Mental Philosophy, and English Literature in

Aberdeen University. His two most distinguished works were The Senses and the Intellect (1855) and The Emotions and the Will (1859). Bain's approach was principally through physiology; he utilized, organized, and interpreted findings of the German experimentalists in a systematic restatement of associationism. Perhaps Bain's most important contribution was his pioneering effort to contain the entire range of human experience within a system of psychology.

These several examples will suffice to indicate the major interests of nineteenth-century psychologists, from which the pioneers in psychological testing had to break away. Yet the work of these early psychologists did significantly influence the types of testing first used in experimental work on individual differences.

The nineteenth century, particularly the second half, had witnessed the development of a number of scientific tools and innovations in physics and chemistry and scientists were of the opinion that those physical methods could also be successfully tried in measuring psychological properties. As a result, psychophysics was born and experimental psychologists began to study the relationship between physical stimulus such as the intensity of light or sound and the experiences or sensations produced by these stimuli. Many new experimental techniques of measurement followed these psychophysical experimentations.

Besides psychophysical methods, some early physiologists were also influencing the development of psychological measurement. These physiologists were mainly interested in measuring the process of seeing, hearing, speed of conduction, etc. As a result, the first laboratory for studying psychological reactions was established in (1879) by Wilhelm Wundt at the University of Leipzig. Although the laboratory was established for measuring and studying psychological reactions. Wundt and his disciples mostly concentrated upon physiological reactions only. Gradually, however, this laboratory flourished and developed into an excellent centre for the measurement of human reactions and invited the attention of several experimenters from abroad too.

Darwin's theory of evolution also provided a big impetus to the growth of psychological measurement. Although it originated in biology, it influenced the thinking of many scientists working in the field of psychology too. One of the basic notions of the theory of evolution was that members of the same species are not alike, that is, individual differences exist among members of a species.

Sir Francis Galton, a half-cousin of Charles Darwin, was quick to pick up the idea of individual difference and gathered data on the individual differences of physical and psychological characteristics. He wanted to measure the basic individual differences among human beings and for this he singled out "human ability" as a possible dimension of study and in doing so laid the foundation stone of that branch of psychology which is today known as psychometrics. Later, Karl Pearson developed several sophisticated techniques for statistically analysing the data on individual differences of human ability, which provided a good stream for psychological measurement. The product-moment method of computing the correlation coefficient was one such technique.

Apart from the above two main streams of psychological measurement, clinical studies growing out of medicine, psychiatry and social welfare institutions in western countries also provided immense impetus for the growth of measurement. Clinical interest in the feeble-minded, insane and misfit was first evoked about 1990 in France. Psychologists working there were deeply interested in developing tests and instruments which could measure maladjustment and locate the possible reason for insanity. Alfred Binet in (1905) gathered data based upon the intelligence of school-going children in this context, which were later on manifested in terms of the development of different intelligence scales.

Development in the Twentieth Century : The first 60 years of the twentieth century may conveniently be divided into four equal parts, so far as the recent history of psychological and educational measurement is concerned. We may designate the period from 1900 to 1915 the pioneering phase. This was the period of exploration and initial development of methods. It saw the emergence of the first Binet intelligence scales and their American revisions. Standardized achievement tests in different subjects began to appear, exemplified by Stone's arithmetic tests, Buckingham's spelling tests, and Trabue's language tests. Thorndike developed his first handwriting scale. Otis and others were initiating work on group tests of intelligence.

The next 15 years, 1915 to 1930, can perhaps be called the "boon" period in test development. The pioneers had shown the way, and in the hands of enthusiastic followers tests multiplied like rabbits. Standardized tests were developed for all the school skills and for the content areas of the school programme.

Achievement batteries made their appearance, Starting with Army Alpha of World-War I, group intelligence tests were produced in great numbers. Also starting with a wartime product, the Woodwerth Personal Data Sheet, a whole line of personality questionnaires and inventories came into being.

The rapid development of testing instruments and methods was pushed by a group of enthusiasts. They were converts who had "gotten the word." Their enthusiasm was contagious and extended not only to the production of tests but also to their use. Tests of intelligence and achievement were administered widely and some what indiscriminately. Test results were often accepted unhesitatingly and uncritically and served as the basis for a variety of frequently unjustified judgements and actions with respects to individuals. In the expansive flood of enthusiasm for objective measurement, some enthusiasts were not inclined to be critical of their instruments or the interpretation of results from them. Many sins were committed in the name of measurement by uncritical test users.

The critical attack had the healthy effect of forcing the test enthusiasts themselves to become more critical of their assumptions and procedures and to broaden their approach to the whole problem of psychological and educational appraisal. From about 1930 to 1945 may be considered a period of critical appraisal, devoted to taking stock, broadening techniques and delimiting interpretations it was a period in which the centre of attention shifted from measuring a limited range of academic skills to "evaluating" achievement of the whole range of educational objectives. It was a period in which the holistic, global projective methods of personality appraisal came to the fore.

It is difficult to view with any perspective at all events that have taken place as recently as the 1950's. History may eventually characterize the period quite differently than do we, standing so close to it. However, we will venture to predict that the period from 1945 to 1960 will be characterized as the period of test batteries and testing programmes. Partly as a result of their successful use in World War II, integrated aptitude batteries for educational and personnel use multiplied during this period. And the large scale external testing programmes, such as those administered by the College Entrance Examination Board, though stemming from much earlier in the century, expanded in size and multiplied in numbers at a striking rate. We have experienced a second boon period-not so much in test development and construction, as in test administration and use. The mid-twentieth century is a period in which standardized testing is a widely experienced and widely accepted phenomenon of our American culture.

Finally, we may sense in the past few years the swing to a second cycle of criticism. In an age of computerized technology, when an individual is identified by number-social security number, draft board number, student number-rather than by name, there is a resurgence of reaction against quantification and the use of numbers to express psychological assessments. Subscribing to an egalitarian philosophy, which is sometimes carried to the extreme of denying the existence of individual differences, many thoughtful people are concerned over the social implications of testing programmes for our society.

Under these circumstances it is particularly important that construction, use, and interpretation of these instruments be well understood by teachers, guidance workers, and psychologists for whom they are daily tools of the trade. It is also important that the phenomenon of standardized testing be understood by the citizens who are exposed to it in their search for employment for themselves or education for their children. Therefore, let us try at this point to formulate a philosophy or measurement that will take into account the lessons of the past, and will serve to guide our attack on measurement problems and our use of measurement techniques in the years ahead.

The beginning of the twentieth century was marked by a tremendous growth of psychological and educational tests, and the development of measurement tools and techniques started almost on a war footing. The first psychological test to appear was the Binet-Simon Intelligence Scale. It proved to be one of the most promising instruments for measuring the intelligence of children. Later on its several American revisions appeared. Besides this, several other achievement tests including the famous Thorndike Handwriting Scale appeared. In 1918, Woodworth's Personal Data Sheet appeared, which was the first personality inventory. During the two World Wars the two well known tests, the Army Alpha test and the Army Beta test were developed. Several group intelligence tests and achievement tests also made their appearances. The outcome of all these enthusiastic developments in the sphere of psychological tests was a rapid development of psychological and educational measurements. During the last 30 years or so, a different trend has become evident. Much emphasis is now being placed upon the methodology of development and use of measurement in almost all branches of psychology. Newer methods of development of psychological and educational tests have become the main centre of interest for psychologists. They are frequently found criticising the old methods and placing arguments for the adaptation of a new method. This methodology is known as the psychometric theory which mainly includes the basic principles of test construction.

Development in a Particular Manner

Beginnings of Experimental Psychology: The modern scientific era was first ushered into the physical sciences in the seventeenth and eighteenth centuries. Scientific interest and method soon spread over to the biological sciences, and by the early nineteenth century experimental physiology was a centre of active research interest in the experimental laboratories in Germany and other European countries. Experimental physiologists became interested in the operation of the senses, studying intensively seeing, hearing, and the other senses. Physiologists also became interested in measuring the speed of simple motor responses.

In 1879 the first laboratory for experimental psychology was established Wilhelm Wundt at Leipzig. Early experimental psychologists were interested in many of the same measurements that had concerned the physiologists. These were measures of seeing, hearing, feeling, and speed of response. But gradually they extended their concern to more clearly psychological matters, such as measurement of perceptual span-the amount that the individual can "take in" at once, of rate of learning, of the timing of complex mental tasks, and so forth.

One area of particular interest for its contribution to the broad field of psychological and educational measurement was that known as psychophysics. The experimental psychologist was much interested in exploring the relationship between physical stimulus intensities, for example, of light wave or of sound wave, and the experienced intensity of the resulting sensation. The designing of effective experimental procedures for studying these problems gave rise to a set of techniques that have proved adaptable to a wide range of problems of psychological measurement.

From experimental psychology came a legacy of respect for careful experimental method and precision of technique, a number of experimental designs, and statistical techniques that could be carried over to more general psychological and educational measurement problems.

Early Study of Individual Differences : A second stream contributing to psychological measurement was Darwinian biology. In 1859 Darwin brought out his Origin of Species. The basic concern in Darwin's work was with variation among the members of a species, that is, individual differences. Darwin's work was followed up in England and applied to distinctively human affairs, particularly by Sir Francis Galton. Whereas German psychology had focused on finding the general facts true of all people, Galton became interested primarily in the differences among people. Stimulated by Darwin to study the inheritance of traits, he gathered data both on physical and on psychological characteristics. The study of these individual differences required better statistical tools, and the British group, under the leadership of Karl Pearson, developed improved techniques for analyzing and describing the patterns of individual differences.

These, then, were the two main contributions of the British group to the growth of psychological measurement; a deep concern for studying the differences among people as interesting and significant facts and the invention of appropriate statistical techniques and tools for carrying out this study.

Clinical Study of Deviates : During this same period, a third stream was gathering strength. This was concern for the individual who was not functioning successfully. Humanitarian concern for the insane, the feebleminded, and the general misfit led in the nineteenth century to active research and investigation aimed toward understanding their condition and improving their lot. This clinical interest in the maladjusted individual was particularly strong in France, and it was here that it bore fruit for the field of measurement. As psychologists worked with these unfortunate deviates, the need became more and more apparent for some uniform way of expressing the degree of their defect, particularly in the mental sphere. It was in this context of concern for the child who was not getting along in school that Binet and his colleagues developed the series of intellectual tasks that ultimately grew into the whole array of measures of intelligence.

Early Educational Testing : The appraisal of educational achievement in the United States before 1850 had relied very largely upon oral examination.

During the latter half of the nineteenth century, oral examinations by boards of visitors were replaced by set written examinations as a basis for promotion or admission to an academy or college. Outside examination in turn yielded to evaluation by the classroom teacher. Whether carried out by an outside examiner or by a teacher, however, the technique was that of the essay examination, in which a pupil responded in his own words to a question set by the examiner.

The written examination had advantages over the oral examination of (1) presenting the same tasks to each member of the group and (2) letting each pupil work for the full examination period. However, though the task was made uniform, at least for the members of a given class, appraisal of each individual's response to the task remained highly subjective, depending upon the standards and prejudices of the particular scorer. Only since 1900 has there been any general development of objectively scored tests in which a pre-established key can be routinely and uniformly applied to the responses made by each pupil, Only since 1900 has the idea emerged of a general norm of performance for an age or grade, with which the performance by any class or any individual may be compared.

Great Contributions

Francis Galton's Contributions : It is clear from the foregoing brief account that until the last quarter of the nineteenth century there was scant recognition of individual differences as a subject worthy of study and research by psychologists. This difference, no doubt, retarded the development of psychological tests that would be necessary for their measurement. Galton, though interested in and influenced by the psychological work of his predecessors and contemporaries, was even more strongly influenced by the development of the biological sciences then ascendant among British scientists. Consequently, his efforts were devoted largely to investigations of individual differences more from biological interests than from psychological. In the introduction to his Inquiries into Human Faculty (1883), he states,

"My general object has been to take note of the varied hereditary faculties of different men, and of the great differences in different families and races, to learn how far history may have shown the practicability of supplanting inefficient human stock by better strains, and to consider whether it might not be our duty to do so by such efforts as may be reasonable, thus exerting overselves to further the ends of evolution more rapidly and with less distress than if events were left to their own course."

This quotation is evidence of Galton's sustained interest in developing a science of genetics and eugenics. It also indicates a problem with which psychologists have since been concerned-the roles of heredity and environment (or, as Galton named them, "nature and nurture") in the development of man's intelligence. For the study of this problem, objective psychological tests have been indispensable.

Prior to the appearance of the volume mentioned above, Galton had published the results of his earlier studies in Hereditary Genius (1869), and English Men of Science : Their Nurture (1874). His Inquiries into Human Faculty was followed by Natural Inheritance (1889) and Noteworthy Families (1906), the last with Schuster. In addition to these larger works published during this period of about forty years, Galton produced numerous articles on the general subjects indicated by the titles of his book. At the same time, his statistical techniques for the analysis of data provided the basis for the elaborated, extended, and refined statistical methods used by such men as Karl Pearson, British biometrician, Charles Spearman, British psychologist who was one of the earliest and most noteworthy men to engage in the analysis of human abilities.

Galton not only stimulated investigations of individual differences; he also strongly influenced the direction of the experimental efforts to measure intelligence by means of tests of imagery and sensory discrimination. He devised a test for the measurement of the delicacy of weight discrimination; he invented what is now known as the Galton whistle for measuring sensitivity to high tones. In addition, he suggested devices for testing visual and auditory discriminations, reaction time, and muscular strength.

Galton assumed, apparently that the simpler and measurable sensory capacities should be significantly correlated with intelligence. That this was his hypothesis is shown by the fact that as subjects for study he selected persons of extreme differences in mental ability in order to learn whether their differences in sensory discrimination corresponded with the known differences in their mental abilities. Although it has long since been learned that sensory and sensory-motor tests have very little value for the study of the higher and more complex processes called intelligence, Galton's work, nevertheless did strongly affect the course taken by test experimenters until about 1900, when the influence of Alfred Binet, the French psychologist, was felt.

Binet's Contributions : It is impossible in a short space to present a full review and evaluation of the character, range, and importance of Alfred Binet's contributions to individual psychology. An attempt will be made, however, to indicate his supreme importance in the field of mental measurements and individual differences.

Young has quite properly said that "the contribution of Alfred Binet stands supreme for its general originality and the fact that he synthesized the growing movement into his now well-known scale." Dinet and his collaborators objected to the types of psychological testing which followed Galton's work, on the ground that they were too simple in nature and would contribute little to the understanding of differences in the complex and higher mental processes; for it is in these higher processess that individual differences are most marked, and it is these which distinguish individuals most significantly and characteristically in daily activity, whereas it is in the simpler sensory and motor processes that persons differ least. Binet was quite ready to admit that the simpler processes lent themselves to more precise measurement and, therefore, yielded more nearly constant results. Yet his interests were strongest in individuals rather than in the study of sensations or ideas. Thus he was ready to sacrifice the greater quantitative precision of sensory-motor tests in order to obtain a more nearly accurate study of the integrated mentality of the individual. He argued that in the measurement of the higher functions, the greatest precision, though desirable, was not as essential as in measuring the simpler functions, because of the very fact that individual differences are more marked in the former. Binet made it clear, however, that his proposed scale would not measure in a physical sense, in the same way, for example, that a line is measured. It would, however, yield "a classification, a hierarchy among diverse intelligences; and for the necessities of practice this classification is equivalent to a measure." He and his collaborators were interested, consequently, in establishing the extent and nature of variation of the mental processes from one individual to another and in determination of the inter relations of the various processes within the individual. Binet and Henri proposed, therefore, to study the following function : memory, the nature of mental images, imagination, attention, comprehension, suggestability aesthetic feeling or appreciation, moral sentiments, muscular strength and strength of will power, motor skill and visual judgement. They believed 'faculties' which differ much from one individual to another.

Binet had an opportunity to apply his principles with regard to differentiating of individuals and to make a great contribution to study of individual differences in mental ability. The French Minister of Public Instruction appointed a commission to recommend means of educating subnormal children in the schools of Paris because these children were unable to profit from regular instruction. It was to meet this problem that the first intelligence scale was constructed by Binet-Simon scale in 1905. It measures the mentality of children. This principle is that we may identify differences in mental development-in degree of brightness or dullness with reference to average capacities of children of various ages. This is Binet's final contribution to the field of mental measurement revised in 1911 and he died in the same year.

In 1911 he published his standardization of Binet's 1908 revision, with which he had been acquainted since 1909. At that time, he was director of the laboratory of psychology at the Vineland (New Jersey) Training School for Feeble-minded children.

In 1937, a revised and much improved edition in two forms was published in collaboration with M.E. Merrill. The last edition appeared in 1960, again under the co-authorship of Terman and Merrill, although Terman had died in December 1956. The 1916 and 1937 editions have been widely used in clinics schools and other agencies, and the 1960 edition, it is reasonable to assume, will also wide publicity in area of mental measurement.

Various Tests Developed

Individual Tests : It has been discussed under heading of Binet's contribution that he developed an intelligence test in 1905 which is administered individually. One subject can be tested at time. The details of its development has already been discussed at length.

Group Tests : Shortly after 1916, the most significant occurrence in psychological testing was the development of group tests. The

Binet and its several revisions are administered to each person single, the length of time required varying with the age, brightness, and responsiveness of the individual being tested. As a result, it is costly in time and money to test large numbers of persons one by one, and in some instances it is impossible to do so. Therefore, if many people are to be tested at once, as is the case in the schools and the armed forces, a group test will have distinct advantages if it yields sufficiently accurate and dependable results.

Psychologists had already begun to study, by group tests, some of the mental processes required in school work. So it was not a very long or entirely new step to try devising a single scale in which a variety of items, testing several mental processes, would be combined. This tendency in group testing received its greatest impetus in 1917 with the entrance of the United States into World War I. At that time the government agreed with the views of a group of psychologists that it would be desirable to examine the newly drafted men to determine their general mental capacity and vocational fitness by means of the best available psychological methods. The need was a pressing one, and a group testing method was imperative. This army problem enlisted the interests and cooperation of many psychologists, some of whom had already made contributions to the field of measurements, and some of whom were already experimenting with group methods. Pooling their efforts and resources, they emerged with the well-known army tests. Alpha and Beta, the former being verbal in content and the latter non-verbal.

With their army data, these psychologists opened up numerous fields in which group tests might be used, and at the same time gave rise to a number of controversial questions. Among these were the relative influence heredity and environment, racial and national differences, and the age at which maximum mental capacity is reached.

In the ensuing years, a large volume of research on these and other problems was published. For present purposes, it is sufficient to note that this use of tests in the army and the results achieved demonstrated the possible values of group scales and supplied the impetus for their use in other areas, especially in the schools.

There are today a large number of group tests designed for use at educational levels from kindergarten to university. Of these, some are highly reliable and have reasonably good validity whereas others do not withstand scrutiny and evaluation.

Performance Tests : Not long after the introduction of the Stanford-Binet scale, its emphasis upon language was criticized by some psychologists and educators. It was maintained that this scale, valuable though it is, needed to be supplemented by tests which do not require ability to deal with words, numbers, and abstract concepts. Accordingly, "performance tests" were developed to meet this criticism and to provide means of testing individuals with language handicaps, as well as the deaf, the blind, and others for whom an adequate rating could not be obtained with tests that depended largely on language, numbers, and abstractions.

A performance test provides a perceptual situation in which the subject manipulates items such as form boards, blocks, pictures, and disassembled, objects instead of reasoning with symbols. Some psychologists apply the term also to "pencil-and-paper" tests that utilize non-verbal materials such as printed geometric forms, pictorial representations, printed cubes, substituting digits for symbols, and the like. It seems preferable, however, to designate these simply as "non-verbal" tests because they do not involve actual manipulation of objects as do performance tests. Both types of test materials, performance and non-verbal pencil-and-paper, are now used extensively. Some scales, such as the Arthur and the Pintner-Paterson, are built entirely of performance materials; other scales combine one or both with verbal materials.

Aptitude Tests : Another type of instrument, the development of which received impetus in World War I, is the aptitude test. Each of these, unlike tests of general ability, is intended to measure an individual's ability to perform a task of a limited or specific kind, for example, clerical, mechanical, or musical aptitudes. Interest in and development of aptitude testing may be ascribed to several causes: the army's need, during World War 1, to select men for tasks requiring specific skills; the desire, in vocational guidance and personnel assignment, to find the right person for a specific job; the opposition of some educators and psychologists to what they called the "super-faculty" of general intelligence; and the belief of some of them that only specific aptitudes, such as mechanical and clerical, could be satisfactorily measured. As a matter of fact, tests of general intelligence and those of specific aptitudes do not and need not stand opposed; they are supplemental.

Aptitude tests have been developed to predict educability and performance in music and drawing in mechanical and clerical occupations, in engineering, in medicine and law, and in other areas as well. Others in this category are intended to evaluate aptitudes for the study of specific types of subject matter, such as science, foreign languages, and mathematics.

Occupational Interest Inventories : To supplement tests of aptitude and those of intelligence, several self-answering occupational preference questionnaires, or inventories, have been devised to provide information regarding an individual's interests in a variety of activities; for these, it has been found to have some relevance to and predictive value for certain broad vocational areas or for certain specific occupations.

Tests of Educational Achievement : Closely associated with the testing of aptitudes is the measurement of educational achievement and the construction of objective measures for that purpose. These are not designed primarily for prediction; instead, they are intended to measure the individual's actual learning in educational subject matter after a period of instruction. They have proved to be highly valuable in the determination of individual difficulties in learning, in the discovery of strong scholastic interests, in the discovery of special abilities or disabilities, and, in combination with other factors, in plotting the educational career of the individual child.

Educational achievement tests have other values as well; they provide objective measures of progress, as opposed to teachers ratings that may be too subjective; they permit intergroup comparisons based on a reasonably objective determination: and they facilitate experimental evaluation of varied teaching methods.

Test Batteries : During World War II many test "batteries" were constructed. Those that made use of specific 'aptitudes and subject matter knowledge- especially the former were most important. Batteries were devised for the selection and training of personnel in a great variety of assignments in the several branches of the armed forces; radio and radar operators, pilots, navigators, gunners, flight engineers, and other specialities. The development of these batteries in the armed forces stimulated research on and use of similar tests for the selection and training of personnel in civilian occupations.

Multifactor Tests : These also called "differential aptitude tests, are relatively recent developments in psychological measurement and evaluation. Interest in them has increased markedly since about

1945, although research on the subject began as early as the 1920's, when T. L. Kelley and later L. L. Thurstone published their work of factorial analysis of human abilities. Factorial analysis provided the statistical tools for the development of multifactor tests, which isolate and measure relatively "pure mental operations (factors) or "constellations" of closely related factors, rather than general intelligence or general ability. In other words, multifactor tests isolate the elements that constitute mental operations. The psychological principle upon which these instruments are based is the theory that the factors, or elements, are relatively independent of one another; hence, it was concluded that they should be measured independently.

Multifactor scales were expected to be especially valuable in educational and vocational counselling because they consist of separate tests of numerical operations, space relations, form perception, verbal reasoning, rote memory associations, and others restricted in complexity and range of mental operations. Each factor, or test, is thought to have special educational and vocational relevance and predictive value in itself, and a combination of factors is thought to have predictive value for specific areas of learning or occupations. The use of multifactor scales, therefore, would yield a "profile" of scores for each of the several factors or "constellation" of factors, rather than a general, over-all rating for the entire scale, such as those derived from the Stanford-Binet, the Wechsler, and numerous group tests.

Personality Tests : Efforts to evaluate and test non-intellectual traits of personality were apparent in the nineteenth century beginning with Gallon in 1879 and followed by Pearson who devised questionnaires and rating scales. During the last decade of that century and the first of the twentieth, word-association tests were tried out by Jung of Switzerland and Kent and Rosanoff in the United States in an effort to expose some of the deeper personality traits and, if possible, to assist in differentiating among the various mental disorders. Although word-association tests are still used today in psychological clinics and elsewhere in diagnosing personality traits, they are much less frequently employed than inventories and projective techniques.

With widespread use of individual tests of intelligence in schools, clinics, and hospitals, it became increasingly clear that in some cases an individual's performance on a test, his successes and failures, and the content and quality of his responses, were not only evidence of intellectual functioning, but were also affected, in greater or lesser degree, by non-intellectual traits of personality. The recognition of this fact, in addition to the growing interest in the scientific and clinical study of personality perse, provided the stimulus for the development of the several varieties of personality tests. Personnel problems during World War I provided impetus for their growth as well.

Today the tests are used extensively for the analysis of desirable and undesirable traits in a wide range of civilian and military occupations. In addition, psychologists employ personality tests in studies of differences between subgroups within the same general, society and of differences between various cultural, national, and racial groups.

The large current crop of personality tests now available varies in quality from those that are poorly conceived, inadequately validated, and therefore useless, to those having considerable value in the hands of competent psychologists.

Rating Scales : The earliest device employed, the rating scale, is a means of obtaining the judgments of a number of respondents with reference to a limited number of traits of a given individual. They were tried out and used during World War I, well before they were formalized and scaled both by statistical methods and by psychological analysis of personality and behaviour traits relevant to specified situations.

Typical Inventories

The first self-report, questionnaire type of personality inventory is the Personal Data Sheet, devised by R. S. Woodworth for use in World War I and published in 1919. Employed with moderate success, its purpose was to identify men who would prove to be poor prospects for military service because of undesirable personality and behavioural characteristics. This questionnaire consists of a list of items in the form of questions about himself, to be answered by the individual. The aim of the questionnaire is to detect personality and behavioural symptoms that are regarded as indicative of mal-adjustment. The questions on the Data Sheet took the place of an individual interview. Men whose responses indicated a sufficient number of undesirable symptoms were later interviewed individually. The types of questions asked and the aspects of personality sampled were forerunners of many of those included, with very little modification, in subsequent inventories.

Since the appearance of the Woodworth Personal Data Sheet, dozens of personality inventories, representing several different types, have been published. In general, the emphasis of the items questions or statements in these instruments is on what the individual respondent actually does in various kinds of situations and on how he feels about what he does in these situations. Relatively few of these inventories, however, have survived scientific, analysis and practical use. Until the early 1930's these were, however, the principal instruments used to evaluate personality traits in a systematic and scientific, or quasi-scientific manner.

Projective Tests : In the early 1930's a newer type of instrument became prominent in American psychology ; the projective test of personality. This instrument is much more subtle than the self-rating inventory ; it presents more or less equivocal undefined "unsaturated" stimulus situations, usually in the form of pictures, inkblots, or incomplete sentences. Thus, the person being tested has a greater opportunity to impose upon the test his own private and particular personality traits than would be exposed by means of the questionnaire type of inventory.

The best known of the projectives is the Rorschach Inkblot Test, first published in Switzerland in 1921, although not introduced into the United States until the early 1930's. Rorschach, a Swiss psychiatrist, began his experimentation. In the course of his work (1911-21), he perceived the possibilities inherent in the inkblot test as a device for differentiating among various kinds and traits of personalities. Although Rorschach's work on inkblots was the most extensive of any up to that time, he was not the first investigator to discern the possibilities of inkblots in psychological experimentation. As a matter of fact, these had been used for some years in psychological laboratories to study fertility of imagination and of invention. Since the introduction of what has come to be known as "the Rorschach", it has been extensively used in private psychological practice, in clinics, and in hospitals for diagnostic purposes ; in business and industry for some types of personnel selection ; in researches in cultural anthropology ; and in researches on personality theory. Interest in and use of the Rorschach can be inferred from the huge number of professional publications on the subject, which did not begin to appear in appreciable numbers until about 1935.

Another projective instrument of major importance is the Thematic Apperception Test, introduced by H. A. Murry and C. D. Morgan in (1935). This test consists of thirty rather ambiguous pictures, each on a separate card, and one blank card. The person being examined is asked to make up a story of his own each picture. The psychological principle involved is that in his stories the examinee will probably unwittingly, give expression to his needs, values, attitudes, and feeling about persons, situations, and the world around him, as well as to the pressures he is experiencing from sources outside of himself. This instrument, too, has been and is being widely used in a variety of psychological settings. While the number of publications on the TAT, as it is professionally known is not so great as that on the Rorschach, it has, nevertheless, been the subject of many studies and researches.

Since the appearance of the Rorschach and the TAT, a variety of other projective devices and techniques have been made available. Some of these are special adaptations of the two foregoing tests ; others offer rather different approaches for the same general purpose, that is, to elicit responses which will reveal aspects and traits of personality that inventories and rating scales are incapable of eliciting. Since 1945 and to the present time, projective tests have occupied a position of primary importance in practical applications and in research.

The types of techniques for obtaining evaluations of aspects of personality thus far mentioned do not exhaust the list. Among other and more tenuous kinds of procedures used are story telling and story completion, drawing and painting, and "situational tests," in which an individual's behaviour is observed and rated in a setting that stimulates reality. Contrived play activities, usually of one child who is being observed, are used for two purposes ; to permit the child to project some of his inner traits and to serve as a form of psychotherapy. Sociometric methods, whereby an individual's social currency or acceptability is obtaied from ratings made by his peers, is an adaptation and extension of the older rating scale.

Although all of these procedures are used in their appropriate settings, they are much less commonly employed in personality evaluations than are self-rating inventories, the Rorschach, and the TAT, because, being tenuous, they are not susceptible to standardization and objectification. To be sure, personality inventories and the more widely used projective tests present their own problems in standardization. However, progress has been and continues to be made with these and their development has proceeded far enough to provide sufficient common ground and research information, so that in the bands of qualified psychologists they are of value.

Indian Scene

Psychological Tests : The main Indian contributions in psychological tests is the adaptation of foreign tests. Even today very little original work is done in this area. The testing work was initiated by Rice in 1922. The development of psychological tests in India has reviewed topic wise as follows :

1. Development of Intelligence Tests,
2. Development of Personality Tests,
3. Development of Aptitude Tests, and
4. Development of Adjustment Tests.

The historical perspective of these tests have been summarized in the following paragraphs.

Intelligence Tests

The adaptation of foreign intelligence was done to a large extent rather than original contributions.

(1922) Hindustani Binet Performance Scale by A.K. Rice.
(1938) Bint and Terman's Group Test adopted by Jalota.
(1938) Group Intelligence test' by L.K. Shah of Lucknow.
(1940) Adaptation of Binet test by Kamath of Bombay.
(1942) Developed Verbal Intelligence Test by Sohan Lal.
(1943) Developed Intelligence Test by S.M. Mohsin.
(1955) Bhatia's Performance Battery of Intelligence' by C.M. Bhatia.
(1960) Koh's Block Design Test' adaptation by Bureau of psychology Allahabad.
(1960) Group Test of Intelligence by M.C. Joshi.
(1962) Intelligence Test' by R.K. Tondon and K. Ray.
(1962) Verbal Intelligence Test by Prayag Mehta.
(1963) Group General Mental Ability Test by S.S. Jalota.
(1964) Group Test of Intelligence by B.L. Kaur.
(1965) Cattel's Culture Free Intelligence Test adapted by R.N. Singh of Ghazipur.
(1967) 'Non language Test of verbal intelligence test' by S. Chatterjee and M. Mukherjee.

(1967) Hindi Version of Hundal's General Mental Ability Test by A. Singh.

(1968) Group Non-verbal Intelligence Test by Joshi and Tripathi.

(1973) Verbal and Non-verbal Creativity Test by Baqur Mehdi.

Personality Tests

There has been similar trend of adaptation of foreign test in Indian situation. The original contribution is not significant.

(1922) Hindustani Binet Performance Scale by A.K. Rice.

(1951) Varbal Projective test by Shamugban.

(1952) Personality Inventors by Shamughan.

(1958) Personality Questionnaire by M.S.L. Saxena.

(1960) Thematic Apperception Test adapted by H. Chaudhary developed by Henry A. Murry and Morgan.

(1965) An Anxietly Scale by D. Sinha.

(1966) A Projective Technique to Measure the Social Distance by Pratibha Deo and Arora.

(1967) Neurotic Personality Inventory by R.N. Kundu.

(1967) Taylor's Anxiety Test Adapted by B.N. Singh.

(1968) Textile and Audiory Projective Test by Bhattacharya.

(1968) Junior Personality Inventry adapted by S. Kalara developed by Eysenk.

(1969) Comprehensive Test of Anxiety by A.K.P. Singh and Singh.

(1969) Children Manifest Anxiety Test by T. N. Raina.

Aptitude Tests

These is also similar trend of adaptation of foreign test in Indian conditions.

(1948) Aptitude Test by K.L. Agarwal, Allahabad.

(1950) Clerical Aptitude Test by W.N. Parikh.

(1951) Mechanical Aptitude Test Battery by Bureau of psychology Allahabad.

(1965) Engineering Aptitude Test by Dev.

(1965) Aptitude Test, Battery for Differential Prediction by M. Mukherjee.

(1966) Mechanical- Aptitude Test by R. N. Saxena.

(1967) Educational Aptitude Test by Maya Deve.

(1970) Scientific Knowledge and Aptitude Test by S. Chatterjee and M. Mukherjee.
(1970) Teaching Aptitude Test's by K. P. Pandey Meerut.
(1972) Clerical Aptitude Battery-M. Gupta.
(1972) General Scientific Ability by Jai Prakash.
(1973) Numerical Aptitude Test by B. Chatterjee and M. Mukharjee.
(1975) Scientific Aptitude Test by K. Agrawal.
(1981) Engineering Aptitude Battery by S. Pratap.

Adjustment Inventory

The adaptation of foreign tests and original work have been done in this area.
(1950) Adjustment Inventory by H. S. Asthana.
(1950) Adjustment Questionnaire for Adolescents; and Verbal Group Personality Inventory by Jai Prakash.
(1962) Adjustment Inventory adapted by V. K. Mittal of Meerut developed by Bell's inventory.
(1968) Adjustment Inventory by A. K. P. Sinha and R. P. Singh.
(1970) Social and Emotional Adjustment inventory by T. K. Heregang.
(1971) Draw-A man Test by M. Ghosh.

Interest Inventories

The adaptation of foreign tests and inventories have been developed in the area of interest.
(1957) Interest Test adapted by Ray Chaudhary of Vernon.
(1959) Strong Vocational Interest Profile adapted by Jhingra and Ojha.
(1960) 'Interest Inventory' by Chatterjee.
(1968) Vocational Interest Test by B. N. Singh and, R. C. Thakur.
(1968) A Test of Dependence Proneness by J. B. P. Sinha.
(1969) Interest Inventory by R. P. Singh.
(1970) Vocational and Educational Interest by S. P. Kulshrestha.
(1978) Comprehension Scale Reception Test by U. Chaudhary.
(1981) Study Involvement Inventory by A. Bhatnagar.

The Bureau of Psychology Allahabad has contributed significantly in the area of psychological and educational measurement under the guidance of Harper. Some educational achievement test in Hindi and other subjects were developed. Harper has developed a chart for item analysis based of Davis concept of item analysis. There is still great scope to develop original tests in these areas of measurement.

Current Position

Psychological tests of intelligence, whether based upon the theory of "general ability" or upon one of relatively independent factors (or aptitudes), and tests of specific aptitudes and skills are now at a reasonably advanced stage of development. This is so because they have been in the process of evolution and improvement for many years, a tremendous amount of research has been devoted to them by numerous psychologists, and they have been used in a variety of practical situations where their validity could be evaluated. Another reason is the fact that determination of the mental functions, or operations to be tested, though not simple, has not been as difficult as the determination by testing of non-intellective traits of personality.

Because 'personality' is so all-inclusive a concept, and because its manifestations are often complex and covert, development and use of self-rating inventories and projective tests are as yet not on so secure a foundation as tests of mental abilities of specific aptitudes and skills, and of educational achievement.

The great variety of psychological tests in existence has already been mentioned. The numerous uses to which they are put and the important part they may have in the determination of an individual's educational, vocational, or general welfare have been indicated. It is essential, therefore, that anyone who employs these tests in a professional capacity should understand the basic psychological and statistical principles upon which they rest. It is necessary that everyone -teachers, psychiatrists, guidance counsellors personnel administrators-who interprets the results of test findings should be familiar with their essential theory as well as with the meanings of the technical terms.

Since the end of World War I, the use of psychological tests has continuously increased, because they are needed and because they have improved steadily. Education in the United States has become more nearly universal; individuals of inferior and those of seriously deficient mental abilities are being retained in public schools much longer than was the case in earlier years. Thus, the range of intelligence found in schools extends from the very low to the highest levels, making it essential that each individual's educational potential and promise be known as accurately as available psychological means permit. The general increase in years of schooling, not to speak of the tremendous growth in numbers of students, has extended to college and university, so that the importance of knowledge of individual variations in mental ability at higher educational levels has also grown.

Educational and vocational guidance, at all levels, have consequently assumed increasing significance. With the availability of standardized tests, even with their defects, guidance has been placed upon a more objective basis, instead of remaining a matter of subjective, perhaps even casual advice.

For many years school and, now more recently, colleges and universities have been concerned with the learning difficulties of individuals. Are these difficulties due to inferior general intelligence ? Or are they due to specific disabilities, as in reading or spelling ? Or to defective perception of spatial relations ? Or perhaps to defects of the visual-motor function ? Is an individual's lack of aptitude in shop work attributable to inferior manual dexterity ? Is the individual's learning impaired or retarded by poor ability for recall of rote or meaningful materials although his level of general ability might otherwise be adequate for learning ? Answers to these and other important educational problems have been provided or at least facilitated by the use of psychological tests.

The types and numbers of occupations have multiplied, and specializations within the types themselves have increased. It is unnecessary to detail the vocational changes and developments that have taken place with technological and scientific developments, but it does seem necessary to point out that for purposes of psychological testing and vocational guidance, occupations designated by the same name are not necessarily identical in regard to skills, knowledge, specialized functions, and interests involved. For example, there are various factors that combine in different ways to create not a single, unitary aptitude called "mechanical" ; but rather, there are several different aspects of mechanical aptitude, although all have something in common. "Engineering aptitude" is not a single, unitary function either. There are differences in requirements for learning and achieving proficiency in civil, mechanical, electrical, and chemical engineering, although, of course, their requirements are not mutually exclusive. Nor is "clerical aptitude" a single, unitary function. The fact that each of these general areas of training of employment is complex and divisible gives increased significance to psychological testing and insightful guidance.

Tests of personality are being used in some business and industrial organizations in the selection of management personnel, whereas in certain professions, tests are utilized in selecting individuals to be educated for practice in them. These professions include medicine, in which there have been researches on desirable personality traits of medical students. Some engineering schools would like to identify those non-intellectual traits that distinguish the successful from the unsuccessful students of the profession. Psychologists are desirous of determining personality characteristics of the more promising students of clinical psychology. Some religious denominations require that, candidates for admission to their theological schools take tests of non-intellectual personality traits as well as of mental ability.

Finally, there is the whole area of "mental health" to which so much attention has been given since the termination of World War 11. Schools and colleges are concerned over individuals who present more than ordinary degrees of personality difficulties or of problems of behaviour. Numerous bureaus of child guidance have been established within school systems; there are mental health clinics in many sections of the country; federal hospitals (for example, of the Veterans' Administration) have psychological divisions, as do many state and some private hospitals. In all of these settings, psychological testing of all types, especially involving non-intellectual personality traits, is one of the established practices. And it is not uncommon for private welfare agencies to have on their staffs psychologists whose work consists of psychological diagnosis by means of tests, or of the practice of psychotherapy, which is often based upon or facilitated by diagnostic testing, or of both. Also, many psychologist in private practice make diagnostic testing a significant or a major part of their work.

This brief account of the current and extent of psychological testing should be sufficient to emphasize the development of this branch of psychology since its relatively modest beginnings, shortly after the turn of the twentieth century, when the principal purpose of testing was the identification and special schooling of mentally deficient children.

QUESTIONS

1. Explain the term "Development of Measurement'. Describe its need and importance to study the history of Measurement.
2. Describe periodical development of nineteenth and twentieth century. Indicate the present situation of testing.
3. The concept of 'Individual Difference' in psychology is the basis of Measurement. Describe topical development of measurement in behavioural sciences.
4. Describe the contribution of great psychologists and psychomatricians in the field of measurement, with specific reference to Galton and Binet.
5. Write essay on the 'Development of various type tests' in Education and Psychology. Indicate the present situation in this context.
6. Indicate the major contributions in Measurement in the following periods ;
   (a) (1915-30) (c) (1945-60)
   (b) (1930-45) (d) (1960-81)
7. Write short notes on the following ;
   (a) Alfred Binet's contribution in Measurement.
   (b) Francis Galton's contributions in Measurement.
   (c) Main Land marks in measurement during twentieth century.
   (d) Early study of individual differences.
   (e) Beginnings of Experimental psychology.

5

Formulation of Objectives

In this steps teacher has to identify his teaching objective or development of a student and teaching objectives are one and same thing. Education objective can be broadly classified into two parts:

General Educational Objectives : There are three types of educational objectives :

(1) Cognitive objectives,
(2) Affective objectives and
(3) Psychomotor objectives.

Specific Objective or Content Objective: These objectives are written in behavioural terms, which are related to the content of a subject such as Hindi, Maths, History, Geography etc.,. These specific objectives are also known as teaching objective. Teaching objectives are psychological in nature where as educational objectives are achieved with the help of teaching objectives. In teaching process main emphasis is given in realizing behavioural objectives classified in the following parts:

Knowledge Objective : In this objective the awareness and understanding of concept, facts principles, laws and theories is provided. The students are able to recognise, to recall and to evaluate these things.

Skill Objective : It is the second teaching objective in which the learning experiences provided to enable the students for solving the problem related to their life situation. Student will be able to identify the cause and effect relationship of human activities or situations.

Development of Attitude Objective : It is the third objective of teaching in which right type of attitudes are developed towards the personal, social and national problems.

Knowledge Application: It is the fourth objective which concerns with the application of acquired knowledge in his life situations.

Development of Values : It is the main focus of education, that desirable values should be developed among the students, so that the student will be able citizen of nation. It is the highest objective of education.

The behavioural objectives are used in organizing both teaching and testing activities. The following are the main behavioural objectives.

(a) The student is able to comprehend facts, principle and theory.
(b) The student is able to solve the day to day life problems.
(c) Student is able to understand and observe the facts, and realities of life.
(d) The student is able to evaluate the appreciate the elements of the human life.
(e) The students is able to understand the emotional integration and internationalism.

Experiences in Teaching

It is the.second step of evaluation approach. Those experiences which are helpful in achieving the teaching objective inside the classroom and outside the classroom are known as learning experiences. Thus all the learning experiences cannot be called as learning experiences. The following are the main aspects to the learning experiences:

(1) Teaching objective related to the topic.
(2) Outline of the courses.
(3) Teaching methods and techniques.
(4) Maxims of teaching and teaching aids.
(5) Text books and home work, and
(6) Role of teacher and relationship between teacher and students.

The teaching objectives are achieved by providing learning experiences to the students. The learning experiences are controlled by teaching objectives and text books of the subjects. Teaching can be made effective by creating appropriate learning experiences. These experiences should provide the opportunities to do some activities themselves. The teaching activities should be objective centred, and student should be involved in some activities. John Dewey advocated that a major task of a teacher is to generate learning situation, which will motivate to the students for performing certain activities, which are related to the objectives. A teacher role is to organise and control all the teaching activities.

A teacher has to organise and create learning situations for providing experiences to the students according to their available resources. Teacher should behave to the students like philosopher, instructor and friend.

The learning experiences vary subject to subject. The different schools have the different resources. Therefore teacher has to plan according to his subject and available resources and prepare an outline of his teaching activity. A teacher has also to plan about the evaluative techniques for ascertaining the teaching objectives in presentation of teaching content and preparing test for evaluation purpose, a teacher has to consider the needs and level of students in view of his teaching content.

He has to develop a sequence of teaching activities so that appropriate learning situations can be generated for providing learning experiences to the students. A teacher prepares his lesson plan for learning experiences. Some model of lesson plans have been given in the chapter.

Behaviours under Change

It is the third step of evaluation approach. The change of behaviour takes place with the help of learning experiences. The change of behaviours, are related to all aspects of his personality. It includes both internal and external behaviours. There are three aspects of change of behaviour of students—cognitive, affective and psychomotor. The student achievements is of two types—cognitive achievement and non-cognitive achievement. The non-cognitive achievement includes interest attitude, values and certain skills. These change of behaviours are evaluated in terms of teaching objectives formulated in the first step. A criterion test is used for this purpose.

There are three limitations of present examination system

(a) The examination tests are not related to learning experiences and change of behaviour. The main emphasis is given on rote memorization.

(b) The tests do not cover total teaching content, usually sampling is done.

(c) The tests are not objective. They are highly subjective.

In the evaluation approach these limitations are taken into consideration and following things are considered in preparing test:

(1) The table of specification is prepared in which the content and objectives are outline.

(2) The table provides a guideline for preparing a test on the content and teaching objectives.

(3) An objective as well as essay type tests and other techniques are used.

Evaluation Techniques

There are various techniques which are used to measure the change of behaviour in evaluation approach. The main techniques have been discussed in the following paragraphs.

Observation : This technique is mostly used by the teacher to evaluate the performance interests, values and attitude towards their life problems. This technique is of lower classes mainly. The free and control observation is used.

Rating Scale : The Rating scales are used for analysing, and measuring the attitude, values towards the nation society and the world. The attitudes of the students are evaluated with the help of rating scales. It is used of higher class students.

Oral Examination : It is the one of the most ancient techniques of examinations. It is measuring both cognitive and non-cognitive development of a child. The original thinking of student is best examined by this technique. It is highly used daily in every class at the end of teaching. A provision is made in the lesson plan prepared by the trainees.

Written Examination : These can be classified into two types, (1) Essay type examination and (2) Objective type examination.

These two types of examinations are not contradictory to each other but they are complementary to each other for evaluation purpose. An objective type examination is used for measuring lower objectives of teaching, whereas an essay type is used for higher teaching objectives. The objective type has the objectivity in scoring purpose, whereas essay type of highly subjective and scoring. Thus objective type examination is highly reliable and valid, whereas essay type has poor reliability and validity. The change of behaviour can be best measured by using both type of tests. The essay type examination is defective, but it cannot be removed from examination system. It needs certain improvement and modification, which has been given in controlling teaching.

Evaluation Applied

Yearly and Unit Plan

The application of evaluation approach has been illustrated with the help of Geography teaching examination. In using this approach all the three steps are followed. The content which is taught to the students is analysed psychologically to develop the sequence. The teaching and testing points are also determined. A three dimensional table is prepared for determining these points, one dimension indicate the contents and other dimension teaching objective. The weightage is given on these points with the help of teaching periods. All such informations are shown in a table. Generally these tables are of three types :

Yearly Plan or Semester Plan Table : Under this table information about content and teaching objectives are shown for the whole year or the whole semester.

Unit Plan Table : Under this table details about the teaching points and the objectives are given of an unit of the content.

Lesson-Plan Table: Under this table teaching points and specific objectives are given of a topic which is to be taught a period.

Yearly Plan or Semester Plan

A teacher has been assigned to teach Geography of India to secondary class or six class students. The course content is to be taken from the prescribed syllabus. The objectives of teaching are also determined in view of the need of the students and nature of the content. Thus a yearly plan table is prepared.

Yearly plan table provides the information about the outline of the content of the course, the teaching objectives are to be realised and the total periods of teaching are assigned to the course.

Unit Plan Table

Unit plan table provides the information about the unit of the content regarding the structure of the unit content and teaching objectives are to be realized.

The unit plan is the part of the yearly plan. A unit plan has been prepared for the unit i.e. Physical Geography of India, which is the first unit of yearly plan., The unit plans are also prepared with the help of two dimensional table one dimension indicates the structure of unit content and other dimension the teaching objectives. A unit plan is prepared for physical "Geography of India".

Lesson-Plan Table

A teacher has to plan a lesson to be taught within a period of class room teaching. He has to select a topic which is to be covered within a period of 45 minutes duration. The topic is also analysed in terms of the element of the topic of teaching points. The teaching objectives and their weightage are also determined in terms of time (minutes) is allotted to them.

A topic (mountain region) is to be taught to secondary level students. The above topic is analysed in terms of element and objectives are to be achieved. The weightage to these points is given on the basis of time. A lesson plan table is also known as content analysis table. A content analysis table is prepared for the topic "Mountain region of India."

Content Analysis Table
Topic -Mountain Region of India

Teaching Points	*Teaching Objectives*	*Knowledge*	*Skill*	*Knowledge Application*	*Interest& Attitude*	*Total Time In Minutes*
1.	Location of Mountain	8	–	–	2	10
2.	Types of Mountain	10	–	–	2	12
3.	Advantages of Mountain	5	–	2	3	10
4.	Disadvantages of Mountain	8	1	2	2	13
	Total	**31**	**1**	**4**	**9**	**45 Mts.**

Activities in Coordination

In evaluation approach testing is based on teaching. The learning experiences are provided with the help of teaching activities, and testing is done for evaluating the change of behaviours of the students. Thus the teaching and testing activities are made objective centred. After completing yearly plan and unit plan, the test is administered. The weightage for teaching objectives is given with the help of teaching periods, and same weightage is given in preparing a test with the help of number of items. The concept of evaluation approach in teaching may be illustrated with the help of following table.

Evaluation Approach

Teaching Objectives	*Learning Experiences*	*Change of Behaviours*
1. Knowledge Objective	Lecture or question answer method, home assignment and study	1. Oral test 2. Written test 3. Observation
2. Skill Objective	Demonstration, practical work, reading, writing, speaking, performance	1. Observation 2. Practical test
3. Knowledge Application Objective	Discussion on some problem, use of knowledge words, terms and concepts understand cause-effect.	1. Written Test 2. Oral Test
4. Interest, attitude, value objective	Linking, with life situation, life adjustment Lecture, question-answer discussion.	1. Rating 2. Inventory 3. Observation.

The content analysis table indicates that the topic mountain region of India is taught and completed within 45 minute duration in classroom teaching. The table also reveals that the 31 minutes are allotted for knowledge objective, 9 minutes for Interest and Attitude, 4 minutes knowledge application and one minute for skill objective of teaching. The table also provides the sequence of presentation of elements of the topic.

These tables provide the guidelines to the teacher regarding the course of content, unit of content, and the topic of the content. The yearly plan is completed with the help of lesson plan. These tables are also provide the basis for preparing examination tests' which can be made objective centred. Thus, these table are used for teaching as well as testing, and both can be made objective centred.

In using the lesson plan for classroom teaching, a teacher should also be able to select appropriate teaching methods technique devices and teaching aids, which are appropriate for realizing teaching objectives.

The concept of evaluation is applied with help of yearly plan and unit plan. The testing items are prepared with the yearly plan and unit plan. This concept is illustrated with help of the following table.

Coordination between Teaching and Testing

Teaching Objective	*Unit Plan*		*Yearly Plan*	
	Teaching Pds.	*Testing Items*	*Teaching Pds.*	*Testing Items*
1. Knowledge	3	6	24	48
2. Skill	½	1	4	8
3. Knowledge Application	1	2	5.5	11
4. Interest and Attitude	1½	3	16.5	33
Total	**6**	**12**	**50**	**100**

This table indicates that same weightage is given to testing items as the weightage is given for teaching objectives in terms of teaching periods. The same proportion is to be maintained in testing situation in terms of number of items. Three types-essay type, objective type and short answer type items are included in the test. The higher objectives are tested with the help of essay type of items. A criterion test is prepared rather than achievement test. In using the evaluation approach in teaching, the following precautions should be observed.

Message of Caution

The following precautions should be taken in using the evaluation approach in teaching school subject :

1. The teaching objectives should be identified clearly in terms of Bloom's Taxonomy.
2. Teaching objectives should be written in behavioural term or in terms of change of behaviours.

3. The content should be analysed into elements and these should be arranged in psychological sequence.
4. The teaching and testing point should be determined before hand.
5. The learning experiences should be shown or created which are conductive for desirable change in behaviour of the students.
6. There should be coordination between teaching and testing with the help of teaching objectives.
7. A teacher should have an understanding and ability for selecting appropriate teaching methods, technique, teaching aids, so that teaching objectives can be realised.
8. The three step of evaluation approach-Education objective, learning experiences and change of behaviour are related to each other and also modifiable'
9. The tests used in evaluation approach should be reliable and valid.
10. An appropriate testing situation-Essay type, objective type and short answer type should be used but these tests should be objective centered. Thus criterion tests should be used in evaluation approach.

Limitations of Evaluation Approach

Following are the main limitations of the evaluation approach

1. It requires training and understanding for using in class room teaching.
2. The content analysis and the identification of the objectives is not objective.
3. There is no standard criteria for determining teaching and testing points.
4. The yearly plan and unit plan are prepared by a teacher, so it has subjectivity.
5. The teachers do not take interests in using evaluation approach in class room teaching. It is used only by teacher in training programme.
6. It is difficult to write the objectives in behavioural term of in change of behaviour of the students.

QUESTIONS

1. Explain the term evaluation approach and describe its procedures.
2. "Testing should be based on teaching". Discuss and illustrate this statement.
3. Differentiate between learning experiences and change of behaviour. Describe the main feature of criterion tests.
4. Indicate the need and importance of yearly plan and unit plan for coordinating teaching and testing activity.
5. Write short note on the following
   (a) Teaching objective and Educational objective.
   (b) Achievement test and criterion test.
   (c) Techniques of evaluation.
   (d) Characteristics of evaluation approach.
6. Define the term 'Task Analysis'. Differentiate among Job-analysis, content analysis and skills analysis. Illustrate your answer with examples.
7. Define the 'Objective'. Distinguish between educational objectives and teaching objectives.
8. Discuss the taxonomy of 'Cognative domain'. Describe the procedure for writing objectives in behavioural terms.
9. Describe the RCEM approach for writing objectives in behavioural terms and differentiate with Robert Mager's approach. Illustrate your answer with examples.
10. Write short notes on the following
    (a) Taxonomy of affective domain
    (b) RECM approach for objectives
    (c) integration of mental domain
    (d) Unit plan of teaching
    (e) Evaluation approach to teaching

6

Common Aims and Objectives

The main focus of educational measurement is to answer the following two questions.

(1) What a student can do in a subject ?

(2) Why a student can not do in the subject ?

Both the questions are complementary to each other. The first question is answered by administering an achievement test in the subject and second question can be answered by a diagnostic tests of the subject. In recent time an achievement tests have been classified into two types :

1. Norms-referenced tests and
2. Criterion-referenced tests.

The norm referenced tests are related to the content of the subject that a student can do so much in the subject content. The content of subject is the means to develop the child in his cognitive, psychomotor and affective aspects. Teaching is a purposeful activities, it is organized to realize certain specific objectives, which are obtained by bringing desirable behavioural changes among the students. These changes are measured with the help of criterion test. Each item of the test measures the one specific objective in behavioural terms. Thus, this type of measurement is related to both teaching and testing.

This chapter provides the awareness of objectives and the procedure their measurement.

The planning of teaching is most important task of a teacher. He has to utilize his imagination, creativity and insight in analysing the teaching content into its elements and in defining and formulating the learning objectives in behavioural terms. This step is very scientific in nature because the teacher has to analyse the content systematically and arrange in its elements in a logical sequence that may suit to students-learning and desired objectives can be achieved. Thus, a teacher has to perform three activities in this step :

(1) Analysing the task or content Analysis.
(2) Identification of teaching objectives, and.
(3) Writing objectives in behavioural terms.

The detailed description of these activities has been provided in the following paragraphs.

Assessment of Jobs

Ryle has given this concept of 'Task Analysis'. The focus of training psychology is to analyse the task to be performed. This concept is very useful for developing the understanding and skills for teaching and training. This has emerged against the theories of learning because theories of leaning could not provide substantial solution for the problems of classroom teaching and learning.

The effective teaching can only be organized by analysing the content. This task is educational as well as intellectual in nature because it involves both the process of analysis and synthesis. The task analysis has four characteristics :

(a) Description of learning activities.
(b) Identification of desired behaviour.
(c) Identification of appropriate situation and techniques of motivation and
(d) Developing criterion test for measuring the desired behavioural changes.

The task analysis provides the basis for selecting appropriate teaching tactics and strategies and formulating the objectives of teaching.

Types of Task Analysis: The task analysis is classified into three types. These three categories of task analysis are quite different and they serve different purposes.

(1) Content Analysis or Topic Analysis.
(2) Job Analysis and
(3) Skill Analysis.

Content Analysis : In this type of task analysis, the content or subject-matter is analysed into sub-topics and sub-topics into elements and these are arranged into a logical sequence. This type of analysis is purely educational and intellectual activity. For example, 'Density in Physics, Samas in Hindi, Fundamental Rights in Civics and Change of Season in Geography'. This type of analysis is generally concerned with cognitive aspect of a teacher.

Job Analysis : This type of analysis concerns with tasks which are related to some professional and social activity. It involves psychomotor activities for example : Teacher-tasks, Doctor-tasks, Engineer-tasks, etc.

Skill Analysis : This type of analysis is also related to the psychomotor activities but it concerns with the most specific skills. The skill analysis is included in job analysis. In job analysis mainly skills are analysed, but skill analysis is done for specific activities for example : Questioning, Motivating and Diagnosing, etc.

The pupil-teachers should have the knowledge and skill of content analysis. The content analysis is the basis for preparing instructions and formulating the objectives of teaching. Therefore, detailed description of consent analysis has been given below :

Assessment of Matter

The term 'Content Analysis' has been defined by 1. K. Davies-

"It is the analysis of topic or content unit to be taught, into its constituents or elements and arrange them in a logical sequence".

A content is broken down into its elements. Each element may be performed by using specific tactics and the specific objectives can be realized. The elements are arranged in a logical sequence so that positive transfer of learning can be facilitated. The teacher has to employ his imagination, creativity and insight in synthesizing the elements of the content.

There are various techniques (Glaser 1963, Homme 1962, Macnar 1965) of content analysis. Davies matrix technique is most useful and practicable. A content is broken down into subtopics and each sub-topic is further broken down into elements. The sub-topics are arranged in learning sequence. This has been illustrated with the help of a chart.

The Sources : The teacher has to make use of various sources for a content analysis, then he is able to present the correct structure of the content. The teacher should have the mastery over the content. The following sources are essential for content analysis

(1) Study of standard text-books.
(2) Considering the needs of the learners.
(3) Keeping in view the objectives of teaching-learning.
(4) Considering the examination system.
(5) Use of teaching acids, and
(6) Teacher's own skills of teaching.

Integration of Sources : The mastery behaviour is determined in content analysis. It is based upon the needs of students of level or grade of education. The same content is taught at various levels but the structure of content is determined by considering the level of teaching. The teacher should consult and study the standard books available on the content so that appropriate content-structure can be determined. In addition to that, teacher should review the examination papers. The objective type questions require specific information about content. Therefore, new type content should be analysed in more small or specific elements whereas essay type requires the large elements of the content. The examination system helps in determining the size of elements of the content of structure of the content. The teacher should make proper use of the success in analysing the content of his teaching.

The Characteristics : The following are the chief characteristics of content element

(1) The student can exhibit by his activity that he can understand the element.
(2) The comprehension of an element can be evaluated by a question.
(3) The level of the element can be examined by behaviour of the student. The level of element may be knowledge, comprehension and application, etc.
(4) The understanding of various elements can be tested with the help of student's behaviour.

(5) The emitted response for an element indicates the change in behaviour.

In this way every element is complete in itself. The knowledge and understanding of a concept for a fact may be given by arranging the elements in a sequence.

Arrangement of Elements in a Sequence **:** The logical sequence of the elements can be made on the basis of the following rules :

(a) From Known to Unknown.
(b) From Simple to Difficult.
(c) From Concrete to Abstract.
(d) From Observation to Logical Thinking and
(e) From Part to Whole.

The arrangement of elements based upon these rules increases the probability that logical sequence of the elements may be psychologically valid.

The concept of task analysis is practical in nature. Therefore, it has been illustrated with the help of an example. The pupil-teacher can observe an application aspect of this concept and can use to analyse his own content of teaching.

Example

TOPIC- MANAGEMENT OF TEACHING LEARNING

Sub-Topic 1 - Planning of teaching learning
1-1 Element Task Analysis
1-2 Element Identification of objectives
1-3 Element Writing objectives in behavioural

Sub-Topic 2 - Organizing of teaching learning
2-1 Element Selection of teaching strategies
2-2 Element Selection of teaching tactics
2-3 Element Selection of teaching aids
2-4 Element Decision for rules and techniques of instruction

Sub-Topic 3 - Leading of teaching learning
3-1 Element Arranging for student's motivation
3-2 Element Deciding the techniques of motivation
3-3 Element Use of teaching skills

3-4 Element Use of communication strategies

Sub-Topic 4 - Controlling of teaching learning.

4-1 Element Evaluation of learning activities.

4-2 Element Evaluation of learning outcome

4-3 Element Organizing learning objectives

4-4 Element Providing the feedback to the earlier steps.

It is evident from the above example that managing teaching, learning topic can be divided into four units or steps. Each unit is meaningful and quite different from one another. The four units have been arranged in a logical sequence. This arrangement seems to be effective or workable psychologically. Similarly each unit has been further divided into elements. Every element of each unit also seems complete and meaningful in itself and they are quite different from one another. The elements of each unit have been arranged in a sequence so that learner may understand easily. In this way analysis and synthesis both type of activities are performed in task analysis.

The content analysis provides a guide line in determining and identifying the objectives of learning.

Aims Identified

The teaching objectives are identified after analysing the content to be taught because teaching is a meaningful and purposeful activity. The teaching objectives are determined in the planning step. The teacher can identify his teaching objectives with the help of his knowledge and understanding of educational objectives. Therefore, meaning and definition of educational and teaching objectives have been described here.

The Concept

The objective is a statement or a form of category which suggests any kind of change. The objective has the following characteristics : .

1. It provides the direction to the activity which is designed for achieving an ultimate goal.
2. It helps for the planned change.
3. It provides the basis for organizing activities.

"The educational objectives imply the changes that we try to produce in the child."

The educational objectives are generally in the statement form. These are broad and philosophical in nature. The teaching objectives are specific and psychological in nature. The teaching strategies and tactics are selected on the basis of teaching learning objectives. B. S. Bloom has given a very comprehensive definition of educational objectives :

"Educational objectives are not only the goals towards which the curriculum is shaped and towards which instruction is guided, but they are also the goals that provide the detailed specification for the construction and use of evaluative technique." B. S. Bloom believes that education is a tripolar process.

The learning experiences are provided by teaching activities to achieve educational objectives and change of behaviour is evaluated in terms of educational objectives. Thus educational objectives are the basis for teaching activities and evaluation techniques.

Types of Objectives : The objectives are classified in two major categories :

(1) Educational objectives, and

(2) Teaching or learning objectives.

The educational objectives are broad and they are related to educational system and schools. The teaching objectives are narrow and specific and concern with classroom teaching. The educational objectives are achieved with the help of teaching or learning objectives. ' The educational objectives may be achieved by organizing teaching from primary to university levels whereas teaching objectives may be realized within a period of 40 minutes duration. For example : educational objectives are to develop the feeling of national integration. This includes several teaching objectives : Knowledge, comprehension and application of national integration. The educational objectives may be achieved in a long period. The comparison between educational and teaching objectives has been given in the tabular form.

Comparison between Educational and Teaching Objectives

Educational Objectives	Teaching Objectives
1. They are very broad.	1. They are specific.
2. Social philosophy is the source of the objectives.	2. Psychology is the source of the objectives.
3. They imply the teaching objectives.	3. The educational objectives are achieved with the help of these objectives.
4. They can be achieved within a long period of duration.	4. They can be achieved within a period of classroom teaching.
5. All subjects of school are concerned with these objectives.	5. The school subjects have their specific teaching objective.
6. The examples : personality development, feeling of National integration etc.	6. The examples: knowledge skills interests etc.

The teaching objectives are achieved in terms of change of behaviour of learners. These are specific, direct and practical in nature. Therefore, these are most useful for teachers. The teaching objectives are related to learning outcome or change of behaviour of the learners. B.S. Bloom has classified the learning objectives in three categories :

1. Cognitive objectives.
2. Affective objectives and
3. Psychomotor objectives.

Thus, the change of behaviour is also of three types cognitive, affective and psychomotor. Bloom and his associates on the university of Chicago, have produced a most important classification or taxonomy of congnitive educational objectives (Bloom 1956), affective educational objectives (Krath Wehl, Bloom and Masia 1964) and psychomotor educational objectives (Simpson 1969). The taxonomy arranges objectives in the domains into six categories. A useful way of looking at the domain is the cognitive domain, the teacher is interested in what will the student do, whereas in the affective domain, the teacher is additionally concerned with what does he go to it or with it, and conative domain concerns with how does he do it ? An old educational axiom states that 'growth occurs from within' and this inner growth is demonstrated in the two taxonomies by the way in which they are internally related.

Relationship between the Cognitive and Affective Domains

	Cognitive Objectives	*Affective Objectives*
1.	The lowest level in this taxonomy begins with the stu-dent's recall and recognition knowledge.	The lowest level begins with student's merely receving stimuli and passively attending to it. It extends for his more actively attending to it.
2.	It extends through the comprehension of the knowledge.	Then his responding to stimuli on request willingly responding and talking satisfaction in responding.
3.	To his skill in the application of the knowledge that he comprehends.	To his valuing the phenomena or activity so that the voluntarily responds and seeks out further ways to take part in what is going on.
4.	The next levels progress from his ability to make an analysis of the situations involving the knowledge, to his skill in synthesis of it into new organization.	The next stage in his conceptualization of each value to which he is responding by identifying characteristics or forming judgments.
5.	The highest level lies in his skill in evaluation, so that he can judge the value of the knowledge in realizing specific objectives.	The highest level of the taxonomy in the student's organisation of the values into a system, is characterisation of himself.

The cognitive and affective educational objectives are achieved in classroom teaching. The cognitive objective are realized in military and other training programmes. Therefore, the detailed description of cognitive and affective domains has been given in the following paragraphs.

Taxonomy of Cognitive Educational Objectives and Learning Outcome

Benjamin S. Bloom (1956) has written a handbook of taxonomy formulated to stimulate and systematize the assessment of objectives in cognitive domain. The cognitive domain of the taxonomy consists of six broad categories of cognitive learning arranged in an order to increase complexity : knowledge, comprehension, application, analysis, synthesis and evaluation. For each of these broad categories of cognitive learning, the taxonomy identifies specific learning outcome in behavioural terms and each of these educational objectives may be evaluated.

This taxonomy may assist the teacher in clarifying his educational objectives and modifying his teaching practices so that relevant, important outcome of learning are identified and realized.

Various Objectives

B.S. Bloom has divided the cognitive objectives in six categories. Their description has been given in the following paragraphs :

Knowledge : Knowledge objective involves the recall of specifics and universals, the recall of method and process, or the recall of a pattern, structure, or setting. The recall situation involves little more than bringing in mind the appropriate material. The teacher plans, the situation for the learner to recall and recognize traditional, classification, criteria, principles and theories. The knowledge category includes the following three types of content :

(a) Knowledge of specific, i.e. facts and terminology.
(b) Knowledge of ways and means, and
(c) Knowledge of principles, theories and generalizations.

The material and problems may be of such a nature that little specialized and technical information is required. The pre-requisite of this category is still unknown.

Comprehension : This category indicates the lower level of understanding. It refers to a type of understanding as such that the individual knows what is being communicated and can make use of the material. The comprehension objective includes three types of activities.

(a) Translation of specifics : facts, principles and theories.
(b) Interpretation of the same specifics, and
(c) Extrapolation of the above content.

The translation is the lower level activity and extrapolation is the highest level of comprehension objective. The knowledge category is the pre-requisite of this category.

Application : This category includes the use of abstraction in particular and concrete situations. The abstraction may be in the form of general ideas, rules and theories must be applied. This has also three levels.

(a) Make generalization of facts, principles and theories.
(b) Diagnose the weakness of these contents.
(c) Apply these contents.

This objective develops the predictive ability of the learner. It has the pre-requisite of both the earlier categories.

Analysis : This category involves to breakdown of a communication into its elements such that the relative hierarchy of ideas is made clear. The relationship among them can be expressed. This analysis is intended to clarify the communication. The analysis is attempted at three levels :

(a) Analyse the elements of a communication.
(b) Establish the relationship among the elements.
(c) Formulate some principles to organize the elements.

This category develops the reasoning ability of the learners. It has the pre-requisite of three categories.

Synthesis : This has the pre-requisite of the earlier four categories. In this category all the elements are organized in such a way that they can form a unique whole. The elements are arranged and combined in such a way to form a pattern of structure not clearly observed before. The synthesis category includes the activities of three levels :

(a) Unique communication by arranging different elements.
(b) Suggest new plan by combining all elements.
(c) Establish an abstract relationship among different elements.

This category of teaching and learning objective develops the creative ability of the learners.

Evaluation : All the earlier categories are pre-requisites of this category. It includes quantitative and qualitative judgement about the extent to which material and method satisfy criteria. The criteria may be those determined by the student or those which are given to him. It has two levels:

(a) The internal judgement of the material and methods.
(b) The external judgement of the material and methods.

The two types of criteria internal and external are used for judging the truthfulness of facts, principles, rules and theories. This develops the power of judgement.

Teaching is organized to achieve these objectives. The different objectives are achieved by different cognitive outcome. The following are the major learning outcome.

***Pre-verbal Percepts* :** In achieving knowledge and comprehension objectives.

***Factual information* :** In realizing knowledge, comprehension and application objectives.

***Concept Formation* :** In attaining comprehension application and analysis objectives.

***Generalization and Principles* :** In achieving application, analysis and synthesis objectives.

***Problem-solving and Creativity* :** In achieving analysis, synthesis and evaluation objectives.

***Identification of Cognitive Objectives* :** A teacher identifies his teaching objectives in terms of cognitive categories. There are three important considerations in determining the teaching objectives :

(a) Structure of the content.

(b) Needs of the students and

(c) Level of entering behaviour.

The content analysis and entering behaviour of the students provide the basis and insight to the teacher to decide the level of learning outcome of students. The teacher can easily determine his teaching objectives in terms of cognitive category. The teacher should ensure the pre-requisites of the category that students have acquired in their entering behaviour. The teaching objectives may vary from knowledge to evaluation category under cognitive domain.

Taxonomy of Affective Educational Objectives and Learning Outcome.

Krath Wehletal. (1964) have produced a handbook and taxonomy designed to stimulate and systematize an assessment of objectives in the affective domain, as Bloom's taxonomy has done in the cognitive area. The affective taxonomy is equally important, as cognitive taxonomy for classifying educational objectives and learning outcome.

The correct answer of an affective question depends upon the person queried and response in social situation, but the correct answer of a cognitive question is the same for all respondents.

Situational factors of the examiner and an assessment context have a more significant influence on the results for affective measures they do for ability measures.

The teachers and instructions are appreciating the value of using such a taxonomy when they plan their objectives and examinations, perhaps the overall quality of the work accomplished in the classroom teaching and the examination system will improve and standards can be raised.

B.S. Bloom, Karth Welil and Masia (1964) have classified affective domain in six categories. Their meaning and definitions have been given in the following paragraphs –

Receiving or Attending : The pre-requisite of this category is unknown. In this category the learner is sensitized to the existence of certain stimuli, i.e., he may be willing to receive or to attend the stimuli. This is the first crucial step that learner is to be oriented to learn what does the teacher intend to do ? It includes three types of activities :

(a) Awareness about the stimulus or situation.
(b) Create willingness in the learner to receive it.
(c) Control the attention of the learner.

The level of affective domain increases the sensitivity towards human values.

Responding : The first category receiving is the prerequisite of responding. At this level we are concerned with which go beyond attending to the phenomenon. The student should be sufficiently motivated to respond. This may be interested objective of teaching and instruction. It has three levels of responding

(a) The learner's obedience for response.
(b) The learner's willingness to respond.
(c) The learner gets satisfaction in responding.

This level concerns with enjoyment of self-expression of music, teaching, arts and crafts, etc.

Valuing : The earlier two levels are pre-requisites for achieving this level. This category includes the worth of a thing, phenomenon or behaviour. The abstract worth is a result of individual's own valuing and assessment but it is a social product. The attitude is an objective of teaching. This level has also three types of activities :

(a) Acceptance of value.
(b) Preference of value and
(c) Commitment of value.

The individual's commitment to the underlying value guides his behaviour.

Organization: The above three categories are the prerequisites of the organization category. As the learner successively internalizes values, he encounters situations for which more than one value is required. Therefore, necessity arises for

(a) The organization of the values in a system.
(b) The determination of the interrelationship among them.
(c) The establishment of the dominant value.

The organization category needs the conceptualization of values. It places the values properly. The appropriate organization of values can be done on the basis of conceptualization of them.

Characterization: The earlier four levels are the pre-requisites of characterization. At this level of internalization, the values already have a place in the individual's value hierarchy, are organized in some kind of internally consistent system. The acts are consistently in accordance with the values : (a) generalized set provides the internal consistency to the system attitudes and values.

The affective objectives range from receiving to characterization level. The various type of teaching objectives of this domain are achieved with the help of the following :

(1) Interest as learning outcome may be obtained by achieving, receiving and responding objective.
(2) Appreciation as learning outcome may be obtained by realizing, receiving, responding and valuing objectives.
(3) Attitude as learning outcome is obtained by achieving, receiving, responding, valuing and organizing objectives of teaching.
(4) Value as learning outcome is attained by realizing, valuing and organizing objectives of teaching.
(5) Adjustment as learning outcome may be obtained by achieving the valuing, organizing and characterization of teaching.

After task analysis, teacher identifies the affective teaching objectives in terms of above five categories. There are following crucial factors for identifying such teaching-learning objectives

(a) Structure of the content.
(b) Social needs of the students and
(c) Level of students entering behaviour.

The task analysis, entering behaviour of the learner and their social needs are the basis for identifying the appropriate teaching objectives of affective domain. The objectives are achieved in a hierarchical orders. The higher objectives can only be achieved, if lower objectives have already attained.

Writing Learning Objectives : The identification of objectives in terms of taxonomic categories does not specify the form of teaching and learning activities. Therefore, it is essential to write these objectives in behavioural terms. The behavioural form of the objectives reveals the learning activities.

Need for Writing Objectives in Behavioural Terms : The following are the main advantages of writing objectives in behavioural terms :

(1) Teaching activities are determined and delimited.
(2) Teaching and learning process may be integrated for affective learning outcome.
(3) The appropriate teaching strategies and tactics can be selected for effective learning.
(4) Teaching and testing can be made objective-centred. Thus testing may be based upon teaching. Scafold states the following advantages of the behavioural objectives
    (a) Specification of objectives.
    (b) Selection of items for preparing a test.
    (c) Teaching can be related to learning.
    (d) Integration between learning experiences and change of behaviour and
    (e) Selection of appropriate teaching strategies, tactics and teaching aids.

Methods of Writing Objectives in Behavioural Terms : There are various methods of writing objectives in behavioural terms. It is not a new concept and approach in the field of education but it is an old concept, It has five historical basis :

Drucker (1954) has given a new interpretation of management that it is changeable concept. The activities of management should be explained in terms of objectives. Hence he has given emphasis on the behavioural aspects of the objectives.

B.S. Bloom (1956) has shifted the emphasis from content to the objectives in examination system. He has suggested the reformation in examination system that achievement tests should be objective-centred rather than content centred. Each question should evaluate one specific objective. Thus, he has made an effort to write these objectives in behavioural terms.

Robert Mager's approach (1962) is most popular in the development of programmed instruction. He concentrates OD cognitive and affective objectives, in this approach he gives emphasis on action verbs rather than mental processes. The cognitive objectives can be best realized by programmed instruction strategy.

Robert Miller's approach (1962) is used for writing, psychomotor objectives in behavioural terms. The origin of this approach is from the millitary science. Thus, training objectives can be best written by Miller's approach.

NCERT (1972) Regional College of Education Mysore (RCEM) has also developed an approach for writing objectives in behavioural terms. This approach is applicable for cognitive, affective and psychomotor objectives of teaching and training. It gives main emphasis on mental abilities for writing objectives in behavioural terms.

Various Approaches

Mager (1962) considers that clear objective should be written in the following manner :

(1) Firstly, identify the terminal behaviour by name, we can specify the kind of behaviour which will be accepted as an evidence that the learner has achieved the objectives.

(2) Second, try to further define the desired behaviour by describing the important conditions under which the behaviour will be expected to occur.

(3) Third, specify the criteria of acceptable performance by describing how well must the learner perform to be considered acceptable.

Although the three statements are a very good rule of thumb for beginners that they layout exactly.

Miller (1962) tackles the problem of writing objectives more from the point of view of skill-analysis, and according to him a clear objective should be preferably written to the following manner:

1. An indicator on which the activity, relevant-indication appear.
2. The indication or one which calls for a response.
3. The control objective is to be activated.
4. The activation or manipulation is to be made.
5. The indication of response should be adequate or feedback.

The level of detail, used in writing such descriptions is about the same as would be used for writing a set of technical instructions useful to novice. Indeed, Miller has pointed out that a clear objective is written in the above manner and can be used as a procedure manual for doing the job.

A comparison of the Miller and Mager's formates, will show that they bear a marked resemblance; indeed Mager sometimes prefers to follow the formates now associated with Miller. However, they layout and the greater detail of the Miller-type objectives does have a number of advantages for objectives in the psychomotor domain.

Stating the Behavioural Objectives of Cognitive Domain : In describing the behaviour that is required for a student when he demonstrates his mastery over the subject or the skill, it is an important to identify, in a very clear terms, exactly what will he do. This involves saying how will he recognise the cue or situation which will cause him to commence action or behaviour, as well as how will he recognise that the action have been successfully accomplished. The associated action verbs for different objectives have been summarized.

A list of associated action verbs for cognitive domain has been provided :

Cognitive Objectives and Associated Action verbs

Objectives		*Associated Action verbs*	
Knowledge	Define	Write	Underline
State	Recall	Select	
List	Recognize	Reproduce	
Name	Label	Measure	
Comprehension	Identify	Illustrate	Explain
Justify	Represent	Judge	
Select	Narric	Contract	
Indicate	Formulate	Classify	
Application	Predict	Choose	Construct
Select	Find	Compute	
Assess	Show	Use	
Explain	Demonstrate	Perform	
Analysis	Analyse	Select	Justify
Identify	Separate	Resolve	
Conclude	Compare	Break down	
Differentiate	Contrast	Criticise	
Synthesis	Combine	Argue	Select
	Restate	Discuss	Relate
	Summarize	Organize	Generalize
	Percise	Derive	Conclude
Evaluation	Judge	Support	Identify
	Evaluate	Defend	Avoid
	Determine	Attack	Select
	Recognise	Criticise	Choose

These action verbs should be used for defining the educational objectives of cognitive domain and also for examination questions.

There is no fast dichotomy among these domains, there is significant overlapping among these domains. The purpose of educational objectives is the development of the child in desirable direction. The integration of learning outcome at different levels has been summarized in the tabular form.

Robert Mager has used the taxonomy of cognitive domain of B.S. Bloom. The content of elements and taxonomic category as a teaching objectives provide the basis for selecting appropriate action verbs. the action verbs of each category indicate the level of teaching and learning activities. The objectives can be written in behavioural terms by combining action verbs with an element of action.

Behavioural objective= Element of content+Action verb of the objective category.

Example : Topic of teaching 'Task analysis', objective of teaching; knowledge, comprehension and application.

(1) Behavioural form of knowledge objective. (K)

(2) The learners are able to define the term 'Task Analysis'. (C)

(3) Behavioural form of application objectives. (A)

The learners are able to use or demonstrate the task analysis.

Similarly a pupil-teacher can write his teaching objectives in behavioural terms for his own subject in preparing lesson-plans. The examples of behavioural objectives have been given for the school subjects:

Subject Geography and Topic 'Climate'

1. The students are able to define the term climate
   (Knowledge Objective)
2. The students are able to explain the term climate
   (Comprehension Objective)
3. The students are able to illustrate the concept of climate
   (Application Objective)
4. The students are able to analyse the factors of climate
   (Analysis Objective)

In Physics Topic 'Density'

1. The learners are able to define 'density'
   (Knowledge Objectives)
2. The learners are able to explain or illustrate density
   (Comprehension Objectives)
3. The learners are able to compute the density of given substances.
   (Application Objective)
4. The learners are able to analyse the components of density
   (Analysis Objective)

Stating the Behavioural Objectives of Affective Domain

Robert Mager has also used the taxonomy of an affective domain. He develops the action verbs for each category of this domain which indicate the behaviour which is required for a student to demonstrate. The list of action verbs for different objectives has been given below :

Affective Objectives and Associated Action Verbs

Objectives		*Associated Action verbs*	
Receiving	Listen	Accept	Beware
Attend	Receive	Favour	
Prefer	Perceive	Select	
Responding	State	Select	Record
Answer	List	Develop	
Complete	Write	Derive	
Valuing	Accept	Increase	Indicate
Recognise	Develop	Decide	
Participate	Attain	Influence	
Organization	Organize	Find	Associate
Judge	Determine	Form	
Relate	Correlate	Select	
Characterization	Revise	Accept	Demostrate
Change	Judge	Identify	
Face	Develop	Decide	

These associated action verbs should be used in describing and formulating the educational objectives at different levels of affective domain.

The element of a content and teaching objectives in terms of affective taxonomic category help in selecting the appropriate action verbs for demonstrating the learner's behaviour. The affective objectives can be written in behavioural term by combining elements with appropriate action verbs. It has been illustrated with examples.

Behavioural objectives of 'Task Analysis'.

1. The students prefer task analysis in his lesson-plan. (Receiving Objective)
2. The students develop the task analysis of teaching topic. (Responding Objective)
3. The students accept the important task analysis in their lesson-planning.
(Valuing Objective)

Behavioural Objectives of 'Fundamental Right' in Civics.

The learners accept the fundamental rights.

1. The learners are able to state the fundamental rights. (Responding Objectives)
2. The learners are able to indicate the fundamental rights. (Valuing Objectives)

The teaching objectives of other social-subjects can be written in behavioural terms on similar lines. This is the last termed in planning teaching and learning because criterion test is developed before preparing the teaching instruction. Therefore, behavioural objectives are written usually in present tense. In lesson-planning they may be written in future tense.

Limitations of Robert Mager's Approach

Mager's approach is not a perfect method for writing objectives in behavioural terms. It has the following limitations

1. It gives emphasis on action verbs rather than mental process that involves in performing the actions.
2. Mager is a behaviourist psychologist, therefore, he explains learning in terms of (S-R) whereas all human learning can not be explained by (S-R) learning.
3. This method can be used for writing the lower level teaching objectives, higher level objectives cannot be written clearly.
4. The list of action verbs indicates that there is overlapping of action verbs in different categories. Thus, it may create confusion in the minds of teachers to use the appropriate action verb for specifying objectives.

5. The psychomotor objectives cannot be written by Mager's approach. It is an applicable only for cognitive and affective objectives.
6. There is also overlapping of action verbs provided in the lists of cognitive and affective action verbs. For example, select, list, write, state, analyse, recognize are common in both the lists.
7. Mager's approach can not be effectively used in writing teaching objectives in behavioural terms because teaching objectives are of three types : knowledge, skill, attitude and interest. It can be effectively used in the development of programmed instruction.

The teachers of Regional College of Education Mysore (RCEM) realized the limitations of Mager's approach and they developed a new approach for writing objectives in behavioural terms.

The assumption regarding this approach is that human learning can be best explained in terms of mental process or mental abilities rather than behaviour. It has shifted the focus from product to process. This was very necessary indeed as the list of action verbs designating behaviour was too long and unwidely to have any meaningful application of classroom. Having given a lot of thought to it and having discussed both the system at the Regional College of Education Mysore, the education and content-cum-method experts have formulated the hierarchical structure of expected behavioural outcome.

The RCEM approach has also used the Bloom's Taxonomy of Educational objectives with a little modification. The cognitive has been classified into six categories by B.S. Bloom and his associates. The system has converted into four categories. The last categories : analysis, synthesis and evaluation are denoted by one category, i.e., 'creativity'. These four categories have been further divided into seventeen mental abilities or processes. These abilities or processes are used for writing the objectives of cognitive affective and psychomotor domains in behavioural terms. These seventeen mental processes have been summarized in the following chart :

Taxonomy of Educational Objectives in the RCEM Approach

Bloom's Taxonomy of Objectives	*The RCEM Taxonomy of Objectives*	*Mental Process or Abilities (17)*
1. Knowledge	1. Knowledge	1-1 Recall
		1-2 Recognize
2. Comprehension	2. Understanding	2-1 Seeing relationship
		2-2 Cite example
		2-3 Discriminate
		2-4 Classify
		2-5 Interpret
		2-6 Verify
		2-7 Generalize
3. Application	3. Application	3-1 Reason out
		3-2 Formulate
hypotheses		
		3-3 Establish hypotheses
		3-4 Infer
		3-5 Predict
4. Analysis	4. Creativity	4-1 Analyse
5. Synthesis		4-2 Synthesize
6. Evaluation		4-3 Evaluate

It is evident from the above chart that there are seventeen mental process of abilities; two for knowledge, seven for understanding, five for application and three for creativity. The comprehension category is termed as understanding. An outline has been given here for writing objectives in behavioural terms.

Writing Objectives in Behavioural Form by RCEM Approach

This method also requires the structure of the content and objectives are identified in taxonomic category considering entering behaviour of the learner. An appropriate mental process is selected and the element of content is combined with the mental abilities to produce the behavioural form of the objectives.

Characteristics of RCEM Approach

It has the following advantages in writing the objectives in behavioural terms :

1. This method is very easy and useful.

2. This method is more specific and definite than the Robert Mager's approach.
3. It does not have any doubt or confusion in preparing criterion test items.
4. This method is applicable for cognitive, affective and conative objectives.
5. The method explains the human learning in terms of mental processes or abilities.
6. It has shifted focus from product to process in writing objectives in behavioural terms.
7. This method has been developed in Indian situations therefore, it seems to be most useful for writing objectives in behavioural terms in our schools subjects.

Limitations of RCEM Approach

This method has the following advantages :

1. All behavioural objectives can only be written in seventeen mental abilities whereas Guilford has extracted 120 mental abilities.
2. These seventeen mental processes are employed in writing the behavioural objectives of the three domains. Hence it is difficult to differentiate among cognitive, affective and psychomotor objectives on the basis of behavioural objectives.
3. It is generally very difficult to select appropriate mental process for a content element.
4. There are seven mental processes for understanding, two for knowledge, five for application and three for creativity. In this way, there is no proper balance in mental abilities assigned to different categories.
5. There are only three mental abilities in creativity objective whereas Torrence and others have given five types of activities.

The teaching is organised for the development of a child. The child's development is concerned with cognitive, affective and psychomotor domains. Therefore, Mager's approach can not serve the purpose of writing teaching objectives in behavioural terms. It can be used in planning instructional material. The RCEM approach is useful for writing teaching objectives. There is no fast dichotomy among the three domains. The higher objectives of teaching and learning outcome are complex and are integrated in these domains.

The concept of evaluation approach is given by B.S. Bloom. His main emphasis was that testing should be based on teaching and both these activities should be objective-centred. Today teaching is organised by using the evaluation approach. Under this approach yearly plan and unit plan are prepared. The education process is considered as tri-polar process. There are three fundamental elements : 1. The educational objectives. 2. Learning experiences and 3. Change of behaviour of evaluation approach.

The evaluation approach and educational process are closely related to each other. The effectiveness and appropriateness of educational process is ascertained by evaluation approach. All the activities of teaching are evaluated in terms of student performances, which is known as change of behaviour. In this approach criterion tests used rather than achievement tests. A criterion test is always objective-centred. Therefore, in the present chapter main feature of evaluation approach have been described in detail.

Meaning and Definition of Evaluation Approach : The evaluation approach is a new concept in the discipline of education, which has revolutionalized the process of education.

In this approach main emphasis has been given in realizing the objectives of education in behavioural terms.

Quillen and Huna have defined the term evaluation approach in the following manner:

"'Evaluation is the Process of gathering and interpreting evidences on changes in the behaviour of the students as they progress through school".

In evaluation approach teaching and testing activities are performed side by side. The term evaluation is used in broader sense. It does not confine only upto student achievement but it includes the total process of teaching and learning. All the activities of teacher and students are evaluated qualitatively and quantitatively. The evaluation of a student performance does not confine to cognative domain but it also includes the affective and psychomotor domains., The total change of behaviour of student is evaluated for development their personality. The term change of behaviour includes cognative affective and psychomotor behaviours. The educational process is evaluated in terms of change of behaviour of students. Three types of activities are done in the evaluation process.

(1) How far the teaching objectives have been realized ?

(2) How far the learning experiences are effective ?

(3) What are the changes of behaviour have occurred in the students?

These three steps are closely related to each other and are performed in a sequence. The teaching and testing activities go side by side and these are objective-centred. It is the main assumption of this approach that failure of the student is due to the inappropriateness of learning experiences of teaching. Because it is the main responsibility of a teacher to bring desirable change among the students. Thus the change of behaviours are evaluated in terms of teaching objectives.

All the school subjects which are taught to them for providing learning experiences. Other activities which are organised in the school, are ment for learning experiences, but these should be directly related to the teaching objectives. In the following paragraphs an example has been given for using evaluation approach in teaching Geography.

Application for Evaluation Approach in Teaching **:** The following steps are used when teaching is organised with the help of evaluation approach.

(1) Formulation of teaching objectives.

(2) Providing learning experiences for realizing the teaching objectives, and

(3) Evaluating charge of behaviour of the student in the light of teaching objectives.

7

Evaluation of Knowledge

Measurement process is very important in the learning system. The measurement has more administrative utility in education than evaluation. An evaluation process is useful in modifying and improving learning system and instructional procedure. The measurement is precise and objective than evaluation. Hence, it is mostly used in measuring the learning outcome.

The Meaning : Measurement is a process of quantification. It means precision and quantification of a phenomenon or variable.

According to Bradfield, "Measurement is a process of assigning symbols to the dimensions of phenomenon in order to characterize the status of the phenomenon as precisely as possible."

Measurement is always done of a quality, attribute or variable of a thing or a person. We never measure a thing or a person. The psychologists and educationists are mainly concerned with the variables and attributes. The process of measurement converts the variables into variate which is used for drawing the inferences. For example, intelligence is quantified in terms of I.Q. and achievement variable is measured in terms of scores.

The Essentials : Measurement in any field always involves three essentials :

(1) Identifying and defining the quality, attribute or variable that it is to be measured.

(2) Determining the set of operations by which the attribute or variable may be made manifest and perceivable, and

(3) Establishing a set of procedure or definitions for translating observations into quantitative statements of degree, extent or amount.

System at Work

Lee J. Cronbach (1949) has classified all applications of mental measurement under the following three main functions

1. Prognosis function.
2. Diagnosis functions and
3. Research function.

Prognosis Function : The first of these functions is that of prognosis function. Any test tells about some differences among people's performance at this movement. All decisions involve prediction when psychological test is mentioned, so called I.Q. test administered to students in school to predict their academic performance come to mind. The measurement provides the extent of a variable which has the specific purpose of predicting future behaviour.

The prognosis has the administrative function such as classification, selection, promotion and gradation of students. The college students ask a counseller to help them choosing the best curriculum or job. Thus, the guidance and counselling service are also based upon the prognosis function of measurement. The effectiveness of method, instruction and treatment evaluated on the basis of students achievement.

Diagnosis Function : The second major function of measurement listed by Lee J. Cronbach is that of Diagnosis. The prognosis function reveals the level of student with regard to certain characteristics whereas the diagnosis function identifies the weakness of the student-learning. The remedial instruction can be prepared on the basis of diagnosis. It also implies the prediction but there is considerable justification in listing diagnosis of a separate function of measurement. The diagnostic function establishes the cause-effect relationship but prediction implies the simple relationship. The instructional procedure can be improved by this function of psychological measurement.

Research Function : The third major function of measurement listed by Cronbach is that of verification of scientific hypotheses of research. The use of measurement for research purpose, however, is not as great as for prediction and diagnosis. There is good reason for this as measurement is usually considered as completely valid measure of certain human characteristics. An investigator must treat test scores in this experiment as accurate quantification of real and useful variable. Measurement provides a more objective and dependable basis for comparison than dots rough impressions. Thus, the valid generalizations are made on the basis of accurate measurement.

In fact, the quantification is generally considered essential for the progress of education particularly at more advanced level. The scales of measurement have also been discussed below :

Measurement by Scales

There are four basic ways for quantifying a variable. They are also called levels of measurement and are commonly referred to as

(1) Nominal Scale.
(2) Ordinal or Rank Scale.
(3) Equal Interval Scale, and
(4) Ratio Scale.

Nominal Scale : The nominal scale is the least precise or crude among the four basic scales of measurement. It simply implies the classification of an item into two or more categories without any extent or magnitude. There is no particular order assigned to them. The frequency of numbers are used to give a name to something that may be used for determining per cent mode. For example, boys and girls; pass and fail; rural and urban etc.

The classroom observation, the measurement is done at nominal scale. The teaching and instruction are organized considering the mode of the students because a teacher cannot pace with each and every student in his teaching and learning process.

Ordinal Scale : The ordinal scale is precise than the nominal scale. It allows the teacher to assign values by placing or arranging the observations in relative rank order. No value is assigned to the distance between positions of ranking. The scale assigns observations to categories by number and arranges them in a logical order. It does not require the relationship of equivalence but also requires one observation to be greater or lesser than the other.

This scale is used frequently in the schools for prize distribution and to provide the motivation by the technique of competition. In asking the questions, teacher considers the place of a student in the class.

Equal-interval Scale : The equal-interval scale is more precise and refined scale than nominal and ordinal scales. This scale has all the characteristics and relationship of the ordinal scale, besides this distance between any two numbers on the scale are known. The zero point and the unit of measurement used on the scale are arbitrary or assumed. A linear relationship is established in the equal-interval scale.

The equal-interval scale has the greater use in teaching- learning situation, educational administration, educational guidance and counselling and educational research. The effectiveness of any instructional procedure can be evaluated precisely by collecting the data on this scale. The measurement in education is usually done on equal-interval scale. The dependable inferences are drawn in educational research by collecting evidences on equal-interval scale.

Ratio Scale : The ratio scale is the most refined among the four basic scales. It has all the characteristics, of equal-interval scale. In addition to that, it has an absolute zero point representing complete absence of the property being measured. It is used in physical sciences and less frequently in behavioural sciences. In school it is used in maintaining the cumulative records of the students. The cognitive and affective objectives can be assessed by using earlier scales of measurement. The ratio scale may be used for measuring the psychomotor objectives.

The measurement on various scales is done by using different types of measuring instruments. The questionnaire and observations yields ordinal data, educational and psychological tests provide scores or marks and physical measurement yields the data on ratio scale. The characteristics of a good measuring instrument have been described here.

Significant Features

A good measuring instrument or test requires some technical knowledge. It includes the knowledge and understanding of the various kinds of errors which influence the process of measurement. These are known as errors of measurement, and can be classified into four categories:

(a) Personal errors.
(b) Variable errors.
(c) Constant errors and
(d) Interpretive errors.

Personal Errors : In the field of measurement, the term objectivity is used to designate that the characteristic is related to personal error. The persons observing exactly the same responses are likely to assign different scores, because they can see the performance only from their own views or biases. The same person examining the same responses on two different occasions is likely to vary. This is known as personal error. It is termed as degree of objectivity.

Variable Errors : This kind of error may occur in psychological and educational measurement. The variable errors are those arising from accidents and inaccuracies due to many causes. A person making the observation which influences from time to time, test to test and individual to individual, is accountable to variable error. This is termed as degree of reliability.

Constant Errors : Most of the measurement of education and psychology are indirect. It is neither possible nor desirable to open a person's skull, to look inside. An instrument measures what is claim to measure which is related to the trait or characteristics.

Testing the problem of constant error is the problem of validity. It is necessary to know whether a test really measures what is claim to measure.

Interpretive Errors : The test score of an individual has no meaning until it is interpreted in terms of the performance of the other individuals or the performance of the group. Interpretive errors are those which result from understanding as for one or two things :

(1) With what sort of group of the individual is being compared.
(2) The way in which the comparison between the individual and the group performance is expressed.

Interpretive errors may be stated that is the problem of translating the raw scores into the norms. This problem of interpretive errors is taken in care through a process called standardization. This type of error is measured through norms.

The earlier three types of errors are usually considered in constructing the criterion test but the last one is interpretive error which is not taken in consideration because the criterion test evaluates the learning objectives in terms of group performance. This error involves when an individual's score is interpreted. Thus, the characteristics of a good measuring instrument may be summarized in the following forms :

1. It should be objective.
2. It should be reliable.
3. It should be valid.
4. It should be comprehensive and precise. and
5. It should be usable and practicable.

The usability implies the following features:

(a) Ease in administering the tool.
(b) Ease in scoring the answer scripts.
(c) Ease in interpreting scores. and
(d) It should be economical from time, energy and money point of view.

Different Tests

Tests are tools of measurements and measurements guide us in evaluation. Different types of tests are in vogue to facilitate the realization of the different purposes of education in the varying contexts of use. They may be categorised along three lines of approach. The approaches may be :

(i) purpose-specific categorisation of test-types;
(ii) mode-specific categorisation of test-types; and
(iii) process-specific categorisation of test-types.

A world of caution is necessary here.

The categorisation of test-types should not mislead you into thinking that the tests of one type form a variety absolutely distinct from those of every other type. It should not surprise you to find tests of different types requiring the very same kind of task and sometimes even repeating the very same item. That is to say that it is quite possible to find an item recurring in tests which otherwise belong to different types, or even different categories. What distinguishes the test-types, then, is not what is obvious in them but what guided them into being what they are. It is not in the choice of test-tasks, not in the realisation of these tasks in the form of test-items that we are to find the difference. We are to notice the difference; in the overall design of the tests, the purpose that guided them in their construction and sometimes, in the nature and extent of coverage of a given area of learning. With this understanding we can now discuss the features of design of the different test-types.

Purpose-specific Category: Purpose-specific category includes tests designed to achieve a specific purpose of evaluation. Generally four test-types are identified in this category

1. diagnostic tests.
2. aptitude tests.
3. achievement tests and
4. proficiency tests.

The features of each of these are as follows-

Diagnostic Tests : These help us identify the areas of learning in which learner needs a remedial course. They give us a profile of what the learner knows and does not know in a given area of learning. To present such a profile, a diagnostic test has to be a battery of a number of sub-tests each covering one area fairly thorough.

Aptitude Tests : These tests serve a predictive function. They help us identify potential talents. They identify the prerequisite characteristics which are essential for one to be competent to performs given task. Presenting items on such sub-skills which may eventually be developed into expert complex skills, these tests identify those who can do well in a field of study or a profession and those who cannot. These tests are generally used while selecting people for special course/careers.

Achievement Tests: These tests aim to measure the extent to which the objectives of a course have been achieved. The scope of these tests is governed by the objectives of the given course and they cover only the areas of learning demarcated by the given syllabus.

Proficiency Tests : These tests aim to assess the general ability of a person at a given time. Its scope is governed by a reasonable expectation of what abilities learners of a given status (say, matriculates or graduates) should possess. It is not restricted by considerations of the areas covered in any specific course-objectives or syllabus as in the case of achievement tests. While the usual end of course-examination in a school or college may be taken as a typical example of an achievement test, a national level selection or admission test for candidates coming from different states and/ or university jurisdictions can be taken as a typical example of a proficiency test.

Mode-specific Category : Under mode-specific category, we identify test-types on the basis of the mode/attitude that governs the construction and use of test. Under this category, we present six pairs of test-types along six dimensions.

Formal Assessment vs. Informal Assessment : Formal assessment is applicable to a situation where a body answerable to the public is holding a test for a selection or an award. Assessment in such a situation has to ensure objectivity, credibility and relevance. To ensure these, it will have to follow the set standardised norms/procedures of test construction administration and interpretation. Informal assessment is applicable to situations where an individual or a voluntary body is holding a test to obtain some information to fulfil some personal requirements. The informal assessment also needs to be objective and reliable, but the evaluator is not bound to satisfy the public of these qualities of his assessment. Hence the process of assessment need not follow very strictly the set procedures of evaluation.

Formative Assessment vs. Summative Assessment **:** Formative assessment is concerned with identifying learner weaknesses in attainment with a view to help the learner and the teacher overcome/remedy those, while summative aims at certifying and grading the attainment of the learner at the end of a given course. Tests for formative assessment are given at regular and frequent intervals during a course, while the tests for summative assessment are given at the end of a course or at the end of a fairly long period, say a term or a semester or a year. In a course that extends over six months, a test at the end of say, every fortnight will be a formative test, while the test at the end of the six months will be summative.

Moreover, the level of generalisation sought by the items of a summative test will be much higher compared to that sought by the items of a formative test. For instance, if the items of a formative test check the ability to apply a given rule or principle to a given unfamiliar situation, the items in a summative test may check the ability to apply one or more of the appropriate rules/principles from among the many given in a variety of situations.

(i) The account of formative assessment and summative assessment given here belongs to the context of EIEP. Yet the terms are also applied to the context of EOEP. However, in the context of EOEP, the functions of formative and summative assessments are different. Formative assessment here includes tests and other forms of measurement which are intended to give a measure of success of the parts of a course even as the course is in the process of development. Summative evaluation includes such forms of measurement that would give a measure of success of the course as a whole.

(ii) In education yet another term is in use, besides formative assessment and summative assessment. It is 'developmental assessment'. It is used in the context of course development and refers to the evaluation of the preliminary versions of courses with representative sample of learners. It is treated generally as a part of the course development schedule. Formative assessment in this context refers to the evaluation made of a course with larger group of learners. The purpose of such assessment is not to help the process of course development (as with the developmental assessment) but to help the activities of maintenance and revision of courses already developed.

Continuous Assessment vs. Terminal Assessment : While progress or achievement in learning is the concern of formative vs. summative mode of assessment, it is the purpose of grading learner achievement which guides the continuous vs. terminal mode of assessment. Continuous assessment seeks to spread the basis of grading on a number of tests with regular even intervals instead of placing it on one end of the course test (terminal test). Continuous assessment, thus, allows for more intense accommodation of the learning-content in the test process than the terminal assessment normally does. Scores on a series of continuous assessment test, taken together can serve for summative assessment. Taken individually, a continuous assessment test may be used formatively at the time of its administration. In the same way a terminal assessment may serve the purpose of formative assessment for follow-up courses.

Course Work vs. Examination : Learner assessment can be based on course work(s) performed by him during or at the end of a course, or, it may be based on examination(s) taken by him during or at the end of the course. Evaluation of course work or examination at different points of time during a course can be compiled at the end of a course to serve the purpose of summative evaluation.

Process vs. Product Assessment : The basis for evaluation may be either the final product or the result of a given task or the performance at difference stages leading to the accomplishment of the task (as in a research work). While evaluating a learner, one may look for the correct solution to a given problem or may take into consideration the correctness of the successive stages followed to solve the given problem (as in problem-solving tasks). If we do the former, we are supposed to be engaged in product assessment, if we do the later, we are supposed to make process assessment.

Internal Assessment vs. External Assessment : The mode of assessment is external when the evaluation of a learner ability is made by an outsider a person who is not related with the actual process of teaching. The evaluator and the learner are anonymous to each other in this case. When the assessment is made by a person, responsible for effecting the learning being measured, it becomes internal assessment. Formative and summative assessment of both scholastic and non-scholastic abilities is possible in the case of internal assessment. External assessment serves only summative evaluation of scholastic abilities.

These are actually different perspectives along which assessment of learner ability can be thought of and planned accordingly. It is possible to practically combine two or more of these perspectives in one's approach to assessment. For example, one may include both course work and examination as the basis for learner-assessment and these two may constitute the units of continuous assessment. Or, one may opt for formative assessment of the process of course work. Or, one may include both internal and external assessment to serve the purposes of formative and summative evaluation.

Process-specific Category: Sometimes test-types are identified on the basis on the process of test-construction. We can talk, of two pairs of constrastive test-types here

(a) Teacher made test vs. Standardised test, and

(b) Norm-reference test vs. Criterion-reference test.

Teacher Made Test vs. Standardised Test: Standardised tests are commercially produced tests adhering meticulously to certain procedures to meet the demands of objectivity and accuracy. They are finalised through the construction procedures of formulating objectives, designing test-blueprints, employing item try-outs, item-analysis and item-revisions. The teacher made tests, on the other hand, are not governed rigidly by such processes. The teacher who makes the tests uses his direction in matters of the scope of test area and choice of task-types and items. Standardised test derive their name by the fact that they ensure standardisation of the procedures of administration, scoring and interpretation through elaborate specific instructions.

While a teacher made test is designed to operate within the restricted situation of a given classroom (in terms of test- purpose, construction and use), a standardised test is designed for a larger operational situation crossing the barriers of a classroom an institution or even a region. A standardised test may be chosen for use by different teachers/institutions in different classrooms, on different occasions and in different regions.

Norm-referenced Tests vs. Criterion-referenced Test. In a norm-referenced test (NRT) the purpose is to discriminate between the high-achievers and the low-achievers. Its focus is not on what one has learnt or low much one has learnt of a given chunk of learning. Its focus is on where one stands in relation to the others of his calibre/level. It assesses the ability of one against the standard 'norm' of achievement of one's fellow testees.

The purpose of criterion-referenced-test (CRT) is to assess the objectives. It is the objective based-test. The objective type test is objective-centered. The objectives are assessed in terms of behavioural changes among the students. It assesses the ability of student against the criterion-behaviour of the learners.

A Particular Item

An item or a question is an 'instrument' that we use measure 'learning-outcome'. One's learning is measurable by another only when it is demonstrated in observable behavioural patterns. So an item, intended as an instrument to measure learning, should make a learner 'act' or 'behave', or 'respond' so as to demonstrate his mastery or otherwise with regard to the select bit of learning. To make the learner act observably the question/item has to present a stimulus to the learner. The stimulus may be in the form of a task. The task may require the learner to do a descriptive and/or 'practical' activity. Descriptive activities may be oral or graphic. Practical activities may involve the use of some tools and materials and they may be performed in realistic or simulated conditions.

Practical Demands

An item or a question is -primarily a specification of a task- the response to which is expected to put a desired bit of learning to demonstration. This involves two distinct activities on the part of the item-writer.

(i) devising a task to meet the specific objective of the test, and
(ii) specifying the task precisely and adequately.

The devising of task has to be done carefully so as to ascertain that the performance of the given task requires the learner to display the desired quantum of knowledge of a chosen content or the ability to use a skill in a desired way. The specification to task also has to be done with great care. The specification may defeat its purpose :.

(i) When it is not adequate, and
(ii) When it is not 'communicated' clearly.

The specification will not be adequate if it does not point out the conditions under which the task to be performed (say, for instance, the props-tools, materials, guidelines, facts and information etc. to be provided and the stages at which they are to be provided to the learner). It will not be adequate also when the level of accomplishment to which the task is to be performed is not mentioned in clear terms.

And even when an adequate specification is conceived, its purpose may not be served if it is not 'conveyed', or 'presented' to the learner properly. This means a language, or some graphic signs, or gestures, or some other mode of communication has to be employed to 'house' the specification and present the task to the learner. If the mode of communication employed to present, the specification is beyond the comprehension of the learner, then the item, however, adequately conceived, may not be of any use.

To summarise, then, an item, to be an effective instrument of measurement of learning, should meet the following requirements adequately

(i) The task that an item specifies should, in the process of the learner-response to it, demand and reflect only those specific aspects of skills or bits of learning that are being tested.

(ii) It should specify precisely
  (a) what the learner is to do.
  (b) the conditions under which it is to be done and
  (c) to what level/standard it is to be accomplished.

(iii) The medium (linguistic, graphic, sematic etc.) used to present the task specification should be such that there may not be any gap in its communication to the prospective testee i.e., the learner should be able to follow the medium without any misunderstanding of dubious understanding.

Treasure of Items

Development of question/item banks have been another reformative effort in the evaluation procedures in education. In the following sub-sections, we will talk about the concept of question/ item banking, how it is developed and what its various advantages are.

Concept of Item Banks : It is almost like a blood bank where blood from different healthy donors is collected, classified and stored so that blood of required specification can be supplied in no time whenever there is an SOS message from a needy patient. On the same analogy, question/item bank means a collection of questions/items from different sources (of responsible institutions and individuals) arranged in an order and supplemented with adequate information to facilitate retrieval of items of required specification.

The concept of 'question/item bank' is not a revolutionary one. Question banks have been in existence for a long time developed by both institutions (universities and boards of examinations) and individuals (practising teachers). Large number of questions produced in different subject areas over a long period of time used to be stored by these agencies for future use. Most of these questions thus collected did not undergo any scientific process. They had been constructed or selected intuitively because they looked right or because they 'seemed to work.'

They did not carry any precise information about their nature or the level of their use.

Over the years the practice has evolved a scientific process and at present a question bank does not mean just a collection of a large number of questions/items of all kinds pertaining to a subject area. It is a collection of questions/items plus technical information about, the questions/items collected. The information thus provided will be a nature to help the prospective users of the 'bank' to locate and use questions/items to suit their requirements. The information will include the item-writer's assumption about the learning-objective tested by the question/item and the details of item behaviour gathered on the basis of a pretest administered to a sample of population. Each question/item will be accompanied with such specific information as:

1. the content area/topic on which the question/item is based;
2. the specific intellectual ability of the testee that is being tested;
3. time required to answer the question/item;
4. question/item type;
5. mark allotted for each question/item;
6. the difficulty value (DV) and the discriminative power (DP) of the question/item calculated on the basis of the performance of the sample population; and
7. the key to the question/item.

The statistical information (DV and DP) and the key will be precise for all objectives type questions/items.

But for short answer type or essay type or problem solving type of questions, the statistical information will be crude. The key will cover a list of main points of answer and marks to be given for respective points.

Need of Item Bank **:** The concept of question banks has come to stay with various bodies responsible for providing examinations perhaps due to the heavy burden being thrust on them of late. The increasing burden of work load is due to different factors like.

1. the rising number of learners taking up various courses;
2. the constant check on the learning content of course material;
3. the development of new courses comprising modules (i.e., parts) of different other courses; and
4. the continuing use of examinations for one purpose or the other (like course evaluation, learner diagnosis, educational guidance, etc.)

The volume of examination-related work that has to be accomplished as a result of the joint operation of the above factors is very huge. It is in this context that development of a question bank is considered an expedient way of reducing the burden of work at least on one front, namely test-construction.

The question banks have a more special relevance to distance education.

The concept of distance education includes a provision for its learners to pace and time their studies to suit their individual convenience. If this provision is extended to its logical end, then distance education must be able to offer its learners the opportunity to take examinations as and when they find themselves ready to take them. That would mean a situation where distance education must be equipped to meet demands for more frequent examination opportunities. To meet such an exigency, requiring repetitions of the whole cycle of examination activities for different courses and involving large sums of money and time, we need to look for some expedient method. Holmberg (1985) makes a precise reference to the likelihood of such an exigency and the relevance of question banking procedure :

"If the liberal approach is accepted and students are offered the possibility to start, interrupt and finish their study when they want, to pace themselves and generally to organise their study as they see it, there must be a great demand for frequent examination opportunities in all subjects in which formal qualifications are required. A mastery- learning system, allowing individual students to be examined when they feel they are ready for an examination... would seem to be called for. This requires a bank of validated test items."

Procedure Development : The development of the question/ item bank involves the following five distinct phases of activity :

Phase I : Collecting questions/items : At this initial stage questions/items are collected from among existing questions used by the universities, the boards of examinations and individual teachers plus those that are written a new by trained item writers.

Phase II : Pre-validating the questions/items : Pre-validation includes the following activities :

(i) Checking whether the questions/items meet the general and specific criteria of valid questions/items and deciding whether to retain/reject/modify them.

(ii) Categorising questions/items in terms of the content (subject and topic) being tested; the abilities/ outcomes/objectives being tested; the type of question/item and the level at which the question/ item is intended for use.

(iii) Specifying for each question/item details of the marks allotted, and of the time that the learner may require to answer.

Phase III : Post-validating the questions/items : Tests of collected items are administered to a sample population; item-analysis is carried out and decisions are taken as to which items to retain which to reject and which to modify on the basis of the DV and the DP of each item.

Phase IV : Supplementing Operational Characteristics : A represen-tative portion of the collected items are tried out under actual examination conditions to obtain operational characteristics of questions/items and the information obtained on the field trial with a sample of population is supplemented.

Phase V : Storing the questions/items : The questions/items are published in the form of the 'brochures', each question/item with the information on them is presented in a standard proforma,

Or

the question/item with the information pertaining to them are typed out on 5' x 8' cards for storing them in Kardex trays,

Or

the questions/items are coded and stored in the memory of a digital computer.

Advantages : Besides being a ready-source for test-construction purposes and thereby making test construction less time consuming and less onerous, a properly developed question/item bank serves a number of other pedagogic purposes.

The field trial of the question/item with a sample population (with the computation of statistical information on facility value and discrimination index as part of its process) makes possible a concurrent comparability of different groups of learners with the sample of population. This may help in the promotion and maintenance or common standards across geographical, regional and academic boundaries.

A well-developed question/item bank may also help us in bringing about a much desired change in the present education pattern where all teaching is geared to the terminal examination. We could perhaps succeed with the question/item banks in 'matching the examinations to the curriculum that is taught' as against the present practice of matching the curriculum to set patterns of examinations.

The development of question/item bank involving, as it does, a thorough exploration of the learning content and learning activities, may lead to precise specification of course objectives and offer a clearer direction to curricular development.

Costwise also question/item banks are claimed apparently to make the cheapest examination method and comparability procedure. As no comparison of cost effectiveness of various examining and comparability procedures is available as yet no concluding evidence is available in this regard.

Methods of Ranking

Grading is a means for reporting the result of measurement. The performance of the learners is scored, we need to tell people concerned with the test i.e., (the testees, the parents the educational administrators, the selection agencies and such others) how good or bad the achievement of a testee is. The scores on a test put together cannot do this function.

Say, for instance, we administer a test of 50 objective type item and two of the testees score 31 and 17, respectively. What does the score 31 out of 40 or 17 out of .40 on this test mean ? What does the quantitative difference between the two scores signify qualitatively ? Is the first score 'good' or the second one 'bad' ? if 'good', how good it is, or 'bad', how bad it is? When we attempt to describe scores thus-trying to indicate the quality of performance corresponding to particular scores-we are attempting to 'grade' them. Such grading can be done differently-using symbols and verbal descriptions. Before we go any further on the issue under consideration, let us consider the traditional practice of marking and see the relative merits and demerits of grading and marking.

Age-old Exercise

Traditionally we have been resorting to 'marking' to report 'learners' performance and we have been using a 0-100 scale. The assumption behind such wide scale was that learner's ability can be plotted accurately between 0 and 100 with a precision to the value of 1/101 unit. To put if differently, we assume that the performance of a learner, mostly a three-hour performance, covering the learning acquired our three to ten or more months, can be analysed into a hundred constituent bits of equal 'weight', each one of which can be recognised individually and given credit for.

How far is this assumption tenable ?

This assumption is false because :

(i) All learner-tasks cannot be analysed into exactly hundred and exactly one-to-one equivalent constituent bits.

(ii) Even if the condition above were fulfilled, all the hundred 'bits' cannot be recognisably displayed and therefore, cannot be taken into credit individually because these bits may belong in different proportions to the three realms of human ability, the cognitive, the psychomotor and the affective. "Mathematical precision is an almost impossible goal to realise" in the measurement of achievement or human ability. So human ability cannot be measured with sensitivity and precision as assumed by a 0-100 scale.

Fault Possibility

Besides this false assumption, this practice suffers from two kinds of error caused by :

(i) marker variability and

(ii) subject variability.

Marker Variability : Besides the improbability of precision n measuring human ability, there is also room for marking errors on a 0-100 scale. Our tests have, all these days, been consisting either exclusively of free response items, or, as of late, a combination of free-response and fixed-response items. Scoring in the case of fixed-response items such objectively in scoring is not possible because :

(i) fixing a rigid predetermined list of bits to constitute a response is not possible;

(ii) there is room for individual variation in the learner responses and also individual variation in the marker-assessment of those responses. It is difficult to get the subtle variations in the responses distinguished fairly and consistently even within the evaluation of one individual marker.

So, scoring free-response items is subject to differences in marking, when they are marked by different examiners (or, the same examiner on different occasions).

The statistical analysis studying the chance of error in marking has established that :

"When an examiner assigns a mark to a script, there is 50% chance that his error is greater than 5%. This means where a candidate is awarded a raw mark of 41, the true mark may be either above 46 or below 36 in 50% of the cases."

The UGC Report on Examination Reform-A Plan of Action (1973) reports the above finding and concludes that

"Under these circumstances, the 101 point scale where candidates are distinguished in steps of one mark, loose all its significance."

But the traditional practice has been to fail those who got 39 marks and pass those who got 40 and to classify those with 59 marks in second class and those with 60 in first class.

***Subject Variability* :** Though the 0 to 100 scale is used in marking performances in different disciplines, in reality the distribution-spread i.e., (the actual range of marks being awarded) varies from discipline to discipline. While a subject like mathematics (perhaps excluding a few branches in it) enjoys a full-range distribution within the scale (that is to say, in Mathematics scores may easily vary from 0 to 100), subjects like History and English Literature are restricted to the use of a limited range distribution within the scale, say from 15 to 60 (that is however good a performance is in these subjects, it is seldom given the maximum marks in the scale, even the best being given something like 60-marks).

The difference in the utilisation of varying ranges within the scale affects the comparability of scores in the different subjects. While 55 may be an appreciably good score in English literature it may be an average score in Mathematics. But to the recruiting agencies or the public, these have not been scores of different values. Worse than situations of this type has been the practice of educational institutions to sum up the scores in different subjects as though scores in all subjects are of equal value to arrive at the aggregate total obviously little realising that such an aggregate is more often than not deceptive.

To summarise we can identify three serious errors in the traditional practice marking :

(i) false assumption about achieving precise measurement of human ability

(ii) wide inter-examiner differences in marking and

(iii) falsity of score comparability between different subjects.

Advantages : The recent movement in grading has been the result of an honest confession of our inability to measure with precision the human qualities with all their intricate levels of variation and mix-up of observable and non-observable attributes. It has reduced the wide 101 point range of scale to a viable short range. It gives only rough estimates of learner ability, no doubt; but the estimates are more realistic and reliable than the false precision in terms of marks. That is to say, it reduces considerably the chances of error of judgement though it suffers from inaccuracy, which even otherwise cannot be overcome. The possibility of an error in judgement in awarding one grade-point in the place of another is relatively much less than compared to the possibility of awarding 59 marks instead of 60 marks of vice versa. Thus the narrow range scale used in grading minimises the inter-examiner differences in evaluation. Besides, when narrow-range scale is applied chances of utilising the whole range are more than when a wide-range scale is used-irrespective of the subject-variation. The narrow range scale may, thus, lessen the disparity in the value of scores in different subjects. Thus, the practice of grading tends to overcome the errors of the traditional marking system which we identified in the previous subsection.

Different Bases : Whatever be the mode, all grading involves, the use of a set standard. When you say something is 'good', the judgement implies an implicit or overt rating against a set standard – a physical or conceptual model. Similarly when you grade scores, you describe them to be good, or average, or poor-on comparing the scores with some standards. The standards may be what the others in the class concerned have scored; or, what the performance is, expected ideally to be. Thus, basically, grading may be done along two lines, using two different kinds of standards :

Relative Grading Standard (i.e., keeping the performance of the whole group of testees on the given task as a standard) and

Absolute Grading Standard (i.e., keeping an ideal conception of what a good performance on a given task should be as the standard).

Relative Grading Standard : When a Relative Grading Standard is applied, the learners get grades according to their ranks in r elation to the other learners taking the same test. The classical form of relative grading proceeds from a pre-determined plan of learner distribution. It begins with a specification of what percentage of learners are to be grouped under each of the different grades of a chosen scale (the scale may comprise five or seven or nine grades).

Limitations of Relative Grading. This kind of normative distribution of grades will be useful to Universities, Boards of Examinations, Recruitment /Selection Boards, and other Testing Agencies who have to deal with a large number of candidates (say, tens of hundreds at a time) and have to make pass-fail/select-reject decisions and do not have to find 'what' the candidates have mastered or how much of a subject they have mastered. The later considerations are typical the concerns of a class teacher both in formative and summative evaluation and applied in these situations the relative grading following normative distribution is bound to have the following limitations :

Relative grading of a learner-performance in a class-test will be inadequate in its message to the learner, the teacher, the parents and whosoever, is concerned with his/her learning or progress in learning. The position of a learner on the normal curve is determined by the overall performance level of the class. So a grade without any information about the performance of a class as a whole will not convey much sense pedagogically. A learner who gets 'A' in one class may, when placed in another, get 'F' ! So the A's and F's are meaningless, unless they are accompanied by some information about performance ability of the group to which they belong.

Under 'normative distribution' (another description of relative grading) scheme, each grade has to be assigned to a fixed number of learners in the class. This makes farce of the idea of a teacher attempting to help the 'poor' performers do better or the high-achievers improve their performance. Besides, it also tends to create bad attitudes among learners. When a learner - manages to come up from a lower grade, it naturally pushes down someone else to a lower grade. A learner may, therefore, develop negative attitudes and be tempted to hope that his classmates do as poorly as possible so that his efforts will better in comparison. This can inhibit learners from helping one another and can even hurt social relations among them.

Having discussed the relative grading standards at length, we shall now look into the absolute grading standards.

Word Absolute Grading Standards. While applying relative grading word standards, we fix for each grade the number of learners to be assigned. But when we apply absolute grading standards, we fix for each grade a range of scores for a learner to credit with, in order to claim the grade mentioned against them. In another form of absolute standards, one may fix the quantum of content and/or the level of mastery of given skills in, a relative hierarchy of the groups of relevant attributes (like creativity, intelligence, imagination, resourcefulness, simplicity etc., besides relevance and appropriacy of content and form expected of the responses) for each grade to be awarded. The grading scheme following such absolute standards in terms of qualitative (in the place of percentage) values is sometimes called criterion-referenced grading.

While the percentage standards can be applied to grade the performance on objective (fixed-response) items, the qualitative standards facilitate grading the performance on subjective (free-response) items.

The absolute grading standards are ideal to evaluate and grade students. But there are some difficulties in putting them into practice. The fixation of standards (numerical as well as qualitative) has to be flexible and accommodative as the learners' scores depend on the facility level of the test administered. Formulating reasonable bases for the standards is also not easy at all levels and all types of courses. They may be done with relative case at higher levels and in vocational type of courses rather than at lower levéls and in non-vocational courses.

Allotting Division and Position

The attempt to develop a narrow range grading, consequent on the realisation of the weaknesses of marking on a 101-point scale, has led to the suggestion for grading on different scales and of adopting different approaches. The approach which is given in the following pages is quite suitable to the type of composite tests made up of different item-types most commonly in use today. It allows the use of different short-range scales to suit the types of responses expected of different item-types. It is more reliable also because the choice of scale for each item-type is governed more or less by the number of test-point it presents.

For instance, in an objective type item the response can be either right or wrong. There cannot be any range of quality within which the responses can vary. So responses to such questions can be graded only on a two-point scale (0-1), where '1' represents an acceptable response and '0' an unacceptable one. And, in the case of short answer (free-response) type question, the range of coverage of the subject matter may be restricted to a few value points, say, 3 or 4. In such a case both a 7-point scale and 2-point scale may tend to enhance imprecision. The levels of quality of the response may not vary so much as to warrant a 7-point scale and at the same time, the responses may not be totally devoid of variations so as to allow for a binary operation of a 2-point scale. So a scale in between has to be applied say, a 3-point scale (0-2), where '0' can mean an unsatisfactory response, '1' an answer of mediocre quality and 12' an answer of appreciable quality.

QUESTIONS

1. Define the term 'Evaluation and Measurement'. Differentiates between measurement and evaluation.

2. Describe the role of evaluation in an educational programme. Indicate the purpose and functions of evaluation.
3. Enumerate the functions of Measurement and Scales of Measurement. Describe the characteristics of a good measuring instrument.
4. Indicate the type of errors in Measurement. Describe the types of Tests used in evaluation.
5. Explain the term 'Item' of a test. Describe the functional conditions of an item.
6. Explain the concept of 'Question-Bank'. Describe the need and procedure of question-bank development. Enumerate its advantages.
7. Explain the term 'Grading System'. Describe its need and procedure of grading system. Enumerate the advantages of grading system of evaluation in education.

8

Procedure of Evaluation

Perfect Evaluation

Evaluation is always with reference to the objectives of education and is not in a vacuum. Evaluation has to be comprehensive in a system of education which aims at the many-sided development of the personality of a child. "The school of today concerns itself not only with the intellectual pursuits but also with the emotional and social development of the child, his physical and mental health, his social adjustment and other equally important aspects of his life-in a word, with an all round development of his personality", writes the Secondary Education Commission.

Gone are the days when education was considered in terms of 3 R's i.e. Reading, Writing and Arithmetic-denoting traditional subjects. Now it is concerned in terms of 7 R's i.e. Reading, Writing Arithmetic, Rights, Responsibilities, Relationship of Rights and Responsibilities and Recreation.

Evaluation has to be comprehensive as it is an important part of any process of learning and teaching. As observed by the National Policy on Education, 1986 and as amended in 1992, "as part of sound educational strategy, examinations should be employed to bring about qualitative improvement in education."

Two Dimensions

Evaluation in its broader concept includes examination of academic and examination of non-academic aspects of education. According to Wrightstone, "Evaluation is a relatively new technical term, introduced to design a more comprehensive concept of measurement than is implied in conventional tests and examinations evaluation involves the identification and formulation of a comprehensive range of the major objectives of a curriculum; this definition is in terms of pupil behaviour, and the selection or construction of valid, reliable and practical instruments for appraising the specified phases of pupil behaviour." In examination and measurement the emphasis is upon the academic subjects only whereas evaluation includes all the changes that take place in the development of a balanced personality and measures the qualities of head, hand, health and heart of an individual.

H.H. Remmers and N.L. Gage point out, "It is the felt need that has caused the shift from the term 'measurement' - implying mathematically precise mensuration of knowledge - to the term 'evaluation' which widens the areas to be studied to include subjective opinions and qualitative changes as well as objective and quantitative changes, to include changes in attitudes, appreciations and understanding as well as acquisition of knowledge and skills."

Writing about the scope of evaluation, National Curriculum Framework for School Education: A Discussion Document (NCERT, 2000) states, "Evaluation as carried out today is quite restricted in scope, purpose and utility. Although the educational objectives are formulated keeping in view the all-round development of the learners covering both scholastic and non-scholastic dimensions. In practice evaluation rarely goes beyond the scholastics aspects (cognitive development). While curriculum provides for guidelines with regard to the systematic organisation of experiences which may lead to physical and socio-emotional growth and development along with cognitive development of the learners. Non-scholastic (non-cognitive) aspects of learners' growth are not given due emphasis in schools as these are not considered as evaluative entity."

The Areas : These are as under:

1. Scholastic achievement.
2. Personal and social attributes, attitudes, work habits, etc.
3. Physical and health development.
4. Performance in skill areas.
5. Products produced by the students.

A Continual Exercise

Continuous evaluation implies a process of continuous efforts to assess desirable attainment/change/progress/performance taking place in the learner in accordance with the educational objectives.

Need for Continuous Evaluation. Evaluation is an important tool in the hands of the teachers to help the learners to improve their achievement in the scholastic and non-scholastic areas. It is not merely testing him to find out his progress. It is to enable him to improve his performance on the basis of testing which points out his limitations. The National Policy on Education (1986) as amended in 1992 has laid special stress on improving the evaluation process and examination process by "continuous and comprehensive evaluation that incorporates both scholastic and non-scholastic aspects of educations, spread over the total span of instructional times."

The Purposes

Continuous evaluation is expected to serve the following purpose:

1. To appraise the status of and changes in pupil behaviour.
2. To locate pupil's needs and possibilities,
3. To aid pupil-teacher planning.
4. To expand the concept of worthwhile goals beyond pure achievement.
5. To serve as a means of improving school-community relation.
6. To familiarize the teacher with the nature of pupil learning, development and progress.

7. To relate measurement to the goals of the instructional programme.
8. To facilitate the selection and improvement of measuring instruments.
9. To appraise the teacher's competence.
10. To appraise the supervisor's competence.
11. To serve as a method of self-improvement.
12. To serve as a guiding principle for the selection of supervisory techniques.
13. To keep an eye on the continuous improvement in the student.

Techniques and Tools. Comprehensive evaluation cannot be imagined without continuous evaluation.

Both are the two sides of the same issue. Thus tools and techniques are also the same. These are as under:

Techniques

(a) Written examination
(b) Oral examination
(c) Practical examination
(d) Interviews
(e) Observation
(f) Projective techniques
(g) Sociometric techniques

Tools

Tests - These include

(i) Intelligence tests, (ii) Teacher made tests, (iii) Standardized achievement tests, (iv) Unit tests, (v) Terminal tests, (vi) Annual test, (vii) Diagnostic tests.

Development of Tools. Sometimes teachers themselves may be required to develop some of the tools. These need not be very sophisticated. Nevertheless, these tools should be valid, reliable and practicable.

The Advantages

1. Continuous evaluation is helpful to know the extent to which the student progresses regularly.

2. Continuous evaluation is helpful to diagnose the weaknesses and strengths of the individual student.
3. Continuous evaluation provides feedback to the teacher and others connected with the education of the student.
4. Continuous evaluation is helpful to the teacher to organise effective and inspirational teaching -learning strategies.
5. Continuous evaluation is useful to the student himself who comes to know about his limitations, weaknesses and strengths.
6. Continuous evaluation keeps the parents informed of the progress of their wards.
7. Continuous evaluation is helpful in impressing upon the students that their regular attendance in the school is essential for their progress.
8. Continuous evaluation is helpful in seeking cooperation of the parents of the students. It becomes clear to them that they must ensure the regular attendance of their wards in the school and provide instructional material in time.
9. Continuous evaluation brings to light the need for remedial instruction,
10. Continuous evaluation helps to ascertain the areas of aptitudes and interests etc. of the students.
11. Continuous evaluation helps in the guidance programme.

Aims of Evaluation

NCERT Discussion paper (2000) on National Curriculum Framework for School Education has outlined the role of evaluation in raising standard of attainment as stated below:

Main purpose of evaluation as envisaged by the Education Commission (1964-66) and reiterated in NPE, 1986 is to help determine and gradually raise standards of attainment at State and National levels. Evaluation should therefore be construed as a powerful instrument for improving the quality of education in general and that of improving teaching learning in particular. One of the main ingredient, of quality education is quality of learners' achievements which should be effectively realised through feed-back mechanism to be employed for the benefit of learners, teachers and parents. Now-a-days evaluation is practised as a mandatory requirement of the system which is accomplished through end of year examinations and some tests etc. during the year. In order to have proper evaluation of learners' progress examination alone should not be relied upon. Other modes of assessment such as observation during individual and group tasks, sociogram and peer ratings etc. may be put to use. The outcomes of this evaluation convey the achievement of students at particular times as revealed through the testing devices put to use. This exercise is done more as a ritual rather than a device of specific feed-back to learners, teachers and parents. Corrective measures particularly in terms of remedial instructions are a rare phenomenon. In order to derive full advantage of examination and evaluation the outcomes need to be interpreted in the following manner:

1. By the learner to know his/her strength and weaknesses and get inspiration to make up the deficiency at the earliest.
2. By the teacher to have an assessment of students performance on one hand and assessment of the efficacy the teaching learning strategy employed by him/her. This should be analysed with a view to providing differential treatments to different categories of learners so that students may be engaged as under:
   (a) Bright ones may be engaged in goal directed learning through enrichment programme.
   (b) Average ones may be involved in peer learning by assigning specific tasks in small groups.
   (c) The weaker ones may be diagnosed properly and remedial teaching may be organised before embarking upon new teaching units.

The aforesaid practice of evaluation will constitute part of continuous, periodic and comprehensive evaluation and may help learners attain mastery of competencies, basic skills, desirable attitudes and values which may help them to settle in life and become good and contributing citizens of the country. Necessary steps may be taken to reduce the element of rote memorisation of information from books to application of the learned concepts, skills and competencies in practical situations. Besides, this the textbooks, instructional materials will have to be re-oriented towards this goal, teachers will have to be motivated and empowered to undertake such tasks in right earnest. Need for a serious monitoring mechanism cannot be undermined.

The recommendations of the Education Commission 1964-66 though made in the 1970's still hold good. Therefore, these are given below:

Evaluation at the Lower Primary Stage. The Education Commission 1964-66 stated, "One of the main purposes of evaluation at the primary stage is to help the pupils to improve their achievement in the basic skills and to develop the right habits and attitudes with reference to the objectives of primary education. These objectives and their implication for evaluation should be made clear to the teachers."

The lower primary stage covering Classes I to IV should be treated as an ungraded unit, because this would help the children coming from different backgrounds to advance at their pace. As the conditions in most primary schools, however, are not favourable to the general adoption of this procedure, it has recommended that the experiment should be tried out in the beginning in classes I and II, which should be regarded as a single ungraded unit. The two year block may be divided into two groups, one for slow learners and the other for fast learners to enable different pupils to proceed at the level of their ability and move from one unit to another. Such a division, however, will be practicable only in a large sized school with more than one section in each class.

Advantage Climbed. This will put an end in the existing practice of detentions in Class I and to the drop-outs and wastage resulting therefrom, and will also provide for continuity and flexibility in the educational programme of the first two classes. If the experiment regarding the upgraded unit succeeds in Classes I and II, it may be extended to the remaining classes of the lower primary stage.

Preparation of the Teachers. Teachers should be prepared for the ungraded system through the regular training course and orientation programmes and should be helped with a supply of diagnostic tests and remedial material. The orientation may be given by the State Institutes of Education. Observation techniques, which are more reliable for assessing the pupil's growth at this stage than more formal techniques of evaluation, should be used by teachers in a planned and systematic manner.

Evaluation at the Higher Primary Stage. Due importance should be given here also to oral tests, which should form a part of the internal assessment.

The teacher should be helped in such assessment with a rich supply of evaluation materials prepared by the State Evaluation Organizations, including standardized achievement tests.

Diagnostic testing is necessary here and indeed throughout the school stage. In most cases, such testing will be through simple teacher-made diagnostic tests.

Cumulative record cards play a vital role in indicating the growth and development of the pupil at each stage, his academic and emotional problems, and his difficulties of adjustment, if any, and the directions, in which remedial action is to be taken to solve his problems of difficulties. In the first instance, the cards should be introduced from Class IV onwards in about 10 per cent of the selected schools as an experimental measure; but once the majority of teachers are trained in evaluating certain important aspects of the child's personality and the proper maintenance of the records, the use of the cards may be gradually extended to all the higher primary and, as a next step, even to lower primary schools.

No Compulsory External Examination at the End of Primary Stage. The Commission has advanced two arguments against external examinations:

(1) It is not necessary or desirable to prescribe a rigidly uniform level of attainment for all the primary school pupils in a State or even a district, through an external examination.

(2) Instead of creating incentives for better teaching, the external examination intended for all will saddle teachers

with standardized programmes and encourage the process for rote memorization, which is the besetting evil of teaching and learning methods in our schools today.

Periodic Surveys of the Level of Achievement. While not in favour of a compulsory external examination, the Commission believes that for the proper maintenance of standards, periodic surveys of the level of achievement of primary schools is necessary. The Commission recommends that such surveys should be conducted by the district educational authorities to assess the standard of performance of the schools in a given area by means of standardized or highly refined tests prepared by specialists in the State Evaluation Organisations.

Advantages Claimed. This procedure will enable the education officers to pick out the weaker schools and help them to improve their performance. It will also assist the schools in finding out the weakness of their pupils for purposes of remedial work.

Common Internal Examination for Inter-School Comparability. The Commission recommends that by making use of the standardized or refined test material referred to above, the district educational authorities may, if they so desire, arrange for a common examination to be taken by the pupils of all the schools in a district at the end of the primary stage. Though the question paper will be set by the district educational authorities or by special paper-setters appointed by the State Evaluation Organization, the performance of the pupils of each participating school will be done by the teachers of the school themselves, and not by any external examiners.

Advantages of Such a Common Examination. (1) As the question papers will contain standardized tests and highly refined and professional tests items, the evaluation will be more valid and reliable than what is possible through the kind of annual and final examinations conducted in the ordinary primary school. Through such a common test inter-school comparability with regard to levels of performance in the district can be obtained, and this would be helpful, as shown above, both to the education officers and to the schools.

Question Papers of Short Duration. Question papers in the different subjects at this common examination should be of short duration, each of not more than one hour or one hour and a half, so that the entire examination should be completed in two or three days.

This proposal aims at reforming the existing examination by making it less formal, reducing its burden on the pupils' minds, and increasing its validity as a measure of educational attainment. The certificate regarding the completion of the course should be given by the school and not by any external agency, and this certificate should be accompanied by a statement showing the results of the common final examination, if any, together with the results of the internal assessment made by the school of the pupils performance throughout the year, as shown in his cumulative records.

Examinations for the Award of Scholarship. In addition to the common examination, the Commission recommends that special tests may be held at the end of the primary course for the award of scholarships or certificates of merit and for the purpose of identifying talent and pupils may appear for these tests on a voluntary basis. The evaluation of the pupil's performance in these tests will be done by external examiners.

Improvement in External Examinations. (a) The technical competence of paper-settes should be raised through an intensive training programmes sponsored by the State Boards; (b) The question paper-setters should be oriented to testing not merely the acquisition of knowledge but the ability to apply knowledge and the development of problem-solving abilities; and (c) The nature of the questions asked should be improved. (d) It is essential that scientific scoring procedures should be devised so that there may be optimum reliability in the assessment of the candidate's performance. (e) With the ever-increasing number of students appearing for the Board examinations, the task of getting answer scripts properly valued and processing the results efficiently within a given time is becoming more and more difficult. It is necessary that this process should be mechanized so as to make it more accurate and expeditious.

Large Incidence of Failure. The Commission observes, "The matter about which the public at large is most deeply concerned is not the irrationality of the scoring procedures, or the inefficiency of the administrative processes, but the large incidence of failures in the external examination at the end of the school stage. An analysis of the results of the different Board examinations for the last five years shows that about 55 per cent of the candidates appearing for the high school examination and about 40 per cent of those appearing for the higher secondary school examination fail regularly every year. In the case of the private candidates the percentage soars up to 70% or even more. Failure often has a demoralizing effect on the unsuccessful candidates. The failure of such large numbers of students, particularly after they have been screened year after year by means of annual and other school examinations, is a sad reflection on our methods of education as well as on our system of examination."

"We also believe that with the proposed improvement in the curriculum, instructional materials and methods of teaching, and the reorientation in the training of teachers, the incidence of examination failures will be reduced. But we do not think that a student should be branded as a total failure, if he passes in certain subjects but is unable to make the grade in others. There is no reason why he should carry with him the stigma of being declared as unsuccessful candidate if he has partially succeeded in his educational effort."

Certificates Given by the Board and the School. The Commission recommends that the certificate issued by the Board on the basis of the results of the external examination at the end of the lower or higher secondary stage, should give the candidate's performance only in those subjects in which he has passed but there should be no remark to the effect that he has passed or failed in the whole examination. The Board, however, should issue a statement along with the certificate showing his marks or grades in all the subjects.

Permission to Reappear. The candidate should be permitted to appear again if he so desires, for the entire examination or for separate subjects in order to improve his performance.

Certificate from the School. On the completion of the course, at the end of the lower or higher secondary stage, the student should receive a certificate also from the school giving the record of his internal assessment as contained in his cumulative record card. This certificate may be attached to that given by the Board in connection with the external examination.

No Compulsory External Examination. External examination need not be compulsory for all the students of Class X or XI/XII. A student may choose to leave the school with the school certificate only without appearing for the external examination, and seek a job or even an entry into some vocational course on the basis of the certificate and the school records. It must be recognized, however, that since admission to institutions of higher secondary education as well as of higher education will be selective, the authorities controlling such institutions will lay down their own rules of eligibility for admission. A student seeking entry into these institutions may have not only to pass the external examination in the subjects and secure the prescribed grades but also submit himself, if necessary, to certain admission tests required by the institution.

Freedom to Selected Schools to Assess Students. In order to lessen the importance of the domination which the external examinations exercise over school education still further, the Commission recommends that a few selected schools should be given the right of assessing their students themselves and holding their own final examination at the end of class X, which will be regarded as equivalent to the external examination of the State Board of School Education. The State Board will issue certificates to the successful candidates of these schools on the recommendation of the schools. A committee set up by the State Board of School Education should develop carefully worked out criteria for the selection of such schools. For the success of this experiment, it is essential that the schools should not only be freed from the requirements of an external examination but should be permitted to frame their own curricula, prescribe their own text-books, and conduct their educational activities without departmental restrictions.

This suggestion is indeed a bold one in the direction of freedom of educational experimentation and it carries certain responsibilities also. The Commission, therefore, suggests that light given to the experimental schools should be reviewed periodically as institutions invested with such powers should continuously earn their privilege. The Commission envisages that after the experiment is tried out successfully in a few schools, more and more schools will be released from the restrictive influence of the external examination and given the freedom to work out their own ideas in education.

Methods of Internal Assessment. This internal assessment, or evaluation conducted by individual schools is of great significance and should be given increasing importance. It should be comprehensive, evaluating all those aspects of the student's growth that are measured by the external examination and also those personality traits, interests and attitudes which cannot be assessed by it. Internal assessment should be built into a total educational programme of the school and should be used for improvement rather than for certifying the level of achievement of the student. It must be pointed out that all items of internal assessment need not follow quantified scoring procedures. Some of them may be assessed in descriptive terms and results should be kept separately and not combined artificially with other results to form aggregate scores.

The written examinations conducted in schools should be improved on the same lines as the external examination.

Methods Suggested by the Commission to Overcome the Shortcomings of Internal Assessment. The results of the internal assessment and external examination should not be combined because the purposes and techniques of the two evaluations are different and because the results of the internal assessment of the different institutions are not strictly comparable. The results of the external and internal assessment should, therefore, be shown separately in the certificate(s) given at the end of the course.

It should be an important point in the inspections of schools to review the internal assessment made and to examine the correlation between the internal and external assessments. Persistence in over-assessment should be regarded as a weakness in the school programmes. It should be taken due note of while classifying the schools and should also be related to grants-in-aid so that institutions which tend to over-assess their students persistently would stand to lose in status and finance. The grant-in-aid rules should also authorize the Education Department to withdraw recognition for persistent irresponsible assessment.

Creation of a Well-organized Machinery. In the end, the Commission states, "The comprehensive programme of evaluation that we have described in the preceding paragraphs requires for its implementation a well-organized machinery both at the State and the Central levels. The Secondary Boards of School Education that now conduct external examination at the secondary stage will be converted into State Boards of School Education with enhanced powers and functions. At the Centre will be the National Board of School Education that will be responsible for evaluation programme at the national level."

Causes of the Lack of Interest among Teachers

1. No extra pay is given to them for organising non-scholastic activities.
2. Their teaching hours are not reduced.
3. A majority of the teachers does not possess the proper training for organising such activities.
4. Some of the teachers do not see any good coming out of these activities as they do not fully realise that they should aim at the all-round development of the personality of the student.
5. Due to the rigid outlook of the teachers and the heads of schools, the idea of the self-government is not allowed to creep into the minds of the students of the school. They feel that the students are not sufficiently mature and may misuse power invested in them.
6. The vain idea of superiority among the teachers checks them from allowing the students to share responsibility with them.
7. Lack of adequance reliance on the evaluation done by teachers in these programmes.

Developing Motivation Among Teachers

1. Giving credit to the teachers for their participation in the activities while evaluating their work.
2. Making participation in non-scholastic activities as an integral part of school programme.
3. Providing adequate facilities in the schools.
4. Providing adequate training to teachers in such programmes.
5. Making available evaluation tools for measuring non-scholastic areas.

Conclusion. The discussion on the planning of co-curricular activities may be summed up with the views of the Secondary Education Commission : "In the planning of these activities, it is important to remember that they should be as varied as the resources or the schools permit. Academic activities like debates, discussions, drama, school magazine, social activities like the organising of different functions for the school community as well as the local community, sports activities, manual and practical activities, social service projects, art projects, must all be woven into a rich and unified pattern, within which every child will be able to find something to suit his tastes and interests. In the actual working out of these activities, academic, social, practical and sports - the teachers will find that there are really no tight boundary walls between them. Thus by planning a coherent programme of different activities, rich in stimuli, the school will not be frittering away either the time or the energy of the pupils but will be heightening their intellectual powers also side by side while training them in other fine qualities."

Practical Work

N.L. Bossing has observed, "The central position of the assignment in the techniques of teaching has remained unquestioned." G.H. Betts asserts, "Upon the proper assignment of the lesson depends much of the success of the recitation, and also much of the pupil's progress in learning how to study." W.N. Drum suggests, "Teachers generally do not appreciate the importance of the assignment, and the work of the pupils probably suffers as much from hasty or careless assignment as from any other single cause." H.R. Douglass and other are of the view, "The assignment represents one of the most important phases of teaching."

There is no doubt that assignments properly planned and assigned, regularly done by the students and carefully evaluated by the teacher go a long way in improving the attainment of the students. Assignments serve two-fold purpose i.e. they are used as a learning device and a tool in evaluation.

Purposes of Assignments

1. To provide opportunities to students to work independently and thereby to develop in them self-reliance and initiative.
2. To develop habits of reading regularly among the students.
3. To provide opportunities to the students to utilise their leisure time profitably. It is generally seen that our school children waste their precious time in loitering about or making mischief when no such work is given to them.
4. To give them an opportunity to do practice what is done in the school.
5. To finish the prescribed courses in time. The syllabi is too heavy to be finished in the classroom work.
6. To serve as a link in the parent-teacher co-operation. It enables the parents to know that regular work is being done in the school.
7. To develop permanent interests and to train the students in the profitable use of leisure.
8. To enable the child to revise his previous lesson and prepare the next one.
9. To provide remedial measure for backward children.
10. To give chance to every child to progress at his own speed.

Different Types

Classification I

N.L. Bossing has listed the following:

Page or Paragraph Assignment. It is often thought of as the textbook assignment. Unfortunately, this method is still widely used as recent studies have revealed.

Chapter Assignment. This is another form of the textbook assignment though vastly different from the page or paragraph form. Chapters usually are of a unitary nature and involve some elements of completeness within themselves.

Topical Assignment. This type may or may not centre around a single chapter in a textbook. It has a wealth of possibility in the social sciences particularly.

Problem Assignment. Where an arbitrary distinction is set up between a problem and a project the type becomes very valuable form of assignment.

Project Assignment. It is adapted especially to the workshop, natural sciences, and some measure to the social sciences. Its special appeal is through the natural motor activity required.

Experience Assignment. This type is most frequently used in mathematics. It represents the old traditional approach to teaching although if used in combination with other types, this form can be used very effectively.

Individual or Group Report Assignment. Used extensively as a device to supplement other types and to provide for individual differences in interests and capacities within the class, it is very effective.

Unit Assignment. It may apply to any extensive segment of classroom activity that presents factors of cohesion and a relatively complete additional element around which the unit may resolve itself as a core. A rather pretentious problem may serve as this unitary core.

Experimental Assignment. This is a form of the problem and project types characteristic of the science laboratory. Too often in practice, it does not represent either an experiment or a problem in the true sense. It can be made a vital instrument of educational training if properly used.

Practice Assignment. This type represents an assignment of repetitions of activities designed to produce mental or motor skills. Mastery of the simple combinations in arithmetic, memorization of a poem, or practice in speed on the typewriter are examples of this type of assignment.

Classification II

(1)	(2)	(3)	(4)
Extension of the classroom work or home work.	Development of the lesson	Self-evaluation study of specific topics	Detailed

Classification III

(1)	(2)	(3)	(4)
Written	Oral (Skills)	Practical of a project.	Preparation

The Essentials

1. The assignment should be clear and definite.
2. The assignment should be concise but sufficiently detailed to enable each student to understand the task assigned.
3. The assignment should anticipate special difficulties and suggest ways to remove them.
4. The assignment should relate the new unit to past experience.
5. Students should understand the importance of the assignment.
6. The assignment should arouse an interest in advance work.
7. The assignment should provide for differences in the ability and interest of students.

8. The assignment should be motivated chiefly by the hope of worth-while achievements, rather than scholastic reward or the fear of punishment.
9. The assignment should stimulate thought.
10. The assignment should provide necessary and specific directions for the study of the lesson.
11. The assignment should be adjusted to the time and opportunity of the class.
12. Materials of the assignment should be varied and adaptable to the needs and interests of the students.

Difficulties in the Preparation of a Good Assignment. Fleming and Wooding have listed the following difficulties:

1. Insufficient thought and preparation in planning the assignment.
2. Inability to obtain an acceptance by the pupil of a worthy purpose for performance of the task.
3. Simulation in the preparation of the assignments by appealing to the interests of adolescents and by providing for real needs growing, out of pupil experience.
4. Prevention of loss of interest due to too long phase of time between the assignment and preparation.
5. Avoidance of assignments so long that successful accomplishment is impossible in the time available for preparation, with consequent loss of interest.
6. Guarding against too many and too varied activities, resulting in dividing interests with consequent bad habits of work, and unsatisfactory accomplishments.
7. Difficulty in presenting work to be done so that it is clearly understood by the pupils; also, the difficulty of ascertaining whether every pupil understands.
8. Gauging the difficulty of work so that success is possible for each pupil.
9. Determining essential requirements, and differentiation of assignments to suit the various levels and types of ability existing in the class.

10. Inclusion of challenges to mental exploration by the pupil, thereby stimulating real thinking.
11. Provision for continuity of work by presenting new problems as a continuation of previous experience and anticipation of future problems.
12. Correlating with other subjects and outside activities.
13. Focusing attention on important elements in the new problem of task, and directing the attack in such a way as to increase interest rather than lessen it to stimulate effort, and to overcome seeming obstacles to accomplishment.
14. Providing the necessary tools for preparation by training in study procedures and techniques, and in selection, organization, and use of materials, thereby developing effective habits of independent work.
15. Giving to pupils devices for checking the mastery and performance of work undertaken.
16. Evaluating the effectiveness of an assignment by the quality of response during the presentation of the assignment, and by the adequacy of pupil preparation.
17. Providing sufficient time for adequate consideration of the assignment and determining the psychological moment for its presentation.

Suggested Assignment Procedure. The procedure suggested for the preparation of a good assignment is as follows:

1. Analyse the nature of the learning process required in advance unit. This is without exception the first step in a good assignment procedure. Much of what follows in any good assignment depends upon this analysis.
2. Study the various types of assignments available and select the one, or modified form of it, that appears to fit best the learning situation. Some assignment types are admirably adapted to one form of learning for teaching but not to others.
3. Provide the essential background for the advance work where uncertainty exists that such background obtains. At this point too many teachers are likely to assume the

adequacy of this background when in fact it may not exist. Scarcely can one emphasize too strongly the appreciative preparation for the new.

4. Whether this is the next step in the assignment procedure or not, it is obvious that very early in the assignment phase the teacher must throw out a challenge to the student that will enlist his interest and maximum effort in the new unit.
5. Outline in sufficient detail the advance unit to be studied.
6. It is well to remember one caution-do not do for the student that which he may be led to do for himself. This suggests the desirability of leading the class in a cooperative discovery of desirable leads for the general attack upon the new.
7. Where reference to source material other than the textbooks is necessary, this should be made specific. The most satisfactory plan in the large unit assignment is to provide the select list of available sources in mimeographed or hectographed form with chapter or inclusive page references given.

Correction Process

The following methods of correction may be adopted:

1. Correction by the teacher himself.
2. Correction with the help of the bright students in the class.
3. Correction with the help of the blackboard.
4. Correction by interchanging the exercise books among the students.
5. Glance checking and signing by teachers.

At the primary stage, teachers should correct all the assignments without any help from the children. At this stage it is not possible for the children to do any self-correction.

Examples. After teaching a lesson on 'Religions of the World' following assignments may be given to the students as homework. The purpose of the assignments would be to evaluate the attainment of the students and also to evaluate by the teacher the effectiveness of his teaching strategies.

1. 'Jainism and Buddhism were popular social religious revolts against Hinduism.' Explain the main teachings of these two faiths with reference to the above opinion.
2. Throw the light on the teachings of Christ. Compare these with the main principles of Islam and Judaism.
3. Write an essay on the contribution of the religion to the intellectual, social and cultural life of man.
4. Write briefly on the ethical principles of Judaism.
5. Discuss the principles of Islamic teachings.
6. Write short notes on:
   (i) Animism. (ii) Shankaracharya's Advaitvada. (iii) Hinayana and Mahayana. (iv) Torah. (v) Protestantism. (vi) Bhakti Movement. (vii) Sankhya Darshan. (viii) Concept of Non-violence.
7. 'The ethics of Confucious have deeply affected the course of Chinese life throughout the ages.' Do you agree?
8. Arrange the following names of religions correctly against their founders:

Religion	*Name of the founder*
Christianity	Hazrat Mohammad
Islam	Mahatma Buddha
Buddhism	Bhagwan Mahavir
Jainism	Lord Christ
	Saint Confucius

9. Arrange the following dates of birth correctly against the names of the religious leaders:

Mahavira	570 A.D.
Buddha	563 B.C.
Christ	550 B.C
Mohammad	470 A.D.

10. Fill up the blanks selecting the most appropriate word from the lists of words given: India, Mecca, China, Sixth Century B.C., Medina, Jews.
    (a) Judaism is a religion of the ....
    (b) Jainism is confined to ....
    (c) The birth of Mohammad took place in ....

(d) Mohammad fled from Mecca to ....

(e) .... was an age of religious reformation in different parts of the world.

(f) Confucius was a resident of ....

11. Tick mark the correct alternatives in the following:

(a) Ahimsa is practised in its extreme form in Hinduism/ Christianity/Islam/Jainism.

(b) Eight-fold path is the middle path of Judaism/ Confucianism/Buddhisn/Islam.

(c) Moses was an exponent of the philosophy of Judaism/ Jainism/Christianity/Islam.

(d) In the pre-historic ages, the religion of the Egyptians/ Sumerians/Aryans was not guided by fear from the forces of nature.

(e) Christianity was declared as a state religion by Nero/ Constantine/Julius Caesar.

(f) The sermon on the Mount was delivered by Buddha/ Mahavir/ Christ/ Mohammed.

Growth Record

The progress of a student in scholastic and non-scholastic areas is indicated on a sheet of paper/papers or folders and the same is communicated by the school to the guardians of the student for their information and follow-up action. This tool is usually known as the progress report. The progress report contains the strengths and weaknesses of a student in various areas like learning, his attitudes, aptitudes, interest values and personal and social development.

Scores and Ranks

Raw Scores. Raw scores are marks of students in a test. They have no absolute significance. A score of 30 in a test having only 30 items would have a different meaning in a test having 50 items. A raw score of 80 in Mathematics would have different meaning from a raw score of 80 in English. This is on account of the fact that these scores cannot be directly compared, with other scores. Importance of these scores is only relative. According to Smith, raw scores are "direct counts of the number of times a specified event has occurred, such as the number of items answered correctly, the number of books read, the number of errors made in solving a problem, the number of statements endorsed on a questionnaire etc." The scores have a meaning only when additional data are available. The scores do not provide a true measure of a pupil's achievement.

Norms. The term 'norm' has two meanings. It is used in the sense of standard comparison. It is also used in the sense of control tendency of the scores of a group. Raw scores can be understood only by comparison with some reference group or groups. The comparison may be with:

1. A series of age groups (age norms).
2. A series of grade groups (grade norms).
3. A single group, indicating what per cent of that group the score surpassed (percentile norms).
4. A single group, indicating standard deviations above or below the group mean (standard scores).

Each alternative has certain advantages and certain limitations.

To get an index of brightness from age norms, quotients such as the intelligence quotient and educational quotient have been devised. These become meaningful and usable when they have approximately the same standard deviation for all age groups. In that case, they are essentially standard scores and should be thought of as such. Norms represent a descriptive framework for interpreting the score of an individual, a class group, or some large aggregation. However, before a judgment can be made as to whether an individual or group is doing well or poorly, allowance must be made for ability level, cultural background, and curricular emphasis. The norm is merely an average, not a strait jacket into which all can be forced to fit.

Complete Report

If the norms available for a number of different tests are of the same kind and are based on comparable groups, all the tests can be expressed in comparable terms. They can then be shown pictorially in the form of a profile. Profiles emphasize score differences within the individual. When profiles are sued, care must be taken not to over-interpret minor ups and downs of the profile.

Profiles are very useful in the study of achievement, interests, or even personality scores of an individual. By studying these charts, standard scores and their equivalent percentiles can be known immediately.

Marks and Scores

A percentile rank or percentile score indicates a pupil's relative position in a group in terms of percentage of students scoring below him. A percentile rank of 80 means that a pupil's performance surpasses that of 80 per cent of the group.

Record on Card

A Cumulative Record Card is that card which contains the results of different assessments and judgments held from time to time during the course of study of a student. Generally it covers three consecutive years. It contains information regarding all aspects of the life of the child-physical, mental, social, moral and psychological. It seeks to give as comprehensive picture as possible of the personality of a child. "Periodically the significant information gathered on student through the use of various techniques-tests, inventories, questionnaires, observations, interview, case study, case conferences and the like-should be assembled in summary form on a cumulative record," writes Jane Warters.

A Cumulative Record Card is a document in which it is recorded cumulatively useful and reliable information about a particular pupil, at one place, thus presenting a complete and growing picture of the individual concerned for the purpose of helping him, during his long stay at school and at the time of leaving, in the solution of his manifold problems of educational, vocational and personal-social nature and thus aiding him in his best development.

Record in School

The Secondary Education Commission has made the following observation regarding the need for school records: "Neither the external examination, singly or together, can give a correct and complete picture of a pupil's all-round progress at any particular stage of his education: yet it is important for us to assess this, in order to determine his future course of study or his future vocation. For this purpose, a proper system of school records should be maintained for every pupil indicating the work done by him in the school from day to day, month to month, term to term, and year to year. Such a school record will present a clear and continuous statement of the attainment of the child in different intellectual pursuits throughout the successive stages of his education. It will also contain a progressive evolution of development in other directions of no less importance such as the growth of his interest, aptitudes, and personality traits, his social adjustments, the practical and social activities in which he takes part. In other words, it will give a complete picture of his career."

The Advantages

1. A good record contributes to guidance work in general in the following ways: (a) By providing a sound basis for understanding the individual, (b) By showing the significant experiences of the individual, (c) By indicating his readiness for new experiences, (d) By pointing out the routes to new goals, (e) By pointing out his strengths and weaknesses.
2. The card contains information about the home environment of the child, the standard of living of his parents, the society in which he lives, the activities and the hobbies in which he is interested-all these factors have a great bearing on the development of his personality and help in organising the future of the child.
3. It helps in the improvement of the methods of teaching by revealing the needs of the students.
4. It provides a helpful basis for educational and vocational placement.
5. It is an aid in the search for talent. It assists the teacher to find out students who are gifted in abstract verbal ability, science, the arts and social relations.
6. It helps the teacher to find out the slow learners and accordingly he suggests measures.

7. It contains data which may be useful in conferring with certain pupils about behaviour problems.
8. It serves as a link between the teacher and the parents. The teachers find it convenient to write letters or descriptive reports to the parents on the basis of the information contained in the record.
9. The school authorities can make suitable recommendation to the prospective employers and college admission officers.
10. The cumulative records help in furnishing sufficient data for reports to the various authorities engaged in the student welfare field.
11. At the time of the transfer of a student from one school to another, it helps the new school authorities to know about the child and to avoid mistakes and to facilitate the adjustment of the child to the new environment.
12. It furnishes assistance to counsellors in aiding pupils to plan their higher secondary school and post-higher secondary school courses of study intelligently.
13. It provides valuable assistance to the class teacher or the counsellor in understanding the child who presents a disciplinary problem in the class.

Maintenance of the Record. The maintenance of the cumulative record card should begin when the student enters school and should follow the student from class to class within a school and from school to school as he continues his progress.

The class teacher will maintain the cumulative record. In view of the fact that he spends much time with the students he will be in a better position to judge them from different aspects. He will maintain a diary or note-book in which he will note down from time to time his observations about his students. At the end of the year he will make the necessary entries in the cumulative record card. It is very desirable that he consults his colleagues who also know the pupils. These entries should be made after careful consideration.

Though the Secondary Education Commission admits that the introduction of the cumulative records will increase the responsibilities of teachers and add to their work, yet it does not suggest any remedy which may be of help to the teachers who are already over-burdened. Sometimes we fail to appreciate that even a good case is ruined if suitable means are not adopted to achieve the desired ends. By simply saying that the advantages would outweigh the personal disadvantage to teachers, the Commission has not taken a realistic point of view. If we wish to reap the advantages of this system, the teaching load of the teachers has got to be lessened. The teachers and the counsellors must be provided with sufficient time to make necessary entries.

Methods of Popularising This System. The use of the cumulative record in our educational institutions is still in its infancy. It cannot be imposed upon the teachers. The teachers must be familiarized with the advantages of this system. Talks and refresher courses should be organised for this purpose. Faculty meetings should be organised to discuss the nature of the information that these cards should contain. It must be remembered that the maintenance of cumulative records is a co-operative affair in which administrators, counsellors, teachers, clerical staff, students and their parents must participate and all of these must be convinced of the importance of such records.

In order to maintain these cards properly, the teachers will have to be given some training. The Secondary Education Commission suggests that the State Department of Education should provide such training in the Training Colleges for Teachers. The Commission feels that with such training and certain amount of practice and with an occasional check-up by the head of the institute and by the inspectors, the teachers will be able to discharge their duties to the satisfaction of all. The Commission is of the opinion that in his sense of responsibility, the average Indian teacher does not yield to any teacher in any "other country; what he needs is clear direction, encouragement and sympathy."

Roots of Information

Parents/Guardians Data Form. Family background and the personal history of the child may be gathered from the parents who are asked to fill in a form.

Personal Data Form. In order to obtain information regarding the pupil's interests and participation in extra-curricular activities and his vocational preferences, the personal data is of great use. The pupil may be asked to give details of himself. This will supplement the information obtained from the parents data form.

School Records. These include:

(i) Records of achievement tests.
(ii) Records of other tests.
(iii) Admission and withdrawal record.

Other Sources. These include:

(i) Personal visits by the teachers.
(ii) Observations made by the teachers.

Basic Principles

Data contained in the card should be:

1. Accurate.
2. Complete.
3. Comprehensive.
4. Objective.
5. Usable.
6. Valid.

1. Keeping of record is a continuous process and should cover the whole history from the kindergarten to the college and this should follow the child from school. The card will furnish valuable information about the growth of a child and the new school can place him and deal with him to a greater advantage.
2. All the teachers and the guidance workers should have access to these records. Matters too confidential may be kept at a separate place. The child concerned may have an opportunity to study his own cumulative record in consultation with the counsellor. The students themselves should not have access to each other's record.
3. The essential data should be kept in a simple, concise and readable form so that it may be convenient to find out the main points of the life of the child at a glance.
4. Records should be based on an objective data. They should be as reliable as possible.

5. The record system should provide for a minimum of repetition of items.
6. The record should be maintained by the counsellor and should not be circulated throughout the faculty for making entries on it by other members of the staff. These entries should be made by them on other forms and the entry in this card should be made very carefully by the counsellor.
7. A manual should be prepared and directions for the guidance of persons filling out or using the records given in it.
8. It should contain reliable, accurate and objective information.

Information Categories

Identification Data. Name of the pupil, sex, father's name, admission No., date of birth, class, section, any other information that helps in easy location of the card.

Environmental and Background Data. Home-neighbourhood influences, socio-economic status of the family, cultural status of the family, number of brothers and sisters, their educational background, occupations of the members of the family.

Physical Data. Weight, height, illness, physical disabilities, etc.

Psychological Data. Intelligence, aptitudes, interests, personality qualities, emotional and social adjustment and attitudes.

Education Data. Previous school record, educational attainments, school marks, school attendance.

Co-curricular Data. Notable experiences and accomplishments in various fields-intellecutal, artistic, social, recreational, etc.

Vocational Information. Vocational ambitions of the student.

Supplementary Information obtained by the use of standardised tests.

Principal's Overall Remarks.

Forms of Cumulative Record Card. It is used in various forms such as card, sheet, printed folders, cards or sheets contained in an envelope, booklet or some combination of these forms.

9

Examination Aims

In the words of Thorndike and Hagen, "Evaluation of pupil progress is a major aspect of the teacher's job. A good picture of where the pupil is and how he is progressing is fundamental to effective teaching by the teacher and to effective learning by the pupil." They mention the following purposes of evaluation.

(i) Motivating students to develop good study habits to correct errors and to direct their activities towards the achievement of desired goals.
(ii) Diagnosing weaknesses.
(iii) Defining teaching objectives.
(iv) Differentiation of pupils for various purposes.
(v) Certification of pupils.

Evaluation, the Teaching Learning Process, and the Teacher. A clear concept of evaluation on the part of the teacher enables him to understand the various components of the teaching learning process as all these are interrelated. Evaluation as the last phase of this process enables him to find out to what extent he has been able to achieve the instructional objectives and also to know if these instructional objectives need any change.

Evaluation helps the teacher in the following ways—

(i) Evaluation provides the teacher with adequate knowledge concerning the students entry behaviour. The importance of readiness to learn is a well-accepted fact. For teaching effectively, the teacher must find out where a student is, from where to start and where to go. A teacher, therefore, must have estimates of a student's ability for learning and of what he currently knows.

(ii) Knowledge of a student's entry behaviour obviously helps the teacher in setting, refining and clarifying realistic objectives for each student.

(iii) Evaluation helps the teacher to organise appropriate learning activities for the students to realise the objectives.

(iv) Evaluation helps the teacher to find out the extent to which objectives are realised.

(v) Evaluation helps the teacher to improve his classroom procedures and methods of teaching-learning in the light of feedback.

Evaluation and Students. Evaluation helps the students in a number of ways.

(a) Awareness of objectives. Statements of clear objectives enable the students to know clearly what the teacher expects from them and they cooperate with him in realising the objectives.

(b) Increasing motivation. Knowledge about their performance serves as a motivating factor to the students and ultimately facilitates learning.

(c) Encouraging study habits. Evaluation being a continuous process encourages students to develop good study habits. Students pay daily attention to their work and understand that today's work cannot be postponed till tomorrow.

(d) Greater chances for increasing abilities and skills. Constant feedback makes students aware of their strengths and weaknesses. There is enough evidence to show that such feedback improves subsequent performance. Students learn while preparing for evaluation, while being evaluated and after the completion of a particular phase of evaluation.

Reporting Students' Progress. Evaluation serves as a basis for summarising and reporting the progress of students and institutions.

Evaluation and Guidance. For guidance - educational, personal and vocational, systematic, evaluation serves an important basis.

Evaluation and Parents. A systematic and continuous programme of students' evaluation keeps the parents well-versed with the performance of their children and they endeavour to take appropriate action for their further improvement.

Evaluation and the Administrators and Supervisors. Evaluation helps the administrators and others associated with the various aspects of education to take appropriate decisions in planning curricular and co-curricular programmes. Evaluation helps in proper placement of students in ability-grouping or in achievement grouping. Evaluation is useful in enabling the educational personnel to determine the effectiveness of instruction and learning activities.

Evaluation and Various Agencies. Results of evaluation are very useful to different sections i.e. teachers, students, parents, employers, research workers, guidance and counsellors and social workers etc.

Summary. Evaluation results are used for determining grading, promotion and placement of the students in the same school and other institutions. They are also useful in the determination of various kinds of careers also. Evaluation of curriculum programmes also help in modifying the learning experiences. Evaluation proves very helpful in organising co-curricular programmes. In the end, it may be stated that a comprehensive and systematic evaluation and appropriate follow-up leads to better achievement by students.

Significant Motives

These may be summarised as under:

1. Evaluation relates measurement to the goals of the instructional programme.
2. Evaluation appraises the status of and changes in pupil behaviour.
3. Evaluation discloses pupil's needs and possibilities.
4. Evaluation aids the pupil and the teacher in planning.
5. Evaluation expands the concept of worthwhile goals beyond pure achievement.
6. Evaluation serves as a means of improving school-community relation.

7. Evaluation familiarizes the teacher with the nature of pupil learning, development and progress.
8. Evaluation facilitates the selection and improvement of measuring instruments.
9. Evaluation appraises the teacher's competence.
10. Evaluation appraises the supervisor's competence.

Profile of the Teacher

To a teacher with a clear concept of evaluation, changes in the behaviour of the pupils, in their thinking, feeling and actions are the basis for both of his instruction and assessment. Evaluation oriented teacher has two essential tasks i.e. to adopt a child-centred approach and to individualise instruction.

Interrelation of Guidance and Evaluation. Guidance and evaluation are interrelated. They are the two sides of the same coin. Evaluation becomes the basis of guidance. Diagnostic tests reveal the achievements and limitations of the teaching-learning process followed by the teachers and students. Evaluation and diagnosis have no meaning if follow-up action is not taken up. Guidance assists to take up the follow-up action.

Applied Angle

The guidance view of evaluation is that if the child is provided with a continuous flow of experiences on his growth level and in keeping with his needs, there can be no failure. Robert H. Knapp observes that the terms promotions and non-promotions are counterpart of the psychology which justified the arbitrary practice of grading pupils according to grade standards. A great change has taken place in our methods of appraisal. We now fully realize that it is impossible to expect all children grouped in a given grade to grow at an even rate and reach the end of the school year with the same achievement levels, attitudes and emotional and social levels. The pupils cannot be graded rigidly. They learn according to their own speed. Each child is to be motivated to progress at its own individual rate and not at the rates of the other members of the group. In this way we eliminate frustration and failures. It is said, "Gaps in learning are eliminated and repetition becomes unnecessary. Evaluation becomes a series of progressive steps towards maturity."

According to the guidance view examinations and evaluation should serve the following purposes:

1. They should help to measure pupils' strength and weakness in a learning situation and lead to constructive planning.
2. They should help us to classify students in more homogeneous groups so that they may profit most from class instruction.
3. They should continually measure the day-to-day achievements of the students.
4. They should develop wholesome attitudes in the minds of the students for themselves.
5. They should measure the power of understanding, critical thinking and appreciation of the students.
6. They should measure intelligence, special abilities and interest of the students.
7. They should measure the extent to which the students are co-operative, reliable, courageous-the qualities which a man of character should possess.

Various Tests

Diagnostic testing is an important component of evaluation and thereby of the on-going teaching-learning process. It provides the feedback to the teachers as well as to the students regarding their strengths and weaknesses. However, all the instruments of evaluation do not give indication of the performance of students. A diagnostic test has been defined by English and English (1958) in these words, " One designed to locate the particular source of a person's difficulties in learning especially in school subjects, thus providing clauses to what further measures of instruction, guidance of study are needed". Diagnostic testing helps teachers to modify their teaching strategies so as to make them more effective in the light of the feedback.

Development and Essentials of Diagnostic Testing. Following are the main points which should be kept in view by the teacher while planning diagnostic evaluation.

(1) The diagnostic tests should be prepared in accordance with the specific tasks regarding a particular subject or

area of a subject, for instance diagnostic tests for spelling and comprehension etc. would be quite different.

(2) There should be a large number of items/ questions covering various aspects of the relevant subject matter for which test is designed.

(3) The nature of these questions should be such as they can be administered.

(4) Scoring should be easier and quicker.

(5) Variety of questions like very short type and the multiple type should be included in the diagnostic test.

(6) On a particular skill to be evaluated, a large number of items should be included in the test.

(7) In the process of diagnostic testing, several equivalent forms of tests may be used.

(8) Different kinds of tests may be made use of on students of different abilities.

The following points need to be kept in view:

1. The first task of the teacher is to win the confidence of the students and reassure them that the test is to help them in the improvement of their learning rather than for declaring them pass or fail.
2. It should be administered in a relaxed environment.
3. Students should be seated comfortably.
4. Students should be asked not to consult each other while taking the test.
5. If any student is not able to follow something, he should be allowed to seek a clarification from the teacher.
6. The teacher may ensure that the students taking the test attempt all questions.
7. Time schedule should not be enforced strictly. If any student takes a little more time, he should be allowed to do so.

Counselling a Must

Guidance is an essential component of the teaching-learning process. For formulating an effective programme of guidance in the school, a lot of information has to be obtained about the students so that appropriate measures for their optimum development may be taken. This information is obtained by using a variety of evaluation tools.

The tools of evaluation are to be selected in accordance with the aims of guidance.

Guidance is needed for helping the students solve different kinds of problems. In other words, students are to be prepared to meet the challenges posed by different situations. Guidance is not solving problems for the students. Its focus is on providing assistance to develop insight so that the students solve problems through their own efforts.

The role of guidance, based on evaluation which employs a variety of techniques, may be summarised as under:-

(1) Assisting the learner in understanding himself as a learner.
(2) Assisting the learner in knowing his strengths and weakness in different areas (cognitive and non-cognitive).
(3) Assisting the learner in adjusting himself to varied situations within his total environment.
(4) Assisting the learner to realize his own potential.
(5) Assisting the learner in making the best use of his capacities, interests and motivation to fulfil his needs.
(6) Assisting the learner in understanding the problems and to solve them independently.
(7) Assisting the learner in developing the ability to analyse the situations and to make his own decision wisely.
(8) Assisting the learner in making his own unique contribution for welfare of the society with fullest potential.
(9) Assisting the learner in selecting appropriate educational and vocational courses, based on his own potential.

Techniques and Tools or Evaluation Procedures in the Collection of Evidence Data Regarding each Individual for Guidance Purposes. A variety of techniques and tools are used for evaluating the abilities, achievements, interests, attitudes, motives and their rate of development in respect of each individual for guidance purposes.

Prognosis means foretelling, prediction and forecast. The prognostic tests are designed to predict the student's ability or readiness to undertake the study of a school subject successfully.

The Uses. The test scores gained through prognostic testing indicate not only student's present level of achievement, but they also tell or indicate about the possibility of future achievement. Prognostic tests tell the teacher as to what extent his students can derive advantage for further learning experiences. Suppose for instance, a student wants to take up a course in higher statistics. The prognostic testing would indicate if he has acquired the mastery of elementary statistics or not. If the answer is in the affirmative, he is expected to succeed in taking the course. Several types of prognostic tests have been developed in India also.

Let us take another example. If a teacher of mathematics finds that his entire class has missed how to solve simultaneous equations by substitution method, this implies that learning the solution of simultaneous equations has been incomplete. Perhaps the students did not recognise that certain equations can be solved if one does not use this method or perhaps they did not study the method seriously at all. In such a situation, reteaching becomes necessary.

These tests are used generally with children shortly after their entry into the first grade. The objective at this stage is to give the school as accurate an indication as possible of the child's ability to progress in reading. It may be remembered that the reading readiness test is given only to predict ability to profit from reading instruction in the near future i.e. next few months. It is not used to forecast ultimate level of learning.

The Development. These tests with few exceptions are based on some kind of analysis of the main characteristics of the nature of the learning task.

A large number of 'Reading Readiness' Prognostic Tests have been developed in the U.S.A. Following are the main categories of these tests:

(i) Ability to read letters or words tests.
(ii) Oral vocabulary tests.
(iii) Rhyming or matching sounds tests.
(iv) Visual matching of figures, letters or words tests.

Career Guidance

Aptitude Tests and Achievement Tests. An aptitude is a capacity, plus a probability that a student will develop an ability in a specific field. Aptitude, therefore, refers to a rather narrow field of behaviour; for example, to musical ability or to mechanical ability. An aptitude test is designed to measure the probable future performance. Any test that can estimate the probable future performance may be designated as an aptitude test. An intelligence test may be used as an aptitude test and in fact there are many intelligence tests called Differential Aptitude Tests, and General Aptitude Test Batteries.

An achievement test can also be used as an aptitude test. The distinction between achievement and aptitude is not very strictly absolute. The only difference lies in their uses. When an achievement test in Biology is used to find out the present status of the student (the present performance in the subject), we call it simply an achievement test. But when it is used to predict the future performance of the student in some profession, it is called an aptitude test. Such aptitude tests are given to pupils seeking admission to medical colleges.

The tests which are used to measure the results of training are known as achievement tests. But the tests which are used to measure a person's ability before he has been given a chance for special training are known as aptitude tests. The achievement testing looks to the present and the past, the aptitude testing looks to the future. Any test of achievement is in part a test of aptitude and any test of aptitude is in part a test of achievement.

The main purpose of an aptitude test is to predict or to identify individuals who possess a reasonal degree of potential for developing along special lines to profit most by special training.

Examples of Aptitude Tests in the Area of Teaching

1. M.M. Shah's Teaching Aptitude Test, 1962.
2. R.P. Srivastava's Teaching Aptitude Test, 1965.
3. B.G. Pandya's Test for Teaching Traits, 1972.
4. D.P. Patel's Teaching Aptitude Test, 1980.

Designing of Aptitude Tests and Job Analysis. Aptitude tests are often designed on the basis of job analysis.

Meaning of Job Analysis. Job analysis has been defined by Ordway as "the scientific study and statement of all the facts about a job which reveal its content and the modifying factors which surround it."

J.D. Hackett defines job analysis as "determination of the essential elements in the job and the qualification a worker should have for its successful performance."

Job analysis is the procedure by which is discovered the skills, knowledge, abilities and responsibilities required by any worker for successful performance.

A job may be analysed according to mental requirements, physical requirements and working conditions. Thus a man may be rated on the job according to his personality, physique, attitude etc.

Essentials of Job Analysis. There are three essentials of a job analysis:

1. The job must be accurately and completely identified.
2. The tasks of the job must be completely and accurately described.
3. The requirements the job makes upon the worker for successful performance must be identified.

Purposes of Job Analysis. A job analysis serves the following purposes:

1. Job analysis assists in knowing the personnel specifications for various jobs.
2. Job analysis helps in bringing together the right worker for the right job.
3. Job analysis helps in job satisfaction and job efficiency.
4. Job analysis assists in the accurate determination of job opportunities for various types of manpower in the industries.
5. Job analysis helps in planning appropriate training programmes.
6. Job analysis defines labour needs in specific terms.

Blum and Balinsky point out the importance of job analysis as "an attempt to relate the curriculum of both high schools and colleges to a series of job analysis imposed by industries may make for more meaningful and highly motivated education."

10

Evaluation Approaches

The Summatives

Following definitions throw light on the meaning of summative evaluation.

(1) In the views of Ebel, R.L. and Frisbie, "Summative evaluation is conducted at the end of an instructional segment to determine if learning is sufficiently complete to warrant moving the learner to the next segment of instruction."

(2) In the words of Gilbert Sax, "A summative evaluation can provide evidence that the programme is satisfactory and should be continued for next year's students or that student learning and learning attitudes are so negative that a new programme is needed."

(3) Gronlund, N.E. (1985) observes, "Summative evaluation typically comes at the end of a course (or unit) of instruction. It is designed to determine the extent to which the instructional objectives have been achieved and is used primarily for assigning course grades or certifying pupil mastery of the intended learning outcomes."

(4) According to Nikto, A.J. "Summative evaluation describes judgements about the merits of an already completed programme, procedure or product."

(5) Wiersma and S.G. Gurs (1990) state, "Summative evaluation is done at the conclusion of instruction and

measures the extent to which students have attained the desired outcomes."

The Characteristics and Main Features : A perusal of the above definitions shows that the summative evaluation has the following chief elements:

(i) Summative evaluation is done at the end or completion of a particular instructional programme whose duration may vary from a semester to whole year.
(ii) Summative evaluation checks whether there has been learning or not, if the answer is yes, then what is the quantity and quality of the learning in relation to pre-determined objectives?
(iii) The instructional programme should be for the attainment of some objectives.
(iv) It tends to the use of well-defined evaluation designs.
(v) It focuses on analysis.
(vi) It provides descriptive analysis.
(vii) It tends to stress local effects.
(viii) It is concerned with broad range of issues.
(ix) Its instruments are reliable and valid.
(x) For this evaluation, there are external examinations as well as teacher-made tests and rating scales etc.

The Formatives

(1) According to N.E. Gronlund, "Formative evaluation is used to monitor learning progress during instruction and to provide continuous feedback to both pupil and teacher concerning learning successes and failures. Feedback to pupils reinforces successful learning and identifies the learning errors that need correction. Feedback to the teacher provides information for modifying instruction and prescribing group and individual remedial work."
(2) In the words of A.J. Nitko, "Formative evaluation is concerned with judgements made during the design and or development of a programme which are directed towards modifying, forming or otherwise improving the programme before it is completed."
(3) In the views of R.L. Ebel and D.A. Frisbie (1986), "Formative evaluation is conducted to monitor the

instructional process to determine whether learning is taking place as planned."

(4) Wiersma and S.G. Jurs write, "Formative evaluation occurs over a period of time and monitors student progress."

The Characteristics

(i) It is used to monitor the learning experiences of the students during the period of instruction.

(ii) It aims at providing continuous feed-back to both teacher and student concerning learning success or failure during the teaching learning process.

(iii) Feed-back provides specific learning errors and correction.

(iv) Feed-back to students provides reinforcement.

(v) Feed-back to the teachers provides information as to whether any modifications are necessary in his strategies of teaching.

(vi) Formative evaluation involves assessment of class-work, home work, oral questions and quizzes etc.

(vii) Formative evaluation uses mostly teacher-made tests.

(viii) Formative evaluation is used for assessing student learning progress during instruction.

(ix) Results of formative evaluation are not used for assigning course grades.

(x) Formative evaluation is done during an instructional programme.

(xi) The instructional programme aims at the attainment of certain objectives during the implementation of the programme also.

(xii) Formative evaluation is done to monitor learning and modifying the programme if needed before its completion.

(xiii) Its design is exploratory and flexible.

(xiv) It seeks to identify influential variables.

(xv) It requires analysis of instructional material for mapping the hierarchical structure of the learning tasks and actual teaching of the course for a certain period.

The Differences

In his book 'Evaluation Thesaurus' M. Seriven, who is the originator of the terms summative and formative evaluation, explains the difference in these words, "The formative evaluation is conducted during the development or improvement of a product (or person). It is an evaluation for in-house staff and normally remains in-house but it may be done by an internal or an external evaluator (preferably a combination). Summative evaluation, on the other hand, is conducted after completion of a programme (or a course of study) and for the benefit of some external audience or decision maker (e.g. funding agency or future possible users) though it may be done by an internal or an external evaluator or by a combination."

Gloria, Hitchok and others (1986) state the difference between the summative and formative evaluation in these words, "It is fairly straight forward to produce an 'ideal' type of either a summative or a formative profile. It is far more difficult to combine the two into one unified system. The underlying philosophies of the two appear difficult to reconcile."

Alkin (1974) pointed out that a formative evaluation study uses a great variety of instruments which are either locally developed or standardized, it relies on observation and informal data collection devices, mostly locally chosen. In contrast, summative evaluation studies tend to use well defined evaluation designs, as unobtrusive and non-reactive as possible, they are comparative and concerned with a broad range of issues, for example, implications, politics, costs, competing options. The instruments used in summative evaluation are publicly accepted, reliable and valid instruments, reflecting concerns of the sponsor and of the decision maker.

Following are the main differences between these two types of evaluation.

1. Summative evaluation is the terminal assessment of performance at the end of instruction but formative evaluation is the assessment made during the instructional phase to inform the teacher about progress in learning and what more is to be done.

2. The summative evaluation limits the use of profiles and record of achievement but they are regularly used in formative evaluation.
3. The main consideration in summative evaluation is the determination of the extent to which the examinee has mastered the knowledge and skills associated with a course. On the other hand, the main consideration in formative evaluation is to reveal the processes by which the examinee achieved these outcomes.
4. In summative evaluation, the assessment is done to test learning outcomes against a set of objective criteria without revealing the details of the route to the teacher which the student followed in reaching that point. Formative evaluation takes the form of a dialogue between the student and teacher in which the task is determined by both.
5. Summative evaluation relates to the worth whileness of the instructional programme which has already been completed. Formative evaluation, on the other hand relates to worthwhileness of the instructional programme which is still going on and can be modified.
6. A formative evaluator is partisan of the instructional sequence and makes all possible efforts to make teaching learning better. A summative evaluator is non-partisan and uncommitted who passes judgement on the teaching-learning endeavour.
7. Formative evaluation is in-house evaluation while summative evaluation is mostly done by outside agencies.
8. Formative evaluation is day to day evaluation and is intended to bring about improvement. Public examinations and annual tests and semester tests come under the category of summative evaluation.
9. In a broad sense, all classroom assessments which are not used for grading purpose whether these are home assignments, questioning during teaching, classroom observations of students' responses, and informal tools

come under the category of formative evaluation. As for judgement (pass / fail) of scoring, summative evaluation is used.

In House Examination

Internal evaluation implies the existence of the following elements in evaluation:

(1) Direct involvement of the evaluator or the examiner in the teaching-learning process of the class.

(2) Setting of the question paper by the teacher who teaches the class.

(3) Conducting and evaluating the answer books or scripts by the teacher himself.

The Merits. Following are the chief merits of internal evaluation.

1. One of the chief defects of external examinations is that they neglect the evaluation of the pupil's growth in non-scholastic areas. It may be remembered that education aims at developing the ability of applying the acquired knowledge to new situations, to inculcate desirable interests and to develop desirable personal and social qualities leading to a balanced and harmonious development of pupil's abilities and accomplishments in the cognitive, affective and psychomotor domains. Therefore, a comprehensive school evaluation programme is expected to take note of this fact.
2. Internal assessment mitigates another defect of the external examination. In place of basing results on the assessment at any one time, internal assessment can be as continuous as desired.
3. Internal assessment enables us to diagnose pupils' difficulties in learning. It points out the potentialities of an individual and provides opportunities to find out the needs, goals and interests and aptitudes of an individual and shows him the way for their development. This has a motivating effect and this in turn induces him to utilise his resourcefulness which is otherwise cramped.
4. Since internal assessment is continuous, it builds regular study habits among students.

5. Internal assessment by entrusting the teacher with responsibility provides motivation to him.
6. Internal evaluation by providing a comprehensive picture of students' learning, helps in the improvement of the teaching-learning process.
7. Objectives of the affective domain (appreciation attitudes and interests) and psychomotor domain (skills), require for their achievement a long process of continuous observation, testing and recording etc. Obviously such a process can only be followed in internal evaluation.
8. Internal evaluation provides a continuous feedback for undertaking diagnostic and remedial teaching and other measures.

The Importance : The internal philosophy is interested more in what students get out of education and not just in their passing certain type of examination. Education as a whole is not only concerned with the acquisition of knowledge but also aims at developing in the pupils the desired interests, appreciation, habits, attitudes and personal qualities. Written examinations fail to assess these qualities and the teachers' observation and other informal techniques may be called for which can be used only internally.

Internal assessment mitigates another defect of the external examination. In place of basing results on the assessment at any one time, internal assessment can be as continuous as desired.

Internal assessment enables us to diagnose pupils' difficulties in learning. It points out the potentialities of an individual and provides opportunities to find out the needs, goals and interests and aptitudes of an individual and shows him the way for their development. This has a motivating effect and this in turn induces him to utilise his resourcefulness which is otherwise cramped.

Since internal assessment is continuous, it builds regular study habit among students..

The Shortcomings

1. It can be misused by the teachers.
2. It requires experienced and sincere teachers.
3. Its reliability and validity are questionable in view of several elements of subjectivity.

4. It cannot replace external examinations. It can only supplement them.
5. It requires a lot of time to undertake several activities related to internal evaluation.

Suggestive Guidelines : The following points may be kept in mind.

(1) Follow-up work. Every evaluation should be followed by remedial instruction. When pupils are evaluated too frequently, most of the school time is spent in evaluation and remedial work. Consequently, the instruction in new topics does not progress well.

(2) Evaluation within limits. Too frequent evaluation means that the teacher has to maintain records of pupils' progress very often. Maintenance of records in this situation becomes a time consuming and unmanageable job. Evaluation therefore, should not be done very frequently but necessarily at the end of every teaching unit.

(3) Implementation of the programme. A systematically planned and well-thought-out programme of evaluation is not difficult to implement by the teachers, specially when they themselves are actively involved in its development. However, supervisory and guidance facilities should be provided to implement the programme systematically and to help the teachers to cope with the unforeseen problems.

(4) Recording of valuation results. Systematic recording of evaluation results is as important as the evaluation itself. In the absence of such records, fruitful use of the results cannot be made. The form in which the evaluation results are to be recorded and reported should be determined at the planning stage itself. The records should be such that they can give a comprehensive picture of the progress of each pupil as well as the whole class in a simple manner. There should not be any unnecessary duplication and they should be manageable by the teachers.

(5) Use of evaluation results. The use of evaluation results for instructional decisions is the culminating point of the whole process of evaluation and unless it is reached the evaluation process cannot play its role of being an integral part of instruction and tool of improvement.

(6) The results of the internal assessment and external examination should not be combined because the purposes and techniques of the two evaluations are different and because the results of the internal assessment of the different institutions are not strictly comparable. The results of the external and internal assessment should, therefore, be shown separately in the certificate(s) given at the end of the course.

(7) It should be an important point in the inspections of schools to review the internal assessment made and to examine the correlation between the internal and external assessments. Persistence in over-assessment should be regarded as a weakness in the school programmes. It should be taken due note of while classifying the schools and should also be related to grants-in-aid so that institutions which tend to over-assess their students persistently would stand to lose in status and finance. The grants-in-aid rules should also authorize the Education Departments to withdraw recognition for persistent irresponsible assessment.

(8) Internal assessment should not be used as a tool of maintaining discipline in the institution. Discipline should not be secured by threatening the students to spoil their career or ruin their markings in case they question the authority of the teachers or the principal. No other crime can be more serious than this on their part. Internal assessment is likely to result in non-uniformity of standards of marking in different institutions. To mitigate this evil a general procedure of assessment and of different techniques must be laid down.

(9) The entire staff should be associated with the different aspects of assessment of a single child. This would

help in eliminating to a greater extent the subjectivity and misuse of power.

(10) Sympathetic hearing must be given to the genuine grievances and complaints of the students. The students must be convinced of the awards. Of course, the success of this system of internal assessment depends on teachers themselves. They must justify the confidence reposed in them.

Weightage given to Periodical Tests and Annual Tests: Academic Subjects

Test	Approximate
Monthly tests (3)	30%
Term tests (2)	20%
Annual tests (1)	30%
Home assignments	20%
Total	**100%**

Weightage to Evaluation of Co-curricular Work

Activity	Approximate weightage
1. Library work	20%
2. Games and sports	30%
3. Debates, study circle etc.	20%
4. Community service	20%
5. Visits (excursions etc.)	10%
Total	**100%**

Challenge to Teachers. Internal assessment presupposes responsible teachers. It takes for granted that they will realise the sanctity of the trust reposed in them. They must discharge their responsibilities with impartiality and equity. They should rise above their prejudices and petty values. The success of the scheme depends upon their sincerity, honesty and integrity. They should have the moral courage to face the challenge of favouritism and nepotism. They should work honestly and should not cook figures.

They should not create such impression that those students get high marks in the internal assessment who dance on the fingers of their teachers according to their wishes.

The Problems : The report of a Training Course on Evaluation (1991) discussed the following problems for the implementation of an internal assessment programme.

1. How to get acceptance of the programme of internal assessment by teachers, students, public and administration, etc.?
2. How to develop competence among the teachers to undertake internal assessment effectively?
3. How much of minimum facilities need to be provided in the schools for carrying out an effective programme of internal assessment?
4. How to co-ordinate standard of different schools?
5. What sort of machinery is required to be developed so as to keep up and progressively improve the standard of internal assessment?
6. How to relate the external and internal marks?

Programme of Internal Assessment

(a) The analysis of the examination paper, answer books and examination marks to be made and the data to be placed before the people concerned to realise a need for the development of a more adequate measure of pupils' growth.

(b) Experiments to be made in some selected schools to prove the superiority of the system of assessment which is advocated to be introduced.

(c) Developing a sound technique of internal assessment with the help of teachers and taking their full co-operation in the implementation of the scheme leading to their confidence in it.

Competence of Teachers

(a) In the teacher's training courses, the concept of Internal Assessment in Evaluation, its problems and techniques should be included as an integral part of the training college programme.

(b) For teachers already in schools, special refreshers courses or training camps may be held by way of in-service education.

(c) Periodic conferences of teachers and the principals at least twice a year (in the beginning of each term) may be held so that objectives of internal assessment are classified.

(d) A conference of teachers of different schools in the same region may also be held to evaluate and develop the system and form of maintaining records.

Minimum Facilities

(a) The curriculum should be detailed out adequately in the light of objectives of education.

(b) The curriculum should provide ample freedom to the teacher for planning his work in relation to his own environment.

(c) Any rigorous conformity to particular method of work as is generally advocated by the inspecting staff and other authorities should be avoided to be prescribed in order to allow teachers to develop their own initiative.

(d) Teacher-pupil ratio to be brought to a reasonable size of 1 to 30 at the maximum.

(e) Provision to be made for organizing class-libraries according to the standard of the class.

(f) Study and research in these aspects will help in developing maximum criteria for certifying accrediting schools, which will be necessary in course of time.

Co-ordinating Standards among Different Schools and School Subjects to Internal Assessment

1. Advisory bodies of experts in different areas of knowledge may be appointed. They may issue suggestions to different institutions from time to time and also in the form of articles or books for the guidance of the teachers. A complete change in teacher's attitude will be necessary.

It shall have to be brought home to them that these experts are not official supervisors but only advisers to whom they may refer their problems in time of need.

2. A common core-curriculum may be provided for all schools. It shall be sufficiently flexible leaving enough scope for the teacher's ingenuity and skill.
3. Extensive facilities for the training of teachers in the new techniques of evaluation shall have to be made available and government grants to the institutions may be regulated by the qualifications of staff and other educational facilities available in the situation.
4. Assessors to check the teacher's estimates may be appointed and their identity may be kept confidential. They may compare assessments from different schools and also check them against other criteria which they may decide upon.
5. Teachers' estimates may be scaled against the results of external examination and co-ordination established, if possible.

Standard of Internal Assessment

The State Evaluation Unit will be one good agency for the purpose but it may work in co-operation with other agencies such as Curriculum Committee, Guidance Bureau, the Inspection Department, Central Evaluation Unit and the Research Bureau for the purpose.

Inspection of school by a team of subject experts may also prove helpful in this respect.

Internal Assessment to the External Examination

(a) Internal assessment should be in relation to the various aspects of pupil's growth such as his scholastic achievements, his interests, attitudes and personality traits etc.

(b) There should be some minimum standard of pass prescribed for both internal and external examinations in academic subjects and the result should be announced on the basis of pupil's record of achievement in both and mentioned separately.

(c) To make the result comparable it may be desirable to bring both internal assessment and external examination total marks at par so far as academic subjects are concerned.

(d) It should, however, be noted that internal assessment may be in symbols and grades or in qualitative description for assessing pupil's achievement in some fields, and therefore, external and internal results may not always be comparable.

(e) Certificates showing the achievement of students both at the external examination and internal assessment will provide better scope to the employer for making the choice.

(f) This type of certificate will provide the opportunity to carry on some studies to find out whether the internal or external result is more valid and reliable in respect of a particular school.

(g) This will also help in developing criteria for classifying and accrediting schools.

Summary. Internal and external evaluation have their merits and limitations. What type of evaluation is needed depends on the objective of evaluation. If the objective is to bring about improvement in the learner, then internal evaluation scores over external evaluation. However if the objective is the compare the performance of students belonging to different schools, external evaluation is needed.

There have been disputations about the relative virtues of external evaluation and internal evaluation for a long time. However, the fundamental fact is that both types of evaluation are complementary and are needed to accomplish the full range of purposes in educational endeavour.

Examination under Compulsion

An external examination is necessary for (1) maintaining certain uniform standards at the end of the stage; (2) providing a basis for choice of courses at the secondary stage; and (3) creating incentives for better teaching and learning. But all these arguments do not establish a case for an external examination of the formal type to be compulsorily taken by all the pupils in Class VII or VIII.

The Arguments

(1) It is not necessary or desirable to prescribe a rigidly uniform level of attainment for all the primary school pupils in a State or even a district, through an external examination.

(2) Instead of creating incentives for better teaching, the external examination intended for all will saddle teachers with standardized programmes and encourage the process for rote memorization, which is the besetting evil of teaching and learning methods in our schools today.

(3) Again, since full-time education at the lower secondary stage will provide, by and large, general education without any streaming, the argument regarding the choice of courses does not hold good; and for the diversion of pupils to full-time vocational courses to be made available at this stage, an examination which will test merely intellectual ability and academic attainment will not be of much help.

Periodic Surveys of the Level of Achievement. While not in favour of a compulsory external examination, the Education Commission 1964-66 believes that for the proper maintenance of standards, periodic surveys of the level of achievement of primary schools is necessary. The Commission recommends that such surveys should be conducted by the district educational authorities to assess the standard of performance of the schools in a given area by means of standardized or highly refined tests prepared by specialists in the State Evaluation Organisations.

The Advantages Claimed. (1) This procedure will enable the education officers to pick out the weaker schools and help them to improve their performance.

(2) It will also assist the schools in finding out the weakness of their pupils for purposes of remedial work.

A Common Internal Examination for Inter-school Comparability. The Commission recommends that by making use of the standardised or refined test material referred to above, the district educational authorities may, if they so desire, arrange for a common examination to be taken by the pupils of all the schools in a district at the end of the primary stage. Though the question paper will be set by the district educational authorities or by special paper-setters appointed by the State Evaluation Organisation, the performance of the pupils of each participating school will be done by the teachers of the school themselves, and not by external examiners.

The Advantages

(1) As the question papers will contain standardized tests and highly refined and professional tests items, the evaluation will be more valid and reliable than what is possible through the kind of annual and final examinations conducted in the ordinary primary school.

(2) Through such a common test, inter-school comparability with regard to levels of performance in the district can be obtained, and this would be helpful, as shown above, both to the education officers and to the schools.

Question Papers of Short Duration. Question papers in the different subjects at this common examination should be of short duration, each of not more than one hour or one hour and a half, so that the entire examination should be completed in two or three days.

Preparation of Teachers. Teachers should be prepared for the ungraded system through the regular training courses and orientation programmes and should be helped with a supply of diagnostic tests and remedial material. The orientation may be given by the State Institutes of Education. Observation techniques, which are more reliable for assessing the pupil's growth at this stage than more formal techniques of evaluation, should be used by teachers in a planned and systematic manner.

Evaluation at the Higher Primary Stage. Due importance should be given here also to oral tests, which should form a part of the internal assessment.

The teacher should be helped in such assessment with a rich supply of evaluation materials prepared by the State Evaluation Organizations, including standardised achievement tests.

Diagnostic testing is necessary here and indeed throughout the school stage. In most cases, such testing will be through simple teacher made diagnostic tests.

Cumulative record cards play a vital role in indicating the growth and development of the pupil at each stage, his academic and emotional problems, and his difficulties of adjustment, if any, and the directions in which remedial action is to be taken to solve his problems or difficulties. In the first instance, the cards should be introduced from Class IV onwards in about 10 percent of the selected schools as an experimental measure; but once the majority of teachers are trained in evaluating certain important aspects of the child's personality and the proper maintenance of the records, the use of the cards may be gradually extended to all the higher primary and, as a next step, even to lower primary schools.

No Compulsory External Examination. External examination need not be compulsory for all the students of Class X or Class XI/ XII. A student may choose to leave the school with the school certificate only without appearing for the external examination, and seek a job or even an entry into some vocational course on the basis of the certificate and the school records. It must be recognized, however, that since admission to institutions of higher secondary education as well as of higher education will be selective, the authorities controlling such institutions will lay down their own rules of eligibility for admission. A student seeking entry into these institutions may have not only to pass the external examination in the subjects laid down and secure the prescribed grades but also submit himself, if necessary, to certain admission tests required by the institutions.

Large Incidence of Failure. The Commission observes, "The matter about which the public at large is most deeply concerned is not the irrationality of the scoring procedures, or the inefficiency of the administrative processes, but the large incidence of failures in the external examination at the end of the school stage. An analysis of the results of the different Board Examinations for the last five years show that about 55 per cent of the candidates appearing for the high school examination and about 40 per cent of those appearing for the higher secondary school examination fail regularly every year. In the case of the private candidates the percentage soars up to 70% or even more. Failure often has a demoralizing effect on the unsuccessful candidates. The failure of such large numbers of students, particularly after they have been screened year after year by means of annual and other school examinations, is a sad reflection on our methods of education as well as on our system of examination."

"We also believe that with the proposed improvement in the curriculum, instructional materials and methods of teaching, and the reorientation in the training of teachers, the incidence of examination failures will be reduced. But we do not think that a student should be branded as a total failure, if he passes in certain subjects but is unable to make the grade in others. There is no reason why he should carry with him the stigma of being declared as unsuccessful candidate if he has partially succeeded in his educational effort." ,

Certificates Given by the Board and the School. The Commission recommends that the certificate issued by the Board on the basis of the results of the external examination at the end of the lower or higher secondary stage, should give the candidate's performance only in those subjects in which he has passed but there should be no remark to the effect that he has passed or failed in the whole examination. The Board, however, should issue a statement along with the certificate showing his marks or grades in all the subjects.

Permission to Reappear. The candidate should be permitted to appear again if he so desires, for the entire examination or for separate subjects in order to improve his performance.

Certificate from the School. On the completion of the course, at the end of the lower or higher secondary stage, the student should receive a certificate also from the school giving the record of his internal assessment as contained in his cumulative record card. This certificate may be attached to that given by the Board in connection with the external examination.

Freedom to Selected Schools to Assess Students. In order to lessen the importance of the domination which the external examinations exercise over school education still further, the Commission recommends that a few selected schools should be given the right of assessing their students themselves and holding their own final examination at the end of Class X, which will be regarded as equivalent to the external examination of the State Board of School Education. The State Board will issue certificates to the successful candidates of these schools on the recommendation of the schools. A Committee set up by the State Board of School Education should develop carefully worked out criteria for the selection of such schools. For the success of this experiment it is essential that the schools should not only be freed from the requirements of an external examination but should be permitted to frame their own curricula, prescribe their own text-books, and conduct their educational activities without departmental restrictions.

This suggestion is indeed a bold one in the direction of freedom of educational experimentation and it carries certain responsibilities also. The Commission, therefore, suggests that right given to the experimental schools should be reviewed periodically as institutions invested with such powers should continuously earn their privilege. The Commission envisages that after the experiment is tried out successfully in a few schools, more and more schools will be released from the restrictive influence of the external examination and given the freedom to work out their own ideas in education.

Ascertaining Criteria

CRT is meant to measure the achievement of an examinee on a certain domain to find out his level of achievement in that domain. It has little to do with the achievement level of other examinees.

Following are the important definitions of CRT

1. Poham, WJ. and Husek, T.R. in their paper, "Implications of Criterion-Referenced Measurement" published in Journal of Educational Measurement Vol. VI (1969), define criterion-referenced measures as, "those which are used to ascertain an individual's status with respect to some criterion i.e. performance standard. It is because the individual is compared with some established criterion, rather than other individuals, that these measures are described as criterion-referenced. The meaning of an individual score is not dependent on comparison with

other testees. We want to know what the individual can do, not how much he stands in comparison to others."

2. In the words of Gronlund, N.E. (1985), criterion-referenced test is "a test designed to provide a measure of performance that is interpretable in terms of a clearly defined and delimited domain of learning tasks."
3. Sex Gilbert (1989) writes, "Criterion-referenced tests relate a student's score on an achievement test to a domain knowledge rather than to another student's score."

The Characteristics

1. Its main objective is to measure student's achievement of curriculum based skills.
2. It is prepared for a particular grade or course level.
3. It has balanced representation of goals and objectives.
4. It is used to evaluate the curriculum plan instruction progress and group student's interaction.
5. It can be administered before and after instruction.
6. It is generally reported in the form of
   (i) Minimum scores for partial and total mastery of main skill.
   (ii) Number of correct items.
   (iii) Percent of correct items.
   (iv) Derived score based on correct items and other factors.

Uses

(i) to discover the inadequacies in learner's learning and assist the weaker section of learners to reach the level of other students through a regular programme of remedial instruction.
(ii) to identify the master learners and non-master learners in class.
(iii) to find out the level of attainment of various objectives of instruction.
(iv) to find out the level at which a particular concept has been learnt.
(v) to better placement of concepts at different grade levels.

(vi) to make instructional decisions of what to do with a learner in individually prescribed instruction programme.

Limitations

1. Criterion-referenced test tells only whether a learner has reached proficiency in a task area but does not show how good or poor is the learner's level of ability.
2. Tasks included in the criterion-referenced test may be highly influenced by a given teacher's interests or biases, leading to general validity problem.
3. Only some areas readily lend themselves for listing specific behavioural objectives around which criterion-referenced test can be built and this may be an obstructing element for teachers.
4. Criterion-referenced tests are important for only a small fraction of important educational achievements. On the contrary, promotion and assessment of various skills is a very important function of the school and it requires norm-referenced testing.

Interpretation

1. Interpretation should be based on what the items actually measure.
2. There should be sufficient items for each type of interpretation.
   In case there are less than 10 items, they should be combined with other items through lengthening content items.
3. The test should contain easy as well difficult items otherwise it would be difficult to describe what low achievers could do.

Guidelines for Constructing, Administering and Evaluating Criterion-Referenced Tests

Ronald Hambelton and Daniel Eignor (1978) have suggested the following guidelines.

Determination of Objectives

1. The purposes of the test should be stated clearly and concisely.
2. Objectives should be written in such a way that each item could be identified with one objective.
3. There should be appropriate rationale for the inclusion of each objective in the test.
4. The set of objectives of the test should be a true representative of content domain.
5. The classroom teacher should be in a position to adapt the test to meet local situation.

Test Items Invented and Utilised

1. The set of test items should measure an objective for which it has been included in the test.
2. The test items should be valid indicators of the objectives for which they have been prepared.
3. The test items should be in an appropriate form to measure the objectives for which they have been selected.
4. A heterogeneous sample should be used in the test items.
5. Item analysis should be used to detect flawed items.
6. The item review process should be described.
7. The test items should be free from any bias.
8. The test items should be free from technical flaws.

Administration

1. The test manual should specify the role and responsibilities of the examiner.
2. The test administrators should have adequate information relating to the purpose, time limits, answer sheets and scoring of test.
3. The directions of the test should be clear.
4. The test should be easy to score.

Test Layout

1. Test booklet should be attractively printed.
2. The layout of test booklet should be convenient for examiners.

Reliability

1. The test length should be sufficient enough to find out test score reliability.
2. The sample of examinees used in finding out reliability should be adequate and representative.
3. The reliability information should be provided in the test for each intended use of the test score.
4. The reliability information provided in the test should be appropriate for the use of the score of the test.

Cut-off Scores

1. There should be a rationale for the selection of the method for determining cut-off scores.
2. There should be evidence for the validity of the chosen cutoff marks.

Validity

1. The validity evidence should be adequate for the intended use of the test score.
2. The test manual should provide an appropriate discussion on the factor affecting the validity of the scores.

Norm-referenced Test

Norm-Referenced Test is used primarily for comparing achievement of an examinee to that of a large representative group of examinees at the same grade level. The representative group is known as the 'Norm Group'. Norm group may be made up of examinees at the local level, district level, state level or national level. Since the development of norm-referenced tests is expensive and time consuming, they are produced by commercial test publishers. NRT is defined as under:

Bormuth (1970) writes that a norm-referenced test is designed "to measure the growth in a student's attainment and to compare his level of attainment with the levels reached by other students and norm group."

N.R. Gronlund defines Norm-Referenced Test as "a test designed to provide a measure of performance that is interpretable in terms of an individuals relative standing in some known group."

Bormuth (1970) writes that an NRT is designed "to measure the growth in a student's attainment and to compare his level of attainment with the levels reached by other students and norm group.

Main Characteristics

1. Its basic objective is to measure student's achievement in curriculum based skills.
2. It is prepared for a particular grade level.
3. It is administered after instruction.
4. It is used for forming homogeneous or heterogeneous class groups.
5. It classifies achievement as above average, average or below average for a given grade.
6. It is generally reported in the form of Percentile Rank, Linear Standard Score, Normalized Standard Score and Grade Equivalent Score.

The Uses

N. Vasantha Ram Kumar and K.N. Lalithamal (1990), state the following uses of NRT :

(1) in aptitude testing for making differential prediction;
(2) to get a reliable rank ordering of the pupils with respect to the achievement we are measuring;
(3) to identify the pupils who have mastered the essentials of the course more than others;
(4) to select the best of the applicants for a particular programme;
(5) to find out how effective a programme is in comparison to other possible programmes.

The Limitations

According to the above mentioned authors, some of the criticisms raised against these tests are:

(1) Test items that are answered correctly by most of the pupils are not included in these tests because of their inadequate contribution to response variance. They will be the items that deal with important concepts of course content.

(2) There is lack of congruence between what the test measures and what is stressed in a local curriculum.

(3) Norm-referencing promotes unhealthy competition and is injurious to self-concepts of low scoring students.

Process for the Development of NRT. L.M. Carey (1988) has described the following stages for the development of NRT

Design Stage. It is done through:

(i) Curriculum analysis.

(ii) Selecting objectives to be measured.

(iii) Analysing objectives for determining pre-requisite skills.

(iv) Developing table of specifications for test.

(v) Determining specifications for items.

Development Stage. This consists of

(i) Writing items according to specifications.

(ii) Developing needed art work and illustrations.

(iii) Writing response directions and examples.

(iv) Writing administrative directions.

(v) Reviewing items, illustrations and directions.

(vi) Developing test lay-out.

(vii) Developing simple test.

Conducting Field Test. At this stage, test is tried out through :

(i) Selecting representative group.

(ii) Administering test.

(iii) Scoring.

(iv) Analysing information.

(v) Analysing data and selecting items.

(vi) Developing final test form.

Developing Test Norm. Norms of the test are developed through:

(i) Describing characteristics of population.

(ii) Selecting representative norm group.

(iii) Administering test to norm group.

(iv) Scoring.

(v) Converting raw scores to standard scores.

(vi) Creating norm tables.

Writing Test Manual. The test manual is written through:

(i) Describing the design process and skills measured.
(ii) Describing the field test process.
(iii) Describing the development process.
(iv) Describing criteria used to select items.
(v) Describing norm group selection procedure.
(vi) Describing norm group characteristics.
(vii) Describing test characteristics-reliability and standard error of measurement.
(viii) Describing standard administrative procedures.
(ix) Describing scoring procedures and derivation of standard scores.
(x) Describing score interpretation procedures.

Growing Relevance

Test Length Affects Reliability. Other things being equal, the reliability of the test can be increased by increasing its length. Items of similar content also increase reliability. Items of moderate difficulty increase reliability over the items which are either too easy or too difficult. Increased range of performance of the examinees being tested tends to increase reliability.

Increasing Validity of a Norm-Referenced Test

The validity of a norm-referenced test can be increased by:

(i) Constructing items of proper difficulty level.
(ii) Increasing the test length.
(iii) Increasing the heterogeneity of the group.
(iv) Administering the test under proper conditions.

J.C. Starley and K.D. Hopkins (1972) have stated as: " The word criterion in CRT denotes an instructional objective, an expected post-instructional outcome, an intended level of a student's performance, an acceptable level of learner's achievement or a desired standard of product of performance." By norm-referenced testing is meant the measurement of student's achievement in terms of a group, a class, a school or a state which is taken as a referent for interpreting student's scores and for passing judgements. Thus the typical performance or norm of a group is used as the basis for Judging individual students learning.

In CRT, the emphasis is on improvement of student's achievement and in NRT, emphasis is on measurement of achievement.

Common Factors

(1) Achievement domain is measured in both.
(2) Same types of items can be used in both.
(3) Same rules are followed for writing items in both excepting the item of difficulty.
(4) Validity and reliability are needed in both.
(5) Sample of test items should be relevant and representative in both.

The Comparison

	NRT		CRT
1.	It stresses discrimination among individuals.	1.	It stresses what examinees can do and what they cannot do.
2.	NRT covers a large domain of learning task with just a few items measuring each specific task.	2.	It focuses on a delimited domain of learning tasks with a relatively large number of items measuring each specific task.
3.	It contains items of average difficulty.	3.	It contains easy as well as difficult items.
4.	A student is tested after each unit (usually large) of the new material presented.	4.	A student is tested after each unit for mastery of objectives.
5.	A student is assigned the marks or grades to indicate his performance.	5.	A student is allowed to proceed to the new material if mastery is obtained.
6.	A student is given remedial instruction if the material presented is not mastered.	6.	A student is allowed to go to the next unit along with the whole class.
7.	A student is tested again after remedial work, to check for mastery of the material.	7.	A student is presented with the new materials of the next unit.
8.	A student is tested for mastery of objectives.	8.	A student is tested for the new material and assigned marks.

Perfect System

A norm-referenced test typically attempts to measure a more general category of competencies (for example, reading, comprehension), knowledge (for example, familiarity with the unitary government system) or aptitude (for example, problem solving potential).

A criterion referenced test, on the other hand, typically focuses on a more specific domain of examinee behaviours. A 100-item on referenced test may be needed to cover the entire range of a learner's reading comprehension skills as against five separate twenty-item criterion-referenced test, focusing only on five well defined skills within the overall realm of reading comprehension.

CRT and NRT are used to measure the attainment of the learner. The fundamental distinction between NRT and CRT is based on the manner in which one interprets the results of the learner's test performance. In the case of NRT one interprets learner's test performance according to the performance of 'others'. In case of CRT, one interprets learner's performance in relation to well defined norms of knowledge, skills, attitudes and the like.

11

Evaluation Techniques

It is on the basis of techniques of evaluation that the teachers pass their judgements on the performance of students in various curricular and co-curricular activities/learning experiences/tasks. It is, therefore, very necessary for the teachers to acquire adequate knowledge about these techniques.

Varied Significance

Objective techniques of evaluation are more valid than subjective techniques of evaluation since the element of specificity is present in these techniques. Under these techniques, several elements like testing situation, procedure and assessment norms are predetermined and these elements ensure that in their use, different test administrators would arrive at the same conclusions. These tests are free from the influence of like and dislikes or whims of those who administer these tests.

It is very essential that all types of evaluation techniques are used carefully, rationally and scientifically. At the same time, a balanced use of these tests should be made.

The Measurement

Definition and Meaning. With a view to understanding the various elements of a test, it is necessary to study a few standard definitions of a test.

The Classification

Standardised Tests Objective Methods	Non-Standardised Tests or Subjective Methods	Projective Techniques
1. Achievement Tests	1. Anecdotal Records	1. BG Test
2. Aptitude Tests	2. Autobiography	2. Blacky Picture Test
3. Intelligence Tests Test	3. Case Conference or Case History or Case Study	3. Children Apperception
4. Interest Tests	4. Cumulative Record Card	4. Clay Modelling
5. Personal Inventories	5. Interview	5. Cloud Picture Test
	6. Observation	6. Draw-a-Man Test
	7. Parent's Views	7. Graphology
	8. Personal Data Banks	8. Mosaic Test
	9. Questionnaire	9. Phychodrania
	10. Rating Scale or Attitude Scale	10. Rorschach Ink Blot Test
	11. Schedule	11. Sentence Completion
	12. Score card	12. Socio-drama
	13. Sociometry	13. Szondi Test
		14. Thematic Apperception Test (TAT)
		15. Toy and Doll playing
		16. Word Association (Free and Controlled)

(1) A Dictionary of Education (1981) gives the following definition: "A test is a compact task or series of tasks designed to ascertain the merit or quantity of something. Educational tests constitute a series of items for which a score is obtained. Depending on how they are constructed, they can serve a purpose."

(2) The International Dictionary of Education (1981) explains a Test : "1. Any method by which the presence of quality or genuineness of anything is determined. 2. Examination to evaluate the performance and capabilities of a student or class (e.g. knowledge of a subject). 3. Procedure for eliciting responses upon which appraisal of the individual can be based (e.g. intelligence). 4. Process of detecting the presence of an ingredient in a compound, or of determining the nature of a substance."

(3) L.J. Cronback, in his book Essentials of Psychological Testing (1970) defines a test "as a systematic procedure for observing and describing one or more characteristics of a person with the aid of either a numerical scale or a category system."

On the basis of the above definitions a test may be defined as a device or procedure confronting a subject with a standard set of questions or tasks to which the student is to respond independently and the results of which can be treated in such a way as to provide a quantitative comparison of performance of different students.

Important Elements : Following are the important elements of a test as contained in the above definitions:

1. A test often implies the presentation of a standard set of questions to be answered for tasks to be performed by a student.
2. The student is to take the test independently.
3. The test results in a measure (a numerical value of a characteristic of the students).
4. The test often provides a quantitative comparison of the performance of students.
5. It is a technique that yields only a verbal description; for instance, an interview technique is not a test.
6. A test is to be completed in a given time.

Possible Functions of a Testing Programme

Classroom Functions	*Guidance Functions*	*Administrative Functions*
(1) Grouping pupils for instruction within a class.	(1) Preparing evidence to guide discussions with parents about their children.	(1) Forming of and assigning to classroom groups.
(2) Guiding the planning of activities for specific individual pupils.	(2) Building realistic self-pictures on the part of pupils.	(2) Placing new students.
(3) Identifying pupils who need special diagnostic study and remedial instruction.	(3) Helping the pupil with immediate choices.	(3) Helping determine eligibility for special groups.
(4) Determining reasonable achievement levels for each pupil and evaluating discrepancies between potentiality and achievement.	(4) Helping the pupil to set educational and vocational goals.	(4) Helping determine which pupils are to be promoted.
(5) Assigning course grades.	(5) Improving counsellor, teacher, and parent understanding of problem cases.	(5) Evaluating curricula, curricular emphasis, and curricular experiments.

Main Purposes and Functions. Robert L. Thorndike and Elizabeth Hagen in their book Measurement and Evaluation in Psychology and Education (1951) have illustrated the main purposes and functions of a testing programme as given in Table:

General Purposes of Testing

1. To determine the achievement level and progress of the pupils.
2. To obtain data for diagnostic purposes.
3. To identify the interests of the students.
4. To identify the underachievers.
5. To determine the self-concept, attitudes and personality pattern of the students.
6. To ascertain the extent and quality of social development of the students.
7. To identify the gifted.
8. To improve learning techniques.
9. To improve teaching techniques.

Limitations

1. Heavy weightage to verbal ability in many tests.
2. Difficulty in obtaining level norms.
3. Relative narrowness of the traits measured by tests.
4. Indifference, lack of attention, low commitment and generally low motivation of the students, tending to invalidate the test results.
5. Difficulty to follow the directions of the tester by the testee.
6. Undue influence of socio-cultural conditions or environmental influences on the testees or the students.
7. Low validity and reliability in the case of some pupils.

Relative Importance

Tests are used in the guidance programme as they have the following merits as compared with other techniques of guidance:

1. They are handy.

2. They are economical techniques of collecting information.
3. They are less time-consuming.
4. They are objective.
5. They provide significant means of comparing individuals.

The Importance

According to Ebel and Frisbie (1991), "Tests can be and should be, among the most useful instructional tools for planning new learning activities and for monitoring student's progress in attaining the learning goals presented to them. Tests can be used to provide recognition and rewards for success in learning and teaching. They can be used to motivate and direct effort to learn. In short, they can be used to contribute substantially to effective instruction."

Classification of Tests. Tests have been classified in a number of ways. Some of these even overlap. Here we are stating only one classification which seems to be quite comprehensive.

Two Way Classification

Tests vary according to form, use and type etc. Yoak and Simpson give the following classification of tests:

Form

(a) Oral examinations (b) Written examination

Purposes

(a) Prognostic. (b) Diagnostic. (c) Power. (d) Speed. (e) Accuracy (f) Quality. (g) Range.

Organisation

(a) Essay. (b) Objective.

Period or Time of Administering

(a) Daily (b) Weekly (c) Monthly (d) Term. (e) Year.

Duration

(a) Short. (b) Long.

Method of Scoring and Interpreting Results

(a) Non-standardized. (b) Standardized.

Abilities Involved

(a) Speed. (b) Comprehension. (c) Organization. (d) Judgement. (e) Retention. (f) Appreciation etc.

Nature of Material Included

(a) Arithmetic. (b) Language. (c) Reading. (d) Spelling. (e) Writing etc.

Mental Functions Involved

(a) Association. (b) Memory. (c) Recall. (d) Recognition. (e) Problem-solving.

Types of Response Involved

(a) Alternate response: (1) True - False (2) Yes - No (3) Plus - Minus.

(b) Multiple response: (1) Best Answer. (2) Correct Answer.

(c) Completion.

(d) Matching.

(e) Identification

(f) Enumeration.

(g) Essay.

Managing the System

Proper test administration requires training and the test instructions constitute a very important part of the procedure. Following considerations may be kept in mind while planning and administering a testing programme.

Centralised Responsibility. There should be one person in each school who will look after the administrative details given below:

(a) Ordering for relevant tests and test material.
(b) Arranging schedules of time.
(c) Arranging place for testing.
(d) Arranging scoring and recording results.
(e) Taking responsibility for the security and storage of tests when they are not being used.

Testing Schedule. Tests should be given under standard conditions that permit each testee to perform at his best level. Testing schedule should never be made too tight. The unit of time schedule for testing should be reasonably enough to permit its completion. It should provide a realistic allowance for distributing and collecting papers and for giving instructions.

Preparation by Testers. The testers should prepare themselves in advance especially for the following aspects of the testing programme.

(a) The tester should follow the manual verbatim.
(b) The tester should make the procedures and the tasks clear to the testee before administering the test.
(c) The tester should have a stopwatch and he should allow the subjects to work on a particular test for that much time only which is mentioned in its manual.
(d) The tester should go round the class and ensure that the students have followed the instructions carefully and are not copying.

Preparation of Students for Testing. Orientation talks on the usefulness of testing may be given to the students so that they are motivated to take tests and are convinced that tests are genuinely important.

Appropriate Environment for Testing. The desirable environment for testing should satisfy the following conditions:

(1) Examinees are physically comfortable.
(2) Examinees are emotionally relaxed.
(3) Examinees are free from interruptions and distractions.
(4) Adequate space is provided to the examinees so that they are able to manipulate their test material conveniently.
(5) Examinees are seated in such a way as to prevent copying.
(6) Conditions of lighting and ventilation are adequate for testing.

Recording of Test Results. Results should be kept systematically so that these are made use of conveniently by the appropriate agency. Of course results should be kept confidential.

Interpreting Test Results. Tests will prove useful only when they are interpreted properly. Results of tests provide indication of success or failures of educational programmes. Future planning may be determined on the basis of results. Therefore adequate care has to be taken in interpreting results. Following are the various steps in interpreting test results:-

(a) Classification of data.
(b) Tabulation of scores.
(c) Graphical analysis and representation.
(d) Use of norms and standards.
(e) Analysis of errors.

Qualitative as well as quantitative analysis of test results may be used to supplement each other in interpreting the scores.

The Assessment

Like any other measuring instrument, each component of an evaluation instrument needs to be doing its proper job and functioning harmoniously with the other components in the system. One weak component and the performance of the instrument becomes suspect and its validity open to question. The major need for item analysis is to ascertain whether the questions/items do their job effectively. Usually a detailed test analysis and item analysis will have to be done before a meaningful and scientific inference about the test can be made in terms of its validity, reliability, objectivity, difficulty and discrimination.

Typical Techniques

Self-reporting techniques of evaluation are those techniques which are used in evaluation to find out the reaction of the respondents (students) to items concerning their characteristics or behaviour. The students generally are required to express their likes, dislikes, fears, hopes, ideas about religious beliefs and sex etc. Their expressions reflect the way in which they cope with their own needs and demands of the environment they encounter with.

Significance of Self-reporting Techniques. Broadly speaking, self-reporting techniques are commonly used for measuring the following traits of the students:

(1) Adjustment
(2) Attitude
(3) Interest
(4) Personality
(5) Diverse traits

Examples of Self-reporting Techniques. These are as under:

(a) Check list
(b) Questionnaire
(c) Rating scale.

Important Self-reporting Instruments. These are:

(1) Edward's Personal Preference Schedule
(2) The Minnesota Multi-phasic Personality Inventory (MMPI)
(3) Minnesota Teacher Attitude Inventory (MTAI)
(4) Woodworth Personal Datasheet

Self-reporting techniques which come under the category of subjective techniques, provide useful means for extracting the hidden treasure of students, acquired accumulated complex behaviour patterns of personality which are very difficult to discover through other devices. The information obtained through self-reporting techniques may be collaborated suitably with information obtained through other techniques.

Limitations

(i) Being subjective in nature, they are likely to have a biased element.
(ii) The respondents may attempt to present themselves as most favourable by giving fake or untrue responses.

The Precautions

(1) After rearranging the items, techniques may be again used to find out the responses of the students after a short-interval.
(2) 'Lie' scales may be used to check deceiving tendency.
(3) 'Forced Second Technique' may be used in which a student is given a choice to be exercised for performance which appears to be equally good or

bad, e.g. who has exercised greater influence in developing your value system-your mother or father?

(4) Information obtained through self-reporting techniques may be supplemented to the information obtained through other means.

(5) More than one self-reporting technique may be used.

(6) Norms for local population may be established.

(7) Standardised inventories should be used.

(8) Only due faith should be placed in this type of technique.

(9) Only those techniques should be used in which the teacher has received reasonable amount of training.

(10) In administering and interpreting the information, help of trained professionals may be obtained.

Keen Observation

Observation is one of the oldest techniques that man has made use of. Even today it is our common experience to notice that farmers feel the breeze, watch the sky, sun, moon and stars, all to determine what the weather is likely to be and what season is approaching.

The physicians and the psychologists depend heavily on what they observe of the patient's talk, gestures and facial expressions.

Rousseau wrote, "Watch nature long and observe your pupil carefully before you say a word to him".

Observation has been defined as, "measurement without instruments." In education, observation is the most commonly employed of all measurement techniques. In the present as well as in the past, students have been labelled as good, fair or poor in achievement and lazy or diligent in study etc., on the basis of observation. Similarly, teachers have listened to speeches and ranked students 1,2,3 and so on.

The subjective element is very predominant in observation. To eliminate the subjective element, reliance should be placed on a large number of individual observations or on the observations made by a large number of observers.

Behaviour is a reflection of personality. It must be observed very carefully, intelligently and scientifically as observation of behaviour has been recognised as basic to other techniques.

Merits

1. Being a record of the actual behaviour of the child, it is more reliable and objective.
2. It is a study of an individual in a natural situation and is therefore more useful than the restricted study in a test situation.
3. This method can be used with children of all ages; of course, the younger the child, the easier it is to observe him. This method has been found very useful with shy children.
4. It can be used with a little training and almost all teachers can use it. It does not require any special tools or equipment.
5. It can be used in every situation.
6. It is adaptable both to individuals and groups.

Demerits

1. There is a great scope for personal prejudices and bias of the observer.
2. Records may not be written with hundred per cent accuracy as the observation is recorded after the actions of the observed. There is some time-lag.
3. The observer may get only a small sample of student behaviour. It is very difficult to observe everything that a student does or says. As far as possible, observations should be collected from several teachers.
4. It reveals the overt behaviour only-behaviour that is expressed and not that is within.

Requisites of Good Observation

As a research tool good observation is based on:

I. Proper planning.
II. Proper execution.

III. Proper recording.

IV. Proper interpretation.

Proper Planning of Observation

1. Specific activities or units of behaviour to be observed must be clearly defined.
2. An appropriate group of subjects be selected to observe.
3. Scope of observation-whether individual or group should be decided.
4. The length of each observation period, number of periods and interval between periods should be decided.
5. The form of recording should be determined.
6. The instruments to be used should be decided.
7. Physical position of the observer should be demarcated.
8. Proper tools for recording observation should be kept handy.
9. Various terms may be studied.

Proper Execution of Observation

An expert execution demands skill and resourcefulness on the part of the investigators. This depends upon:

(i) Proper arrangement of special conditions for the subjects.

(ii) Assuring proper physical position for observing.

(iii) Focussing attention on the units of behaviour or the specific activities under observation.

(iv) Observing discreetly the length and number of periods and intervals decided upon.

(v) Proper handling of the recording instrument being used.

(vi) Utilizing well the training received in terms of expertness.

Devices Used in Observation are:

(i) Check lists.

ii) Rating scale.

(iii) Score cards.

(iv) Blank form of tally frequencies.

Recording of Observation

Generally two methods are employed for recording observation. Which of the two methods to use depends upon the nature of the activities or behaviour of the group to be observed. The skill of the observer also plays an important role in deciding upon the method.

The first method is to record the observation simultaneously. It is useful in the sense that a time-gap may distort facts. However, at times, this may not be feasible when the action or activity performed is very swift. Moreover, this is likely to distract the subjects.

Facts may be recorded soon after the observation is over. This is helpful as this does not distract the mind of the subjects. The investigator may not be able to recall facts accurately after the interval of a few minutes.

Proper Interpretation

Records of observation should be interpreted cautiously and judiciously after taking into consideration various limitations of planning and processes etc. involved in observation.

Recording Devices of Observation. Following are the major devices of observation:

(1) Check Lists.
(2) Rating Scales.
(3) Score Cards.

Planning Good, Reliable and Effective Observation

(1) Sampling to be observed should be adequate.
(2) Traits to be observed should be defined as accurately as possible.
(3) Methods of recording should be simplified.
(4) Too many variables may not be observed at a time.
(5) Length of observation should be adequate.
(6) Length of each observation period, interval between periods and number of periods should be clearly stated.
(7) Conditions of observation should remain constant.

(8) Observers should be fully equipped.
(9) Interpretations should be carefully made.

Essentials of a Good Observer

(1) Alertness.
(2) Ability to discriminate.
(3) Freedom from preconception.
(4) Emotional balance.
(5) Good eyesight.
(6) Right perception.
(7) Good speed of recording.
(8) Ability to sift fact from fiction.

Types of Observation

Participant Observation	*Non-participant Observation*
(1) Observer becomes more or less a member of the group which is under observation.	(1) The observer takes a position so that his presence does not disturb the movements/activities of the group.
(2) The observer plays a dual role i.e. observer as well as participant.	(2) It is very helpful in recording and studying the behaviour of the members of the group in detail.
(3) He may assume the role of an attentive listener or a full fledged participant.	(3) Non-participant observation is used in the case of abnormal individuals, infants and children.
(4) It is a flexible type of observation.	
(5) It gives more reliable results.	
(6) It is economical and helps in finding out delicate hidden and minute facts.	

Peer ratings imply the preference and non-preferences of colleagues or members of the class or a social group regarding their choice of friendship or leadership etc. on the basis of behavioural characteristics of individuals. In other words, personality traits are evaluated by peers. Peer rating is helpful to assess the individuals. This shows the acceptance or non-acceptance or rejection by members of the group. Interpersonal relationships and socio-emotional climate of the classroom are revealed through peer ratings.

Techniques Used : Following techniques are usually used in peer ratings:

(1) Sociometry.

(2) Guess who Techniques.

Sociogram and Sociometric Tests

These tests were designed by J.L Moreno and Helen Jennings in 1946. In the words of Jennings, "Stated briefly, sociometry may be described as a means of presenting simply and graphically the entire structure of relations existing at a given time among members of a given group. The major lines of communication or the pattern of attraction and rejection in its full scope, are made readily comprehensive at a glance."

William J. Goode and others state, "These and other variants of sociometric techniques offer rather simple methods of ranking individuals on a continuum of 'acceptability' or 'outgoingness' on the part of group members. When their use is justified they may be powerful research tools since they meet the general problems of scaling very well."

Sociometric studies have been made of many types of social groups including classroom groups. Being peer-rating rather than rating by superiors, sociometry adds another dimension to the understanding of social relationships.

Example-Each group consisting of ten students is asked to write his first, second and sometimes third choices about some significant and pertinent type of social setting. He may be asked questions like this:

1. Whom would you like to be the secretary of your debating society?
2. Whom would you like to sit next to you in the class or in the bus while going for a picnic?
3. With whom do you enjoy most?
4. With whom would you like to work in the science laboratory?
5. With whom would you like to walk home?

All those questions are positive questions and hence show social acceptances.

Negative questions may also be given to show social rejections.

Object. To find out the social structure of a group of 10 students.

Material. A Questionnaire asking students: Whom would you like to be the secretary of your club?

Procedure. After taking the students into confidence, one-line questionnaire as indicated above may be given to the students to mark against one of the 10 Roll Nos. Thereafter tabulation of the students responses may be made. On the basis of responses, the following sociogram may emerge.

Interpretation

1. Roll no. 5 is the 'star' as he has been chosen by the maximum number of students.
2. Roll nos. 7 and 9 did not get any choice. This indicates that they tended to be isolated i.e. not being social.
3. Roll nos. 2 and 8 came next to roll no. 1.
4. Roll no. 5 i.e. the star preferred roll no. 2.
5. Mutual choices were: 2 and 5; 3 and 4; and 2 and 10.

Isolates and Stars

1. The 'isolates' and the 'stars' may be looked for. An 'isolate' is one whom nobody chooses. Of course he is not rejected. A 'star' is a member of the group who receives most of the choices.
2. Attempts should be made to discover the causes for such selection.

An individual may be isolated because:

(i) He is a new member of the group.

(ii) He is of a shy and withdrawing nature.

(iii) He does not try to make friendship with others.

(iv) He may belong to a lower or upper socio-economic level and therefore he is not acceptable to the group.

3. Look for individuals who select each other. This might be due to factors like:

(i) Close relations.
(ii) Neighbours.
(iii) Common interests and the like.

4. A triangle shows three persons selecting each other. This may be an evidence of cliques, or sharp divisions in the group.

Role of the Teacher/Guidance Worker. In general, he can work on three points:

1. Providing opportunities for developing friendly relations.
2. Improving social skills.
3. Building up competency for accomplishing something.

Reliable results can be achieved only when all the members constituting a group are fully acquainted with each other. The worker or the counsellor must establish friendly relations with the members of the group so that they may give their frank opinion about an individual or individuals.

Using Sociometric Techniques

1. To study the relationships among members of the group and to improve them.
2. To organise classroom groups.
3. To assist those who have become isolates in the group.
4. To assign responsibility to the members of the group.

Limitations

1. The relationships are not necessarily stable.
2. Some members of the group may not reveal their real relationships on account of some fear or other considerations.

Principles to be Followed in Sociometric Techniques

1. Ratings of variables to be marked must be simple.
2. Ratings should relate to student's world.
3. Language used should be very simple.
4. Confidentiality must be maintained.
5. Students should be allowed the freedom to mention their

A New Technique

This method reveals the peer judgements about social acceptance or rejection of individuals of the groups. This technique was devised by Hartshorne and Mark A. May. It consists of a description of the various roles played by the members of a group and the members are asked to name the individuals who fit the verbal descriptions. Guessing is the main process through which these roles are revealed.

Some examples of verbal descriptions are given below. Students are asked to write names against each question.

Description

1. Guess who is very talkative
2. Guess who is always cheerful

Name of the student who fits in the description

Description

Name of the student

who fits in the description

3. Guess who is always happy
4. Guess who is always worried
5. Guess who is usually lazy
6. Guess who is always active
7. Guess who does not readily mix with others
8. Guess who is most cooperative

Analysis. Result may be analysed to count the number of times each student's name appears in the blanks. Findings may be utilized to assist students who do not display the appropriate interpersonal relationships in the group.

Responses must be kept confidential.

Techniques for Projection

An individual, it is recognised, reveals or 'projects' his personality in a free and unrestricted activity. According to the psychology of unconscious, the quality of personality is greatly affected by the unconscious methods and emotions. Murray writes, "The purpose of this procedure is to stimulate literacy creativity and thereby evoke fantasies that reveal covert and unconscious complexes. The test is based on the well-recognized fact that when a person interprets an ambiguous social situation, he is apt to expose his own personality as much as the phenomenon to which he is attending." Another writer remarks, "The method is designed to penetrate somewhat below the peripheral personality and to disclose latent needs, images, and sentiments which the subject would be unwilling or unable to embody in direct communication."

"The label projective techniques has been applied to settings or materials designed to give a person a chance to reveal his thoughts and feelings while seemingly responding to something in the external environment," write Gates and others. To quote Ruth Strang, "Projective techniques are a method of understanding the inner world of the individual." Rapport describes the aim of Projective techniques as, "to elicit, to render observable, to record, and to communicate the psychological structure of the subject, as inherent to him at any given moment and without study of historical antecedents." According to Anne Anastasi, it is expected that the test material of the Projective techniques "will serve as a sort of screen upon which the subject "projects his characteristic ideas, attitudes, aspirations, fears, worries, aggressions and the like."

"Typically, projective instruments also represent disguised testing procedures in so far as the subject is rarely aware of the type of psychological interpretation which will be made of his response. Projective techniques are likewise characterized by a global approach to the appraisal of personality Attention is focussed upon a composite picture of the whole personality rather than upon the measurement of separate traits."

L.K. Frank was the first person to use the term 'Projective Technique' in an article that appeared in 1939 though such methods had been in use for many years prior to that date.

Projective techniques are very useful with young children, illiterates and persons with language handicaps or speech defects. Non-verbal media is readily applicable to all these groups.

Kinds of Projective Techniques

1. Play Situation
2. Story Telling and Story Completion
3. Incomplete Sentence
4. Original Drawings and Paintings
5. Free Association and Dream Analysis
6. The Rorschach Inkblots Test
7. Thematic Apparception Test (TAT)

Play Situation. Many dolls are given to the child to play with and observation is made of his reactions. These dolls represent a father, a mother, a boy and a girl. These dolls provide the medium through which the child might act out or reveal his thoughts, impulses and feelings about himself and others. Situation should be such as to give a free play to his ideas at the unconscious level. Controlled play techniques are also used.

In a free play, a boy who happens to be jealous of his sister might assign the role of the sister to the baby doll and cause it punished by the father doll or mother doll, or shunt the baby doll to a far corner of the room. This will indicate that the girl is preferred to him in the family.

A great variety of material may be used in play situations.

Story-telling and Story Completion. An incomplete story may be told to the child and he may be asked to complete it. While completing the story, the child may reveal something about his feelings and desires. He may be asked to let his imagination go to show how imaginative he is. The situation selected should be such as touches the emotional life of the child whose personality traits we wish to assess. For instance, the child is asked to relate a story about an innocent child who was beaten by his father. The child is likely to depict his innermost feelings, wishes and thoughts while he narrates the story. Take another case when a child is told about the beginning of a story. Father is ready to take the children to the exhibition. All of a sudden a guest comes. The child may be asked to complete the story. As the child finishes the story, the psychologist comes to know the personality traits of the child.

This method is usually employed in the case of delinquent children.

Incomplete Sentence Technique. The method is very simple. Some incomplete sentences are presented to the child which he completes in any way he likes. By reading the individual's responses, the counsellor records observations which indicate unhealthy or conflicting, positive or healthy attitudes, etc. Stimulus in the form of the following words may be presented to the child:

(a) A baby ....
(b) The world ....
(c) My home ....
(d) My father ....
(e) Money ....
(f) My best friend ....

The child may complete these sentences in this manner:

(a) A baby is very lovely.
(b) The world is full of cruel people.
(c) My home is not a good place to live in.
(d) My father is very cruel.
(e) Money is everything in life.
(f) My best friend is very poor.

The psychologist, by going through these sentences, may get some clue of the repressed wishes of the child.

Original Drawings and Paintings. Original drawings and paintings of the children give an idea of the personality of the child. The theme or subject he chooses, the colour he uses, the masses and the open spaces that the paintings contain, the length, direction, curvature of the lines-all these give an indication of the various traits of the personality of the child.

Free Association and Dream Analysis. Freud used this method to find out the repressed unconscious desires, emotions and feelings of individual men and women. It has been recognised by many psychologists that day-dreams are rather difficult to interpret but they do not just happen. They have their roots in the person's private world.

According to this method, the psychologist first of all develops rapport with the subject and then the subject is asked to take a comfortable position reclining on a sofa and is encouraged to talk about his troubles freely after a black cloth is tied over his eyes. The psychologist or the psychoanalyst records his responses and interprets them. After many such sittings, it becomes possible for him to have a clue of the personality of the subject.

Rorschach Ink Blot Test. Rorschach was a Swiss psychologist who experimented with the use of ink-blots as a means of diagnosing mental disorders. Perceptual approach is the basis of this test. The perception of an individual is influenced by the emotional and social make-up when he is asked to perceive a figure which is not well defined.

Rorschach experienced for years together with thousands of ink-blots and ultimately selected ten ink-blots which proved to have the greatest diagnostic value. There are ten ink-blots, five in black and white, two with splashes of red and three in other colours. These are printed on 7 by 9 1/2 inch cards.

Each card is given to the subject in turn who is asked to tell what he sees in the ink-blots, what that means to him and what that might be. The counsellor notes whatever the subject says. The counsellor then shows the card a second time and through well-worded questions he elicits answers. The success of the counsellor depends to a great extent upon his skill in asking questions that will clarify the free responses. Special techniques have been developed for recording the responses of the subject.

Uses : This technique has the following uses:

1. This helps to distinguish between 'normal' persons and persons in need of psychiatric treatment.
2. This helps to show the potential intelligence of an individual.
3. This helps to predict and plan for academic success and adjustment in college.
4. This may prove to be helpful in indicating personality tendencies significant for vocational success.

Thematic Apperception Test (T.A.T.). Murray's T.A.T. involves a systematic use of pictures representing a number of dramatic events. The pictures are shown to the subject who identifies himself with some picture. The picture presents a stimulus to the child to talk freely. The child makes interpretations in accordance with his own past experiences and present needs and attitudes. To quote Ruth Strang, "To some extent, he reads into the pictures his own experiences-the responses made in the test situation also reveal the person's attitudes and ways of thinking in life situations."

The pictures selected have the following characteristics:

First, no detail in the background is provided so that this may not limit the picture to a certain time or place.

Second, the theme of these pictures is vague.

Third, the action and expression of the characters in the pictures are not very clear and are rather vague and ambiguous.

Fourth, the contents of the pictures do not give the whole story. They are incomplete.

Fifth, home and social situations relate to the ordinary situations of life.

Sixth, characters in the pictures are such as the child can very easily identify himself.

The test can be employed suitably to persons over four years of age whose intelligence quotient is not lower than 80. The counsellor shows one or more of the pictures and puts questions like these. What does the picture mean to you? What can be the factors that have led to that situation? What will be the outcome?

In interpreting pictures, it is important to note not only the turn of the thoughts the child injects into the situation, but also his mood.

Situations where Projective Techniques can be Used. Some of the most favourable situations for the use of projective techniques are given below.

1. To diagnose the behavioural problems of students.
2. To study the personality of children who are not able or not willing to discuss their problems directly.

3. To verify the patterns of personality emerging out of subjective or objective techniques.
4. To study the home and school adjustment of adolescents.
5. To study personality or adjustment patterns of more sensitive persons or of those who tend to give biased responses on tests.
6. To use for clinical work.
7. To test illiterate persons of different language backgrounds.
8. To identify the subject's real concerns, his conception of himself and the way he views his human environment.

The Advantages of Projective Techniques

1. An individual reveals himself in various situations and sometimes he is not aware of this fact. Thus we get reliable information.
2. The connection between diagnosis and the situations is very close.
3. It is not possible for the individual to give readymade, habitual or conventional responses as the tasks presented are novel and unstructured.
4. These encourage spontaneous responses.
5. These enable us to have a total view of the personality of an individual, rather than in piece-meal.

Limitations

From the point of view of the school counsellor, the projective techniques have certain limitations.

First, they are very subjective.

Second, they require a lot of training in their administration. Only trained psychologists can administer them.

Third, they are time-consuming.

Fourth, they are very difficult to interpret. Lastly, there are very few standardized tests.

Current Position

Anne Anastasi observes, "Such devices still represent only raw materials rather than standardized tests. As such, they may serve as aids to the trained and experienced clinician. In his hands, they may provide effective means of/or establishing rapport, as well as a rich source of leads to be followed in the interview. At the same time, current research, such as that of Thurstone and Goodenough, suggests that the projective approach may eventually be utilised in the construction of instruments which can be properly designated as psychological tests."

Teacher's Responsibility

It must be remembered that the projective techniques, by their very nature, should be administered by properly trained personnel. Teachers should be very careful to venture into the use of projective techniques unless they have acquired the necessary training. In view of the complexity associated with the application of projective techniques, it would be safe to refer cases of students showing the sign of severe emotional problems to clinical psychologists.

12

Measurement of Attitude

An attitude has been defined by Thurstone as, "Attitude denotes the ' sum total of a man's inclinations and feelings, prejudice or bias, preconceived notions, ideas, fears and threats and convictions about any specific topic."

Classification of Attitudes. Attitudes are as under:

(i) Acquisitive and work attitudes.

(ii) Play attitudes.

(iii) Inquisitive and scientific attitudes.

Determinants of Attitudes. These are (i) Cultural factors (ii) Psychological factors (iii) Temperamental factors.

Dimensions of Attitudes to be Measured.

(a) Direction i.e. for and against some idea etc.

(b) Degree i.e. amount of favourableness or unfavourableness.

(c) Strength or Intensity: i.e. how strong an attitude is.

(d) Consistency i.e. how does an individual maintain his attitude towards others under different conditions.

The two most frequently used methods for the measurement of social attitude are: "The Method of Equal Appearing Intervals" developed by Thurstone and "The Method of Summated Ratings" developed by Likert.

The first method since its appearance in a monograph published by Thurstone and Chave in 1929 and until 1932, when the Likert Method appeared, had almost a perfect sway over other techniques in this field.

A variety of statements expressing various points of view towards a particular issue are collected, screened and edited in accordance with certain informal criteria to omit the confusing and ambiguous statements. After this, these statements are sent to a number of judges (fifty or more) who are asked to sort them into a number of categories usually eleven to represent a scale ranging from extremely favourable through neutral to extremely unfavourable expressions of opinion about the issue in question. It may be noted that the judges are asked not to express their opinions but sort them at their face value. Tabulations are made which indicate the number of judges who placed each item in each category. The next step consists of calculating cumulated proportions for each item and ogives are constructed. Scale values of each item are read from the ogives, the values of each item being that point along the base line, in terms of scale value units above and below which 50% of the judges placed the item.

Q values provide the statistical criterion for the ambiguity of items. 20 to 22 items are selected for the final test on the basis of the scale and Q values retaining low Q values and with scale values falling at relatively equally spaced distances along the continuum. This enables us to construct two comparable forms of the scale in terms of the scale and Q values. A new group is asked to check the statement in the form with which they agree. The score of the individual is the mean or median scale value of the items which he has checked for agreement. Reliability of the scales is found by correlating scores on the two forms of the scale.

Perfect Method —

The method does away with the necessity of submitting items to the judges. After editing, the items are given to a group of subjects for responding to each one in terms of their agreement or disagreement. The number of favourable and unfavourable statements should be approximately equal. Usually a 1-5 scale of response is used. A score is given for each item depending upon the response made, and a sum of these scores gives the individual score. Final selection of items is done on the criterion of internal consistency. Usually two methods are adopted to analyse these scales.

(i) A simple way is to indicate the percentage responses on each time.

(ii) The actual Likert Scaling Technique has a five-point scale, each position being assigned a scale value. All favourable statements are scored from maximum to minimum as:

Statement	Scale value
(a) Agree	5
(b) Tend to agree	4
(c) Cannot say	3
(d) Tend to disagree	2
(e) Disagree	1

For statements opposing the position, the items would be scored in the opposite order as 1, 2, 3, 4, 5.

In an opinionnaire consisting of 30 items, the following score values would be revealing:

(i) 30 x 5 = 150: Most favourable possible response.

(ii) 30 x 3 = 90: A neutral attitude.

(iii) 30 x 1 = 30: Most unfavourable attitude.

Thus the score of any individual would fall between 30 and 150.

Relative Merits : The Likert method succeeded the Thurstone method and was considered an improvement over the latter. Justifying the need for devising a new method, Murphy and Likert point out, "A number of statistical assumptions are made in the application of his (Thurstone's) attitude scale e.g. that the scale values of the statements are independent of the attitude distribution of the readers who sort the statements-assumptions which as Thurstone points out, cannot always be verified. The method is more over-laborious. It seems legitimate to enquire whether it actually does its work better than the simple scales which may be employed and in that mamo breath to ask also whether it is not possible to construct equally reliable scales without making unnecessary statistical assumption,"

The main conventions of Murphy and Likert regarding the method of summated rating seem to be:

1. "It avoids the difficulties encountered when using the judging group to construct a scale."
2. "The construction of an attitude scale by the sigma method (later replaced by the even simpler 1-6 method) is much easier than by using a judging group to place the statement in pies from which the scale values must be calculated."
3. "It yields reliabilities as high as those obtained by other techniques with fewer items."

Limitations of Attitude Scales

1. An individual may express socially acceptable opinions and conceal his real attitude.
2. An individual himself may not be clearly aware of his real attitude.
3. An individual may never have been confronted with a real situation to discover what his real attitude towards a scientific phenomenon was.
4. Attitudes are revealed through the behaviour of an individual. But behaviour itself is not always a true indication of attitude.
5. Observation of behaviour may not always be possible when a large sample is under study.
6. Social customs or the desire for social approval may make many kinds of behaviour mere formalities which are quite unrelated to the inner feelings of an individual.

Interests Measured

Following definitions help us to understand the meaning of an interest.

Jones defines interest "as a feeling of liking associated with a reaction, either actual or imagined, to a specific thing or situation."

According to Bingham, "An interest is tendency to become absorbed in an experience and to continue it."

Murphy points out, "Interests are conditioned stimuli related to goal objects, and expressed as likes or dislikes of activities, objects, characteristics of people in the environment."

Berdie points out, "Vocational interests, both as measured by tests and as indicated by occupational choices, are expressions of liking and disliking as directed towards activities, objects and characteristics of the environment."

According to Strong, "Interest is an indeterminate indicator of success."

Importance and Measurement of Interest. Generally speaking, one's interest offers the best clue for finding out one's motivation. It has also been experienced that interest ensures achievement as it is combined with aptitude but interest without aptitude sometimes leads to frustration.

We want to know the interest of an individual because it is one of the most impelling motives. A person may have aptitude for a vocation but if he is not interested in it, he is not likely to be successful in that occupation.

Secondly, it is felt that there is some relationship between interests and abilities. Sometimes our interest may give some indication of our abilities and therefore it is important to measure the interest of a person.

Specific Inventories

Interest inventories have been invented to measure interests. They are based on the fact that "Men engaged in a particular occupation have been found to have a characteristic pattern of likes and dislikes which distinguish them from men following other professions."

Strong's Vocational Interest Blank. Strong of Stanford University of the U.S.A. has done a very useful work in the field of measuring interests. Regarding Strong's Inventory, Bingham states, "The most dependable means available for ascertaining the similarity between a person's interests and those of people actually engaged in specific occupations."

There are five forms of his interest blank. One form is for male students and one for female students. Similarly there are two more forms, one for males who are out of school and one for females who are out of school. The fifth form can be used for men whether attending school or not. Each form contains 400 separate questions and the individual concerned is asked to indicate what he likes and dislikes. The average time taken to fill out the blank is half an hour.

'Norms' or the achievement standards have been established and the rating of an individual, who fills out the blank, is determined by comparing with these 'norms'. These forms should be given to individuals who are above 17 years as it is generally felt that interests stabilise at this age. The inventory seems to be of no use for students below fifteen years.

Another important point worth mentioning is that variations do occur if the same individual fills out the blank after some time but as Strong's studies point out, these variations occur in those items only which are relatively unimportant in determining the tests pattern.

Kuder's Preference Record. This test can be used in the case of high school students and adults. It measures interests in ten general areas : (i) outdoor, (ii) mechanical, (iii) computational, (iv) scientific, (v) persuasive, (vi) literary, (vii) musical, (viii) artistic, (ix) social service, and (x) clerical.

Stewart and Barinard's Specific Interests Inventories. There are four forms available, one each for men, boys, women and girls. The forms for boys and girls are meant for age group ten to sixteen years. Each form contains 100 questions and the questions are divided into 20 groups. Each deals with one type of interest.

Cleeton's Vocational Interest Inventory. This inventory contains separate forms for men and women. Its author claims that this is suitable for high school pupils and college students and for the youth who have left school. The form for men contains a total of 630 items to be checked and 40 questions to be answered in 'yes' or 'no'.

Advantages : Jane Warters writes, "Interest inventories are useful for helping a student to make a systematic approach to his problem of choice (choice of curricula, courses, vocations, recreational activities, and the like), for providing teachers and counsellors with information regarding the student's preferences and aversions, and for helping them to acquire a better understanding of the student's problems of choice and his need for further information and exploratory experiences." These inventories can be utilised as a means of widening and enriching the knowledge of the student. They may also be utilised for the purpose of developing an understanding and appreciation on the part of the students of different types of occupational life. They are very helpful for the employers also. They can use the test as an aid in selecting applicants for employment.

Limitations

1. It is very difficult to check the accuracy of the statements made by the individual who reports his interests.
2. Interests of high school student are not sufficiently permanent and as such they may fail to indicate occupational selection.
3. Interests of the Higher Secondary students are not varied and rich. The interests of the students are confined to those activities in which they have some experience. Therefore these interests may not indicate the occupations the students should choose.
4. Interests are not necessarily closely related to abilities.
5. Differences in interest exist between children from different schools and classes suggesting influences by teachers.
6. Children's interests are the result of learning opportunities.
7. Boys and girls begin to show concern about possible vocational choices and goals when they reach adolescence.
8. Different occupations may involve the same or similar activities thus invalidating the efficacy of interests as a measure of selection of some occupation.

Personality Profile

For the discussion of the measurement of personality, it seems essential to know the meaning of the term 'personality'. But the term is used in so many different ways that a detailed discussion is neither possible nor desirable in the present context. However, some of the important definitions are given here which may throw light on the meaning of the term 'personality'.

Warren and Carmichael call personality "the entire organization of a human being at any stage of his development."

McDougall defines personality as "a synthetic unity of all mental features and functions in their intimate interplay."

To Muir "Personality is the whole individual considered as a whole. It may be defined as the most characteristic integration of an individual's structure, modes of interests, attitudes, behaviour, capacities, abilities and attitudes."

According to Allport, "Personality is the dynamic organisation within the individual of those psycho-physical systems that determine his unique adjustment to the environment."

Morton Prince describes personality as "the sum total of the biological innate dispositions, impulses, tendencies, aptitudes and instincts of the individual and the dispositions and tendencies acquired by experience."

William Healy describes personality as "an integrated system of habitual adjustment to the environment particularly to the social environment."

According to A.J. Jones, in simple terms, personality consists of the following:

1. The way you look.
2. The way you dress.
3. The way you talk.
4. The way you walk.
5. The way you act.
6. The skill with which you do things.
7. Your health.

Methods of Measuring Personality. It is difficult to analyse and measure personality. However several methods are adopted to measure it. Some of the important ones are:

Methods of Measuring Personality: Classifications-I

(1)	(2)	(3)	(4)	(5)	(6)	(7)	(8)
Question-naire method	Obser-vation method	Case History	Interview method	Rating scale	Projective Techni-ques method	Auto-bio-graphy	Personal Inventories

Methods of Measuring Personality: Classification-II

(1)	(2)	(3)
Clinical	Psychometric	Experimental

A Typical Method

One of the oldest clinical methods of studying personality is through life history. A psychologist collects the information from the person himself. The task of a psychologist to collect information is very different from that of a biographer or a police officer. Through special knowledge and skill a psychologist handles the relationship with the individual more or less objectively and creates the conditions for a relatively free communication of facts, feelings and ides.

Starting with free association as a method, Jung developed it into the clinical method of word association. The method uses a list of words and these are spoken to the person and he is asked to tell an associated word that comes to his mind. The reaction of the subject is recorded.

Clinical method includes:

(i) Projective techniques
(ii) Interview technique
(iii) Motor technique
(iv) Situational tests of personality.

Characteristics of Clinical Methods

(1) They are observer dependent.
(2) They are primarily qualitative.
(3) Data collected can be analysed in various ways.
(4) Their reliability and validity are not very high.

(5) They require specially trained psychologists for administering, scoring, analysing and interpreting.

Psychometric Methods. These methods do not require the presence of the observer. The responses are self-recorded and art analysed according to a fixed set of rules. These methods aim at qualitative assessment. They are relatively easy to administer.

Whereas most of the clinical methods give a global and complex picture of personality, the psychometric methods tell us only something about specific traits.

Questionnaires and tests of personality come under this category.

Experimental Techniques. This method has helped in contributing to the theory of personality and perception. The controlled conditions in the laboratory have made it possible to study the person under conditions of stress in the laboratory leading to greater understanding of factors responsible for his breakdown and stress.

Development of Personality and Education. Education has to be so arranged that it helps the process of personality development. The personality of the teacher has a great bearing on the development of the personality of the child.

Personality Tests in India. Mr. B. Krishnan of the University of Mysore has standardised a questionnaire for the assessment of personality,

T.E. Shanmugam has standardised a test in personality for use among Tamil-speaking students in Madras. He has developed a verbal projective technique.

Udai Pareek has also done some useful work in this direction.

In Lucknow, a thematic appreciation test has been developed suitable to Indian conditions and an adjustment questionnaire has also been standardised for Hindustani-speaking students.

Personal Measurement Inventory. In a personal measurement inventory, some questions are listed and the subject (respondent) gives his answers. The rater of personality rates the personal on the basis of the answers and norms fixed for these.

Significant and Important

(1) R.S. Woodworth's Personal Inventory - Probably the first inventory prepared in 1918 - during the First World War, for finding out neurotic tendency among soldiers.
(2) Cornell Index.
(3) Bell Adjustment Inventory.
(4) Allport A.S. Inventory.
(5) Bernreuter Inventory.
(6) Heston Personal Adjustment Inventory.
(7) Guilford Inventory.
(8) Thurstone Inventory.
(9) Minnesto Multiphasic Personal Inventory
(10) California Inventory
(11) Shipley Personal Inventory.

Bell Adjustment Inventory. In this inventory items are classified into separate categories and a score is provided for each category. Two forms of this inventory are available, one for high school and college students, the other for adults. However, the student form has been employed more widely. This form has been designed to measure adjustment in four areas: (1) Home, (2) Health, (3) Social, (4) Emotional. An additional score has been provided in the Adult Form to measure occupational adjustment. Answers are recorded by encircling 'Yes' or 'No'.

Inventories for the measurement of behaviour such as social dominance, introversion-extroversion, emotional maturity, self-sufficiency and sociability have also been prepared.

Allport A.S. Inventory. This is also known as Ascendance Submission Inventory. This inventory seeks to assess the individual's tendency to dominate his associates or be dominated by them in face-to-face contacts of everyday life. Each item begins with a brief description of a situation which we usually encounter at a meeting, in school, on a bus or in other familiar settings. The subject is asked to indicate one of the two or four alternative ways listed for meeting the situation. Responses indicate the degree of ascendance or submission.

Separate forms of the tests are available for men and women.

This inventory has greatly influenced the development of many other inventories.

Bernreuter Inventory. This is designed to measure six scores: (1) Neuroticism, (2) Self-sufficiency, (3) Introversion, (4) Dominance, (5) Confidence, (6) Sociability. The last two were added by Flanagan.

This manual provides norms on all six scores for high school, college and general adult population.

Guilford Inventory. This inventory consists of 300 items, 30 for each of these 10 traits. (1) G-General Activity. (2) R-Restraint (3) A-Ascendance. (4) S-Sociability. (5) E-Emotional stability (6) O-Objectivity. (7) F-Friendliness. (8) T-Thoughtfulness. (9) R-Personal Relations. (10) M—Masculinity.

The construction and the use of personality inventories are beset with special difficulties in view of the following:

1. Complex nature of personality.
2. Different definitions of personality.
3. Greater specificity of responses in the sphere of personality.
4. Lack of adequate criteria for the determination of empirical validity.
5. Different actions by the same individual in different situations.
6. It is very difficult to determine validity of an inventory.
7. Items in the personality inventory are sometimes very vague.
8. The subject may not reveal his weakness for fear of its misuse.
9. The subject may not have the proper perspective of his own psychological make-up.
10. We do not have definite norms for ideal personal adjustment or behaviour. What is good adjustment of personality for one individual may be poor for another one.

11. Results obtained through personality inventories may be tentative. These need to be supplemented with other measurement tools.

Personality Measurement and Adjustment Inventories

1. Adjustment Inventory for School Students (Hindi) by A.K.P. Sinha and R.P. Singh
2. Adjustment Inventory (Student Form) by H.M. Singh
3. Adjustment Inventory for College Students (Hindi) by A.K.P. Sinha.
4. Adjustment Inventory (Hindi) by D.N. Srivastava
5. Adjustment Inventory (Hindi) by R.K. Srivastava and V. Srivastava
6. A Youth Adjustment Analyser by M.D. Bangalee
7. Aggression Questionnaire by G.C. Patti
8. Battery of Pre-adolescence Personality Test by U. Pareek, T.V. Rao and others.
9. Children's Personality Questionnaire (Hindi) by Kapoor and Rao
10. Dependence Proneness Scale (Hindi) by B.R. Singh
11. Ego Strength Scale (Hindi) by Q. Hasan
12. Eysench's Maudslay Personality Inventory (Hindi) by Jalota and Kapoor
13. Family Relation Inventory (Hindi) by G.P. Sherry and Sinha
14. Indian Adaptation of Saranson's General Anxiety Scale for School-going Children (Hindi) by A. Kumar
15. Indian Adaptation of Rosenweig Picture Frustration Study, Children's Form (English/Hindi) by U. Pareek
16. Indian Adaptation of 'Adult Form' (English/Hindi) by U. Pareek, R.S. Devi and S. Rosenweig
17. Indian Adaptation of Lowenfeld Mosaic Test by B.B. Chatterji
18. Indian Adaptation of Murray's Thematic Apperception Test, Bureau of Psychology, U.P. Allahabad

19. Indian Adaptation of Thematic Apperception Test by Uma Choudhary
20. Indian Adaptation of Children's Apperception Test by Uma Choudhary
21. Indian Adaptation of Senior Apperception Test by Uma Choudhary
22. Indian Adaptation of IPAT Neuroticism Scale Questionnaire (English) by Kamlesh Kapoor
23. Introversion-Extroversion Inventory (Hindi) by Aziz and Agnihotry
24. Inferiority and Insecurity Questionnaire by G.C. Patti
25. Junior and Senior High School Personality Factor Questionnaires by Kapoor and Mehrotra
26. Jung's Word Association Test (Hindi) by Kapoor.
27. Kent Rosenoff's World Association Test (Hindi) by Kapoor
28. Kundu Introversion-Extroversion Inventory (English) by R.N. Kundu
29. Locus of Control Scale for Children, Adolescents and Adults by Roma Pal
30. Moony Probivin Check-list by M.C. Joshi and J. Panday
31. Multivariable Personality Test (English) by B.C. Muthayya
32. Mohsin Self-concept Inventory (English/Hindi) by S.M. Mohsin
33. Personality Adjustment Inventory (English/Hindi) by C.P. Sharma
34. Personality Need Inventory by C.P. Sharma
35. Personality Need Inventory (Hindi), Bureau of Psychology, Allahabad, U.P.
36. Personality Differential Scale (Hindi/English) by K.G. Agarwal
37. Prolonged Deprivation Scale by G. Misra and LB. Tripathi
38. Personality Inventory (Hindi) by Y. Singh and H.M. Singh

39. Kundu Neurotic Personality Inventory (English) by R.N. Kundu
40. Problem Check-list by N. Bhagia
41. SC (Self-confidence) Inventory (English) by M. Basavanna
42. Self-concept Questionnaire (English/Hindi) by R.K. Saraswat
43. Self-concept Scale (English) by N.K. Chaddha
44. Social Adjustment Inventory by R.C. Deva
45. Sixteen Personality Factor Questionnaires (Hindi) by S.D. Kapoor
46. Student Problem Check-list, NCERT
47. Self-disclosure Inventory (Hindi/English) by Virender Sinha
48. Security- insecurity Inventory by K. Diwedi
49. Sinha's Anxiety Scale (English/Hindi) by D. Sinha
50. Sinha's Comprehensive Anxiety Scale (Hindi) by A.K.R Sinha and L.N.K. Sinha
51. Swatva Bodh Parikshan (Hindi) by G.R Sherry and R.R. Verma
52. Test Anxiety Scale (English/Hindi) by V.R. Sharma

Measurement of Interest Inventories

1. Chatterji's Non-verbal Preference Record by S. Chatterji
2. Educational Interest Record (English/Hindi) by V.R. Bansal and S.N. Srivastava
3. Educational Interest Record (Hindi) by S.P. Kulshrestha
4. Indian Adaptation of Geist Picture Interest Inventory (Hindi) by N.S. Chauhan and Govind Tiwari
5. Interest Inventory, Bureau of Psychology, Allahabad, U.P.
6. Interest Inventory for Girls by T.S. Sodhi and A. Bhatnagar
7. Interest Inventory (Hindi), Vocational Guidance Bureau, Jabalpur

8. Interest Record by R.P, Singh
9. NCERT Interest Inventory (English) (Senior Form), NCERT
10. Study Habit Inventory by M.N. Palsana
11. Vocational Interest Record (Hindi) by S.P. Kulshrestha
12. Vocational Interest Record (Hindi) by V.P. Bansal and D.N. Srivastava
13. Vocational Interest Record (Hindi) by Kamal Dwivedi
14. Vocational Interest Record (English/Hindi) by B. Bansal
15. Vocational Preference Test by M. Joshi and J. Pandey

Attitude Scales

1. Attitude Scale towards Education by S.L. Chopra
2. Attitude towards Communication Jobs (English) by O.S. Rathore
3. Career Maturity Inventory (Indian Adaptation) by Nirmala Gupta
4. Dimensions of Temperament Scale (English) by N.K. Chadha
5. Occupational Aspiration Scale by J.S. Grewal
6. Rao's School Attitude Inventory (English) by D. Gopal Rao
7. Science Attitude Scale (Hindi) by Avinash Grewal
8. Sex Behaviour Attitude Scale (Hindi) by Y Singh
9. Study Habits Attitude (Hindi) by C.R. Mathur
10. Study Habits Inventory (English) by D.N. Sansanwal and M. Mukhopadhyay
11. Study Involvement Inventory (English/Hindi) by Asha Bhatnagar
12. Study Habits and Attitudes (Hindi) by M.C. Joshi and Jagdish Pandey
13. Teacher Attitude Scale (English) by J.C. Goyal
14. Vocational Attitude Maturity Scale by Manju Mehta
15. Vocational Preference (Hindi) by Mera M. Joshi and Jagdish Pandey.

13

Test for Success

An achievement test is an instrument designed to measure relative achievement of students. It is an indispensable instrument in the teaching-learning process.

The following definitions given by experts enable us to have a comprehensive view of an achievement test.

1. Gronlund defines an achievement test as "a systematic procedure for determining the amount a student has learned through instruction."
2. N.E. Gronlund, and R.L. Linn, in their book Measurement and Evaluation in Teaching have observed, "There typically have been norm-referenced tests that measure pupil's level of achievement in various content and skill areas by comparing their test performance with the performance of other pupils in some general reference group."
3. Popham states, "The achievement test focuses upon an examinee's attainments at a given point in time."
4. Thorndike and Hagen observe, "The type of ability test that describes what a person has learned to do is called an achievement test."
5. W James Popham in his book Modern Educational Measurement gives the description of achievement

tests in these words, "Tests in the cognitive or psychomotor realm are often focused on an examinee's attainment at a given time; these tests are usually referred to as achievement tests."

The Characteristics

1. It should contain a sufficient number of test items for each measured behaviour.
2. A good achievement test is tried out and selected on the basis of its difficulty level and discriminating power.
3. It should be divided into different knowledge and skills according to behaviours to be measured.
4. Its instructions in regard to its administering and scoring are so clear that they become standardized for different users.
5. It should have a description of measured behaviour.
6. It provides equivalent and comparable forms of the test.
7. It is accompanied by norms which are developed at various levels and on various age groups.
8. It includes a test manual for its administering and scoring.

Main Purposes and Uses : These can be used for the following purposes:

1. To diagnose student's strength and weakness.
2. To motivate students.
3. To report to the parents.
4. To predict future progress.
5. To reflect teacher's effectiveness.

Uses of Achievement Tests to a Teacher

1. The teacher comes to know about the general range of abilities of students in the class.
2. In the light of above, he can select appropriate materials of instruction so that all individuals benefit from instruction to the maximum.

3. The teacher can determine and diagnose the strengths and weakness of the students in various subjects.
4. The teacher can spot out brilliant and backward children.
5. He can determine the progress of the group in a particular subject over the period of time.
6. By studying the results of the students on achievement tests and intelligence tests, the teacher can determine whether or not the students are working at their maximum capacity.

Uses of Achievement Tests to Administrators

1. Tests help to discover backward children who need help and to plan for remedial instruction for such students.
2. Tests help to select talented pupils for special classes and courses.
3. Tests help to decide proper classification of students.
4. Tests help to get a better understanding of the needs and abilities of pupils.
5. Tests help to select students for the award of special merits or scholarships.
6. Tests help to group pupils in a class so that students are put in such a way that individual differences are as slight as possible.
7. Tests help the parents in recognising the strengths and weaknesses of their children so that they direct their energies on suitable goals only and do not put heavy demands on them.
8. Tests help to determine the efficiency of one school with the others.
9. Tests help to determine the general level of achievement of a class and thus judge the teaching efficiency of the teacher. The level of achievement of a class may be judged on the basis of the achievement of the class in the beginning and at the end of the school year.

10. Tests help to discover the type of learning experiences that will achieve these objectives with the best possible results.
11. To evaluate, revise and improve the curriculum in the light of these results.
12. Tests help to evaluate the extent to which the objectives of education are being achieved.
13. Tests help to classify school objectives.

Achievement Tests

1. Students come to know about their strengths and weakness.
2. Students are motivated to work hard for removing their deficiencies.

Classification of Achievement Tests

Teacher Made	Standardized Objective Type
Essay Type	Teacher Made
	Objective Type
	(Non-standardized)

Tests of Intellect

By an achievement test we mean test of academic achievement such as English or Hindi etc. An achievement test is a measure of learning itself and an intelligence test is a measure of learning capacity. An achievement test attempts to measure education whereas intelligence test attempts to measure educability.

The development of an individual in the future is likely to be along the lines of tests for specific aptitude rather than test of general intelligence. Dunlop writes, "The more 'general' the intelligence test the less its value. By increasing the specificity, we add to its value."

The Construction : There is no agreement among experts regarding the number and nature of steps involved in the construction of an achievement test. Here we mention only a few selected views of experts.

W. Wiersma, and S.G. Jurs have identified the following stages for planning an achievement test:

1. Deciding purposes of the test.
2. Listing educational objectives of different areas of knowledge.
3. Preparing table of specifications.
4. Determining practical consideration.

M. Shipman, in his book School Evaluation (1979) suggests the following stages which can be helpful in planning an achievement test:

1. Stating the objectives in such a form that it will enable their achievements to be verified.
2. Spelling out the actions that are necessary for the attainment of objectives.
3. Spelling out the criteria by which the attainment of objectives is to be assessed.
4. Spelling out personnel whose judgments are involved in each component of the plan.
5. Stating the arrangements for any standardization procedure and the forms of reports and records which are to be maintained.

Gronlund and Linn (1990) discuss in detail the following steps in classroom testing:

1. Determining the purposes of testing.
2. Developing the test specifications.
3. Selecting appropriate type of items.
4. Preparing relevant test items.
5. Assembling the test.
6. Administering the test.
7. Scoring the test.
8. Appraising the test.
9. Using the test results.

Determining the Purpose of the Test. According to purpose, tests may be divided into the following five categories:

(a) Readiness pre-test
(b) Placement pre-test

(c) Formative test
(d) Diagnostic test
(e) End testing-summative test

Developing Test Specifications. Specifications of the test include the following:

(a) A list of instructional objectives.
(b) An outline of the course contact.
(c) A two-way chart.

Following chart explains the specifications of the contents of the test as for weightage to different areas is concerned.

Specifications of the Contents of the Test

Each level of thinking and number of test items.

% Content	*Knowledge*	*Comprehension*	*Application*	*Analysis*	*Total*
Topic No. 1	7	5	4	4	20
Topic No. 2	6	6	4	4	20
Topic No. 3	6	6	3	3	18
Topic No. 4	2	5	5	2	14
Topic No. 5	4	5	5	2	16
Topic No. 6	5	6	1	0	12
Total	**30**	**33**	**22**	**15**	**100**

Selecting Appropriate Types of Questions. There should be a balanced selection of essay type, short-answer type and objective type questions.

Preparing Relevant Test Items. This includes the following steps:

(i) Matching the test items with the learning outcome.
(ii) Selecting most representative items.
(iii) Preparing test items which are of proper difficulty level.
(iv) Avoiding all possible barriers in test items which prevent examinees from responding.

(v) Avoiding providing any clues to answers which may help examinees to answer correctly even if they lack the necessary achievement.

Assembling the Test. After preparing relevant test items, the test constructor should follow the process as indicated below:

(a) Writing each item on a separate card.

(b) Reviewing the test items by the test constructor himself and also by some other teacher.

(c) Arranging the test items according to well defined criteria.

(d) Providing proper instructions to the examinees.

Administering the Tests. Following suggestions are made while administering the test.

(i) Long announcements before or during the test should not be made.

(ii) Instructions, if any, should be given in writing so that uniformity is maintained and all the examinees get the same opportunities.

(iii) The test administrators should not respond to the individual problems of the examinees, otherwise any hint on their part may provide unfair chance to some examinees.

(iv) Test should be administered in an appropriate physical and psychological environment.

Scoring the Test. Scoring may be done mechanically or manually; depending upon the situation.

Appraising the Test or Item-analysis. After scoring, the test should be appraised for each item.

Using the Test Results. Test results are used primarily for the following purposes:

(a) For making decisions about the promotion of students to the next higher grade.

(b) For bringing about improvement in teaching methods and techniques.

An Example of Constructing and Design of an Achievement Test

Identifying Instructional Objectives. Each subject has instructional objectives of its own.

Designing the Test. It specifies the weightage given to: (i) Instructional objectives, (ii) Types of questions, (iii) Units and subunits of the course. (iv) Level of Difficulty, (v) Options if any.

Preparing the Blue Print. Blue print incorporates the policy decisions of the design.

Writing Down Questions. It includes different categories of questions i.e. long answer, short answer and very short answer.

Marking Scheme. The marking scheme prevents inconsistency in marking.

Design of the Question Papers

Subject: History — Max. Marks: 100

Class : XII — Time: 3 Hrs.

The weightage or the distribution of marks over the different dimensions of the question paper shall be as follows:

Weightage to Instructional Objectives/Learning Outcomes

S.No.	*Objectives*	*Marks*	*% of Marks*
1.	Knowledge	30	30%
2.	Understanding	45	45%
3.	Application	15	15%
4.	Skill	10	10%
	Total	100	100

Weightage to Content/Subject Units

Modern India — ***60 marks***

1. Indian States and Society in the 11th century
2. Beginning of European Settlements
3. British Conquest of India
4. Structure of Government and Administrative Organisation of the British Empire in India.
5. Economic, Social and Cultural Policy of the British Empire in India (1757-1857).

6. Social and Cultural Awakening in the first half of the 19th Century
7. The Revolt of 1857
8. Growth of New India: Religious and Social Reforms
9. Administrative Changes after 1858
10. India and her Neighbours
11. Economic Impact of the British Rule
12. Growth of New India: Nationalist Movement.
13. Nationalist Movement (1905-1918)
14. Struggle for Swaraj
15. Map Work on Modern India

Contemporary World ***40 marks***

16. Introduction.
17. The World from about the end of the 19th century to the end of the First World War.
18. The World from 1919 to 1939
19. The Second World War
20. The World after the Second World War
21. Main Features of Development in Economy, Society and Polity
22. Developments in Science, Technology and Culture
23. The Future Outlook
24. Map Work on Contemporary World

Weightage to Types/Forms of Questions

S.No.	*Form of Question*	*Marks for each Question*	*No. of Questions*	*Total Marks*	*%*
1.	L.A.	8	4	32	32%
2.	S.A. I	5	8	40	40%
3.	S.A. II	2	9	18	18%
4.	Map	5	2	10	10%
	Total	20	23	100	100

Note: The expected length of the answers under different types of questions would be as follows:

S. No.	Type/ Forms of question	Marks for each question	No. of Questions	Expected length of each question	Expected time for each question
1.	L.A.	8	4	upto 25 words	17x4=68
2.	S.A. I	5	8	upto 100 words	8x8=64
3.	S.A. II	2	9	20 to 30 words	3x9=27
4.	Map	5	2		5x2=10

L.A. = (Long Answer Type Questions) 4
S.A. I = (Short Answer I Type Questions) 8
Expected time for each question
S.A. II = (Short Answer II Type Questions) 9
Maps 2
Total 23

This is only an approximation. Though students are advised to be as near the approximation as possible, the actual length, however, may vary. As the total time is calculated on the basis of the number of questions required to be answered and the length of their anticipated answers, it would, therefore, be advisable for the candidates to budget their time properly by cutting out the superfluous length and be within the expected limits.

Weightage to Difficulty Level of Questions:

S.No.	*Estimated Difficulty Level*	*Percentage*
(1)	Easy (C)	15%
(2)	Average (B)	70%
(3)	Difficult (A)	15%

Note: A question may vary in difficulty level from individual to individual, as such the approximation in respect of each question will be made by the Paper Setter on the basis of general anticipation from the group as a whole taking the examination. This provision is only to make the paper balanced in its weight rather than to determine the pattern of marking at any stage.

Scheme of Options

(1) There will be no overall option in the form of 'Do any ten questions or so'.

(2) Internal choice (either/or type) on a very selective basis may be given in long answer questions testing higher mental abilities.

(3) The alternate question given by way of choice should be based on the same objective and the same unit. It would have the same anticipated difficulty level and length of answer.

Instruction Marks

Broad hints regarding points to be covered are issued to the examiners so that evaluation of answer books should be as objective as possible. (Based on the CBSE Guidelines)

Scheme of Marks

A marking scheme is an important element in the evaluation process to prevent inconsistency in grading or judging. It includes the scoring key which is prepared in respect of objective type questions in special and all types of questions in general.

Chief Purposes of a Marking Scheme

(1) To bring consistency in judgement.

(2) To ensure objectivity in evaluation.

(3) To eliminate differences in score.

(4) To make results more reliable.

(5) To avoid inconsistency in marking.

(6) To bring uniformity in marking and to reduce variations in marking-both inter-examiner and intra-examiner.

Characteristics of a Good Marking Scheme

1. It should cover all possible areas as demanded by the questions.
2. It should clearly indicate each expected point of each major area.
3. It should indicate marks for each point and part of a question.
4. It should cover all types of questions.
5. In case of objective type of questions, it should provide the complete answer.

6. In case of short answer and long answer (essay type of questions), it should indicate main points which the examiner should keep in mind while marking.
7. It should specify the maximum word limit for each type of answer: (i) Very short answer/objective type, (ii) short answer, (iii) essay type or long answer type.

Examples of Instructions and Marking Scheme

Subject: Social Science **Class: X**
Time Allowed: 3 hours **Max Marks: 100**

General Instructions

1. The question paper is divided into 4 sections namely:
   Section A - History
   Section B - Civics
   Section C - Geography
   Section D - Economics
2. All questions are compulsory.
3. All questions of each section must be attempted together at one place.
4. Write the same question number as given in the question paper while answering a question in your answer book.
5. (i) Answer to questions of 1 mark should not exceed 20 words each.
   (ii) Answer to questions of 2 marks should not exceed 30 words each.
   (iii) Answer to questions of 3 marks should not exceed 60 words each.
   (iv) Answer to questions of 4 marks should not exceed 80 words each.
   (v) Answer to questions of 5/6 marks should not exceed 100/ 120 words.
   (vi) Stencils or templates for drawing outline maps may be used wherever necessary.
   (vii) Attach the maps provided within the answer book.

Broad Classification. Tests vary according to form, type and use etc. Yoakaya and Simpson give the following classification of tests.

1. Form
   (a) Oral examinations. (b) Written examinations.
2. Purposes
   (a) Prognostic. (b) Diagnostic. (c) Power. (d) Speed. (e) Accuracy. (f) Quality. (g) Range.
3. Organization
   (a) Essay. (b) Objective.
4. Period or Time of Administering
   (a) Daily. (b) Weekly. (c) Monthly. (d) Term. (e) Year.
5. Duration
   (a) Short. (b) Long.
6. Method of Scoring and Interpreting Results
   (a) Non-standardized. (b) Standardized.
7. Abilities Involved
   (a) Speed. (b) Comprehension. (c) Organization. (d) Judgment. (e) Retention. (f) Appreciation, etc.
8. Nature of Material Included
   (a) Arithmetic. (b) Language. (c) Reading. (d) Spelling. (e) Writing etc.
9. Mental Functions Involved
   (a) Association. (b) Memory. (c) Recall. (d) Recognition. (e) Problem solving.
10. Types of Response Involved
   (a) Alternate response: (1) True-false. (2) Yes-no. (3) Plus-minus.
   (b) Multiple response: (1) Best answer. (2) Correct answer.
   (c) Completion. (d) Matching. (e) Identification.
   (f) Enumeration. (g) Essay.

Test in Objective Manner

Meaning and Classification of an Achievement Test of Objective Type.

An objective type of question is one which is free from any subjective bias either from the teacher or the student. Its answer is definite.

Classification of Objective Type of Questions/Tests

Recognition Type				Recall type	
(1)	(2)	(3)	(4)	Single	Completion
Alternative Response	Multipurpose Choice	Matching	Classification	Recall	

Examples. Objective tests are of a large variety. However, only seven or eight types of the objective tests are commonly employed.

Matching Test. Under column A, names of certain books and under B, names of certain authors are given. Write down the names of the right authors under column C.

A	*B*	*C*
Meghaduta	Ashvaghosha	....
Raghuvansam	Megasthenes	....
Raj Tarangini	Kalidasa	....
Uttar-Ram Charita	Kalhan	....
Sakuntalam	Bhava Bhuti	....
Budh Charitam	Kalidasa	....
Indica	Kalidasa	....

Multiple Choice Test. Below are given a few questions. Against each are given a number of answers. One of these is correct. Underline the same.

(a) Who was Kalidasa? King, poet or scientist.
(b) What was the capital of Kanishka? Patliputra, Ujjain, Parushpur.
(c) Who built edicts? Chandragupta, Vikramaditya, Ashoka, Samudra Gupta.

True-False Test. Certain statements are given below. Against each statement are mentioned two words, e.g., true and false. Underline the correct one:

1. People used to lock their houses during the Mauryan Period True/False
2. Similar triangles are congruent True/False
3. Supplementary angles are equal True/False

Correct/Incorrect Tests. Some sentences are given below. Against each are mentioned two words, i.e., Correct and Incorrect. Underline the correct one.

(a) He has been absent from the school from last Saturday. Correct/Incorrect

(b) I prefer English to French. Correct/Incorrect

Simple Recall Test. Write in one word the answer of the following:

(a) What is the per capita income in India?
(b) What is the per capita income in the U.K.?
(c) What is the exchange value of the Indian rupee in terms of the U.S. dollar?

Best Answer Test. Put mark against the best answer.

Alexander did not proceed further because

(i) he did not know the route.
(ii) his forces refused to go further.
(iii) he was defeated by some king.

Completion Test. Fill in the blank by appropriate word(s) in the following:

(i) To be wealthy, a thing must have scarcity, utility and ....
(ii) You should refrain .... doing undesirable things.

Classification Test. In each line, underline the word that does not belong there.

(a) Tulsidas, Kabir, Surdas, Napoleon.
(b) Calcutta, Madras, Bombay, Delhi.
(c) Cat, horse, cow, tree.

Construction of New Type of Tests. (1) Prepare a list of all the topics falling within the scope of the examination. (2) Keep in view the most significant items in each topic. (3) Put easy questions first, then moderate and, in the end, the most difficult ones. (4) Put definite questions, brief and free from ambiguity, (5) Do not put suggestive statements. (6) Put items which should have only one correct answer. (7) Include different types of objective tests, e.g., multiple choice, matching, etc. (8) Give reasonable time to the students to answer the paper. Ruch suggests the following time: Recall type- 4 to 8 items per minute. (9) Give very clear instructions.

Advantages

Percival Symonds and others have given the following merits.

First. "The new type examinations are more objective in their scoring, since the responses of pupils are controlled, and since there can be no doubt as to the correctness or incorrectness of their responses."

They are free from the personal factor of the teacher. The mood of the examiner in no way affects scoring. Each question which is asked has only one possible answer. 'Contrast the achievements of Mahmud Ghaznavi with Mohd. Ghori' is a legitimate thought-provoking assignment in the essay type of examination, but there is a great scope for a variability in marking.

Second. "They may be very comprehensive 'and can be made to cover a great deal more material than the old type of examination. Since the pupil does very little writing, he can devote his time to thought and can thereby answer a great many questions than when he has to write his answers out at length."

Chance element is very predominant in the essay type of examination. Only a limited number of questions are set out of the wide field that has been covered. It is not uncommon to find students preparing fifteen or twenty questions in a subject and securing very high marks and students preparing forty questions but failing miserably. How does it happen and how could it be avoided? The answer is very simple. This happens simply because the number of questions set in the paper is so small that quite a major portion of the course covered remains untested. On the other hand, a large number of questions which are set in a new type of test eliminate the element of chance and cover a wide field of course.

Third. "They are very easy to score as compared with the older type of examination. Notwithstanding the fact that the tests are more comprehensive, they may be scored in less time and with less labour. This is of itself a sufficient reason to make them attractive to all teachers."

A key of the various questions may be prepared and then anybody can mark the question papers.

Fourth. "Pupils like them. There is no question as to the accuracy of marks they receive. There is no chance for the teacher to show favouritism or personal bias. The pupils, relieved of much writing, find these tests less tiring."

The pupils like the new type of tests because they think that marking will be fair and judicious. Even the students may be asked to mark the papers themselves if key is supplied to them. The general complaints of leniency of marking in one case and hard marking in the other are eliminated.

Fifth. "They are more educative for the pupils. Let your pupils score their own tests directly after they take them by exchanging papers with their neighbours. It is then that their interest is at white heat. After the papers have been scored, the questions may be discussed. The pupils readily see where they need further study."

Sixth. The new type of tests discourage cramming and encourage thinking, observation and scrutiny.

Seventh. They are more reliable. Same results will be secured whoever may be the examiner. An essay type of question paper cannot give the same results if it is given to different examiners.

Eighth. Objective tests can be standardized by applying beforehand to a large number of students of the same age group before the actual examination. On the basis of the results of these standardised tests, the authorities of a particular institution can compare the standard of their institution with other institutions of the same area.

Disadvantages

First. "The pupil does not have an opportunity to show his ability to organize his thought. He has nothing to do except check over the truth and falsity of statements or fill in the missing words or incomplete sentences. Pupils miss the valuable experience of making comparisons, giving explanations or giving definitions. They are not asked to summarize the material or to make applications of principles, and, of course, these are valuable abilities which we do not want to neglect."

Second. "These new types of examinations are not diagnostic in that they do not tell where the pupil's reasoning process goes wrong or where he stops reasoning altogether and starts guessing."

Third. It is commonly said that new type of tests fail to check cramming. Once the test is standardised the teachers will coach their pupils on the test, thus making it utterly useless. There is every possibility that 'keys' or 'guides' to these tests may find their way in the market. General knowledge guides have made their entry on a large scale in the market.

Fourth. It is often argued that use of new types of tests is very expensive.

Fifth. Like the essay type of tests, these also fail to test the character-building aspects.

Tests Compared

1. The number of questions in the essay or old type of tests is very small, generally five or six questions in the paper. There are a large number of questions in the new-type tests.
2. Answers required in the old type of test are large. The answers are so short in the objective tests as can be written in a word or two or at the most in a sentence.
3. Essay-type questions are usually broad, general and indefinite. The examinees are at a loss to know how much they will have to write as answers. Objective questions are special, narrow and definite.
4. In essay-type tests personal factors like bias, temperament, whims, etc., of the examiner influence marking. Scoring becomes objective in the new type of tests.
5. In the answer of the essay test, there is scope for partial credit. Answers may be partially wrong and right. In the new tests, there is no provision for partial credit. Answers must either be right or wrong and hence full or no credit.
6. In the essay tests, examinees have to devote a long time. Questions can be answered in a short time in the new tests.
7. In the essay tests, questions are selected at random and the entire course is not covered. Some chapters or

questions are completely ignored. The entire course can be covered by comprehensive questions in the objective type tests.

8. Essay tests put premium on expression. Students hardly find any time to think over the question. New tests put premium on thinking.
9. Pupils having linguistic skill are at an advantage in the essay tests. New tests are advantageous to the intellectually smart students.
10. It takes a short time to frame questions in the essay tests. It takes a long time to frame questions in the new tests.
11. Students find it easier to prepare essay questions. They can safely omit many portions of the subject-matter in the essay tests. Students have to devote a longer time to prepare as they have to go through the entire course for clear conceptions.
12. Essay tests are very suitable for testing composition, skills and knowledge of the subject. New tests are not suitable for testing composition and skill as well as appreciation of the subject.
13. In the essay tests there is great scope for 'guessing' questions. Students prepare themselves from 'Made Easy' books. In the new type also, there is scope for guessing answer.
14. Essay tests take a shorter time in examining scripts. Short answers take longer time to examine scripts.
15. Printing cost is small in the case of essay tests. Since there are many questions, printing is costly in the new tests.
16. Answer scripts cost much as answers are very lengthy in the case of essay tests. Answer being very short and usually can be written on the question paper itself, this makes the answer scripts less costly.
17. There is less scope for adopting unfair means by the students in the essay type tests. There is adequate

scope for the use of unfair means by the students in the objective type test.

Concluding Observations. Neither the essay type nor the objective type questions can single serve the purpose of evaluation. A balanced and judicious blend of the two is needed. A third category of tests, namely short answer question may also be introduced.

The Central Board of Secondary Education follows the pattern in its class XII, examination (History) as given below:

	Type	*No. of Questions Question*	*Marks for Each*	*Total Marks*
1.	Long Answer/Essay Type	4	8	32
2.	Short Answer-I	8	5	40
3.	Short Answer-II (Objective Type or questions needing answers in about 20 words	9	2	18
	Map	2	5	10
	Total	**23**	**20**	**100**

Various Problems

General Guidelines : E.W. Menzel observes that whether old-type or new-type, we observe among others the following principles:

1. It will be general and comprehensive enough to test thoroughly the pupil's mastery of the desired skills or grasp of a subject-matter. It will make it impossible for a pupil to get a good mark just because he got a few 'lucky questions' and will not fail a good pupil just because of a few 'unlucky questions'. Very few examinations in India are adequate in this respect.
2. It will reliably grade the pupils into at least six to ten (or more) different classifications according to their ability.
3. It will be as objective as practicable. Some questions of a discussional nature can be given to advantage

but there should also be some work which pins pupil and examiner down to answers which can be quite objectively scored. Even in the essay type of examination, the objectivity can be greatly increased with study and care.

4. Other things being equal, the test which examines most intensively or extensively in the least time and with the least fatigue on the part of the pupil is the best.
5. The test should encourage creative and self-reliant work and discourage mere mechanical rote-memory work.
6. The test should encourage the pupil to put forth his best effort.
7. The test should convincingly reveal to the pupil his deficiencies and encourage him to remove them.
8. The test should examine exactly what it pretends to examine and not handicap pupils for deficiencies in unrelated subjects. The more a test tries to examine in subjects extraneous to the avowed subject, the less efficiently it examines its own.
9. The standards of a test should be based on actual performance and not upon mere opinion of what a standard should be or on an arbitrary percentage work.
10. The more a test makes it possible to compare the performance of a certain group of pupils to that of other pupils the more revealing it is.
11. Keep in mind that no test is infallible. The daily work of the pupil and an observation of his habits of work are equally important in appraising the work and ability of a pupil.
12. Keep in mind that poor results on the part of a group of pupils indicate a faulty test or one that is not graded to the ability of the pupils or deals with matters the children have not been taught.

Managing Examinations

Administering an achievement test is as important as planning or developing an achievement test. Following are the important guidelines:

Time Schedule. The unit of time schedule for testing should be reasonably enough to permit its completion. It should include a realistic allowance for distributing and collecting papers and for giving instructions.

Preparation by Testers. The testers should prepare themselves in advance especially for the following aspects of the testing programme:

(a) The tester should follow the manual verbatim.
(b) The tester should make the procedures and the tasks clear to the testee before administering the test.
(c) The tester should go round the class and ensure that the students have followed the instructions carefully and are not copying.

Preparation of Students for Testing. Orientation talks on the usefulness of testing may be given to the students so that they are motivated to take tests and are convinced that tests are genuinely important.

Appropriate Environment (Physical i.e. Hall-Room etc.) for Testing. The desirable environment for testing should satisfy the following conditions:

(1) Examinees are physically comfortable.
(2) Examinees are emotionally relaxed.
(3) Examinees are free from interruptions and distractions.
(4) Adequate space is provided to the examinees so that they are able to manipulate their test material conveniently.
(5) Conditions of Righting and ventilation are adequate for testing.

Recording of Test Results. Results should be kept systematically so that these are made use of conveniently by the appropriate agency. Of course results should be kept confidential.

Equipment. Provide necessary equipment. Ensure that examinees are seated in such a way as to prevent copying.

Invigilators. Provide necessary invigilators to supervise.

Two Procedures

Grading implies classification of students into a few ability groups or categories according to their level of achievement in the examinations. The achievement is devoted in the form of numerical (1, 2, 3 etc.) or letter grades (A,B,C, etc.)

Types of Grading. Grading is of two types:

1. Absolute grading.
2. Comparative grading.

Absolute Grading. In single words, student's in different subjects, irrespective of the fact whether there is scope for higher scores, for distance in Mathematics in which several students can score 100 per cent marks and in English in which scores are comparatively lower, students are given grades in accordance with the same yardstick. Grading is based on the same cut-off point in both the subjects.

Comparative Grading. Grades are given on the basis of rank order or percentiles. For example, top 5 percent students may be given grade A. Grade A in one subject would be quite different from grade B in another subject. For example in mathematics students scoring 95 or more marks may be given grade A and in English students scoring marks between 80 and 90 may be placed in grade A.

Comparative grading is preferred. Following are the merits of comparative grading over absolute grading:

(1) Comparative grading is based on ranks ordering or percentiles.

(2) It provides better comparability of scores irrespective of the scoring possibility i.e. whether a subject is scoring or non-scoring.

(3) The gap between scoring or non-scoring subjects is done away with for grading is not based on absolute marks but is based on rank order or percentiles.

(4) It provides a more meaningful profile of the performance/ achievement of a student or group.

Discussion

The issue of grading vs marking was discussed the Secondary Education Commission (1952-53). After going into the pros and cons of both the systems, it favoured the grading system and rejected the marking system on the following grounds:

(1) Marking introduces too many subdivisions which are not only useless but cumbersome.

(2) It is indeed difficult to distinguish between two pupils, one of whom obtains, say, 45 marks and another 46 or 47.

The Secondary Education Commission suggested the grading system as in this system, pupils are grouped in broad divisions which are more easily distinguishable than the differences indicated by marks. It suggested the following grading

A Distinction

B Credit

C Pass

D and E Failure or 'Cases Referred Back'. The values of the categories in terms of percentile marks may be determined by the examining authority. Percentile marks may be converted in terms of categories.

Demerits of Numerical Marking

A Monograph on Grading in Universities (1976) gives the following reasons in favour of grading over numerical marking.

1. Numerical marking provides a very inaccurate measurement for:

   (a) The standards of examiners differ widely. There is a standard error of measurement ranging from 5 to 20 marks in different subjects.

   (b) Examiners, by indulging in evaluation rather than measurement, distort results by giving an unusually great number of 35 marks (when 35 is passing mark) and none at all of 34 and 33.

   (c) Examiners in different subjects use different ranges. In some the full scale of 0 to 100 is used, while in many others, scales used are all different.

(d) Marks given by examiners are not scaled.

(e) Marks in different subjects are added up when they should not be. The most important of all these is that it is impossible to have comparability amongst different disciplines (even in different papers in the same discipline) with the result that there is a great irrationality in the choice of subjects by students. This does not reveal the actual aptitude of students but the ease with which high marks can be secured. Finally, every one tends to take marks as absolute and attach a kind of arithmetic value judgement that is to say if three students A, B and C score 58, 61, and 57, they think that 61 is more than 58 and 58 is more than 57. In reality if the S. Errors of measurement is taken as 5 marks, then the true marks of the student with 58 marks is either (58-5)=53 or (58+5)=63. For every 2 out of 3 cases, his true marks which will fall within the range of 53 to 63 includes marks of all the three students. In a sound grading system, all these students are said to belong to the same group of achievement and given a letter grade. Here a single individual mark has no meaning but there is a range of marks to be replaced by single letter grade.

Merits of the Grading System. A grading system ensures fulfilment of the following objectives:

(a) Evaluation which is mainly judgement based on measurement is uniform if all the universities agree to adopt the 7 points scale grading system and establish relationship between various grades and their meaning in qualitative terms. It is possible also for teachers and examiners to do what is called 'direct grading' and this has been found to possess merits over the process of initial marking and conversion into grades.

(b) Comparability amongst various disciplines and within various subjects in a particular discipline is possible with the grading system. Top students in Mathematics (and those securing 95% and above) will be given a letter grade of 0 (outstanding) as also the top students of History (and those securing 58% and above). If students discover that an equally good student of Mathematics or history is likely to get a high grade (no matter what maximum marks they get) the choice of subjects will be rational and dependent more on their aptitude than on the fact that in some subjects getting a higher grade is easier than in others.

(c) If all universities adopt the same 7 points scale, then students can move from one university to another much more easily.

(d) Grading system takes the emphasis away from marks.

(e) Teachers employing many procedures for evaluating achievement (test, oral recitation, quiz, project work, lab/practical work, assignments, tutorials, checklist, rating scales, etc.) will find that a grading system is much more meaningful and feasible than the marking system. It is recommended to various universities wanting to implement a 7-point scale grading system, that wherever possible, there shall be direct grading. Direct grading requires a thorough understanding of the meaning of each letter category in terms of their quality and it is much more. The manner in which the results of an examination should be furnished has engaged the attention of experts all over the world. It appears that in a majority of the examinations in the advanced countries of the world, the trend is towards adopting what is called a Five-point scale. In this technique, all the candidates who appear for the examination are grouped into five grades: grade 1 signifying the best and grade 5 the weakest of candidates. Grouping is also done in five grades.

The strongest argument in favour of grading is that unreliable as the numerical marking is, it is highly unfair to discriminate a score of 33 from 32 by which one student is declared 'pass' and the other 'fail'. This logic is apparently quite sound. But, it means that since the numerical marking scale having 101 points is not very reliable, it may be replaced by another having only five or seven points so that all the candidates falling within the score-limits of a particular 'grade' are clubbed together. Will it not do injustice to good students of the group? It is evident that grading does not necessarily eliminate the chances of mis-classification, especially, in the neighbourhood of cut-scores. The chances of mis-classification increase with the increase in the variability and decrease in the reliability of test scores. Consequently, the abler students are subjected to disadvantage and 'poorer' ones to an advantage because they are lumped together.

It is also argued that 'grading' is more reliable than numerical marking. There is nothing miraculous about it. When we accept broader ranges of abilities to represent the same levels of performance, we are, in effect, accepting larger errors as genuine, thereby lumping errors, with reliability. Moreover, by reducing the number of categories, we also lose the information conveyed by raw scores. Therefore, adopting the system of assigning grades instead of numerical marks amounts to adopting a cruder scale in order to cover up the deficiencies of a more refined scale of 101 points, and those of instructional process.

The standard of marking varies from subject to subject, and in the same subject, from examiner to examiner. For example, the spread of marks in mathematics usually covers the entire scale from 0 to 100, and in social studies a relatively smaller, say 2565, range is covered. This means that the best candidate in social studies gets 35 marks less than the best candidate in mathematics. If 'absolute grading' is done, then, none will get an A in social studies while many may get A in mathematics. This shows that dispersion of marks awarded by the examiner influences the proportion of students placed in each grade. Similarly, in a difficult question paper, very few students will get an A while in an easier question paper many may get As.

The quality of the group of students being tested is also an important factor in determining grades when grading is done on the 'normal curve' or any other presumed distribution. In a group of bright students, many will get As, but some will have to be given Ds and Es to maintain normality. In the same way, in a poorer group some will have to be awarded As.

The 'grading' system to be introduced in the CBSE is going to create problems for the universities and colleges where admissions are made on the basis of performance at +2 stage because, it will be difficult to determine merit when limited seats are to be filled up. Similarly, employers who select workers on the basis of examination results at the school stage, will find it difficult to decide merit. As a coping mechanism then, the universities and employers will have to conduct their own tests for making selections, and the secondary school examination will be rendered superfluous. There are many other similar problems which need to be addressed while taking further action in this matter.

Concluding Observations. In our country, the current practice in most of our Public Examinations is to measure the candidate's performance by assigning marks to answer script. Suppose there is a paper of three hours carrying 100 marks. The examiners are asked to award numerical scores while assessing the answer scripts. The marks can range from 0 to 100. This is called the hundred and one point scale because including 0, there are in all 101 units measurement. The implicit meaning of having such 101 steps in marking is that a candidate who scores 46 is superior to one who scores 45 and so on.

It is generally believed that grading system is more rational than the marking system. In view of the element of subjectivity, marking system is considered to be inferior to the grading system.

14

Aptitude Tests

An aptitude test according to Hull is a test "designed to discover what potentiality a given person has for learning some particular skill."

In the words of Prem Pasricha, "Aptitude tests are expected to measure the potential for specific abilities and skills such as music, graphical arts, medicine, law, engineering, teaching etc."

Aptitude Tests and Interest Tests

Prof. Prem Pasricha has explained the difference in these words, "While the interest tests measure the liking that an individual may have for a particular skill, the aptitude tests tell how well the individual is equipped to exceed in that skill. Cases are common when a person is interested in a certain field but does not have the aptitude for it. He may excel through sheer hard work but not because of the potential talent."

The Uses

Aptitude tests serve the following functions.

Admissions. Aptitude tests can be used in admitting candidates for various types of professional training such as engineering, medicine and training etc.

Guidance. Aptitude tests can be used for the purpose of guidance in selecting subjects for studying in educational institutions.

Selection for Jobs. The employer can use aptitude tests for selecting persons for jobs. Perhaps for the time in India, selection of teachers on the basis of aptitudes (one of the measures) was envisaged by the Delhi Administration.

Right Use of Aptitude Tests

Jones has observed, "An examination of the 'aptitude tests' clearly shows that many of them are not tests of aptitude as defined by most authorities... the study of aptitudes must, in the future proceed on a more individual and clinical basis than is true at present and employ methods that will reveal the integration of the various factors rather than each separately."

Jones further states, "An aptitude test would be one that would measure all the factors necessary for success; this goal is practically impossible. The complete determination of aptitude for any job would require tests of specific abilities, personality, general mental ability, observations by skilled observers and mental and physical records. Emphasis should be given not to weakness and to lack of abilities so much as to strengths and to presence of abilities."

Specific Areas

Among these may be mentioned as under:

1. Art Aptitude Test.
2. Clerical Aptitude Test.
3. Manual Aptitude Test.
4. Mechanical Aptitude Test.
5. Medical Aptitude Test.
6. Musical Aptitude Test.
7. Scholastic Aptitude Test.
8. Scientific Aptitude Test.
9. Teachers Aptitude Test.

Ability, Achievement and Aptitude

Jones has differentiated these terms as under:

Ability is concerned with present. It indicates the combination of skills, habits and powers which an individual now has and which enables him to do something.

Achievement looks to the past. It indicates what has been done.

Aptitude looks to the future and, on the basis of the habits, skills and abilities that an individual now has, predicts what he, with training, may become and what success he may have in a given occupation or position.

Difference between an Intelligence Test and an Aptitude Test. An intelligence test measures general ability of an individual whereas an aptitude test measures special mental ability.

A Particular Type

Traxler has observed, "Tests of general scholastic aptitude have long been known as intelligence test. There is now a tendency to favour the term 'Academic aptitude test', or 'Scholastic aptitude test' rather than 'Intelligence test', because to many people 'intelligence test' implies a measure of native ability."

Observation and research indicate that two kinds of aptitude are related to success in a variety of school subjects and vocations.

1. Verbal or linguistic aptitude.
2. Numerical or quantitative aptitude.

Tests of Aptitude in Special Subjects. Aptitude tests in different fields have also been prepared. For example, to measure aptitude in languages and mathematics, aptitude tests have been constructed. Results of research show that these tests have not been found to be very helpful.

What do Scholastic Aptitude Tests Measure? These tests measure the capacity of an individual to learn. When evaluating aptitude, we try to place the emphasis upon native capacity by posing problems in which the individual has had no formal training.

Uses of Scholastic Aptitude Tests. Scholastic aptitude tests are helpful in giving educational and vocational guidance to students. Frohick and Benson think that we can use the results of scholastic aptitude tests in counselling students regarding vocational opportunities. Reading, writing and speaking abilities are involved in various jobs and a student's scholastic aptitude is a fair measure of his chances for success in such jobs.

Students with superior scholastic aptitude should be preferred in admitting to colleges.

Scientific and classical courses require a higher level of scholastic aptitude on the part of the student.

How Can Scholastic Aptitude be Measured?

Intelligence Tests. Students with super intelligence have greater chances of success in academic subjects of the school curriculum than a subjects with average intelligence. Thus with the help of the intelligence tests we can measure the scholastic aptitude of the student.

School Marks and Scholastic Aptitude. This is the traditional method of measuring scholastic aptitude. It is generally found that the academic achievement is an index of future scholastic achievement. A student securing good marks in a subject would be classified as a student having marked scholastic aptitude for that subject.

Occupation of Parents and Scholastic Aptitude. Different occupations require different level of intelligence. Studies undertaken in the U.S.A. have indicated that there is a positive relationship between the intelligence of the child and the occupational status of the father. The study undertaken by McNemar revealed that children of engineers, doctors, lawyers, etc. had higher I.Q.'s at all age levels than children of clerical, skilled trade and retail business people. The children of day labourers got the lowest I.Q.'s. Thus the occupation of the parent would also indicate the scholastic aptitude of the students.

Teachers Observation

The following points may be observed.

(i) Rapidity in comprehending material of study.
(ii) Rapidity and accuracy in reading.
(iii) Ability in attaching new problems.
(iv) Large vocabulary.
(v) Eagerness to answer questions.
(vi) Deficiency in one or more skills.
(a negative criterion.)

Curricular Activities. Participation of the students in debates, declamation contests, essay competitions etc., may also give some ideas of the scholastic aptitude of the child.

Following are some of the important aptitude tests constructed in foreign countries:

1. Kuhlmann-Anderson Intelligence Test.
2. California Test of Mental Maturity.
3. Stanford Scientific Aptitude Test.
4. Iowa Plane Geometry Aptitude Test.
5. Columbia University's Foreign Language Prognosis Test.

Yale Educational Aptitude Test. The battery contains tests designed to measure a person's relative aptitude or ability in the areas of (1) Verbal facility; (2) Linguistic ability; (3) Verbal reasoning; (4) Quantitative reasoning; (5) Mathematical aptitude; (6) Spatial visualising; and (7) Mechanical ingenuity. On the basis of these aptitude tests, students are admitted to courses like social sciences, pure sciences and mathematics and applied sciences.

Aptitude Testing in India

Madras: St. Christopher Training College, Vepery, Chennai. Tests of the following types are available for distribution:

(a) Two intelligence tests.

(b) Two attainment tests in Tamil.

Banaras Hindu University

1. S.K. Pande's Standardised Tests of Mental Ability (called Samoohika Mansika Yogyata Pariksha).
2. General Mental Ability Test, in English by Shri R.K. Tandon.
3. General Mental Ability Test, in Malayalam by Shri P.G. Pillai.

Patna University

1. Arithmetic Attainment Test in Hindi (A.R Poddar) for classes IV to VI.
2. School Achievement Test Battery (B. Upadhyay) in Hindi for classes VI to VIII.
3. Clerical Test.
4. Stenotypist Abilities Test (in English).

Different Types

1. A Battery of Clerical Aptitude Test by Kiran Gupta
2. A Battery of Mechanical Aptitude Test by A. Sharma
3. A Battery of Mechanical Aptitude Test, Bureau of Psychology, Allahabad, U.P.
4. Engineering Aptitude Test Battery Form A and B (English) by Swarn Pratap
5. Indian Adaptation of Differential Aptitude Test (DAT) Form L.H. (Hindi) by J.M. Ojha

6. Scholastic Aptitude Test by Jai Prakash
7. Scholastic Aptitude Test, NCERT
8. Scientific Aptitude Test for College Students (Hindi) by A.K.P. Sinha
9. Scientific Aptitude Test Battery (Hindi) by K.K. Agarwal
10. Scientific Knowledge and Aptitude Test by S. Chatterji
11. Teaching Aptitude Test Battery (Hindi) by R.P. Singh.

Development of Inventories

Inventory

1. In the inventory, statements are put in the first person. For example, "I am more at ease than the other."
2. It is constructed in the form of a questionnaire. It consists of a series of questions or statements to which the respondent responds by answering 'Yes or No', 'agree' or 'Disagree' etc. 3. An inventory is more exhaustive than the questionnaire.

Questionnaire

1. In the questionnaire, question is in the second person. For example "Do you think you are more at ease than the other."
2. It is a device to secure answers to a question by using a form which the respondent fills it by himself.
3. A questionnaire is less exhaustive than the inventory.

Sometimes both the terms are used interchangeably but there is clear difference between the two.

Guidelines for the Administration of an Inventory/Questionnaire.

1. The teacher should explain instructions very clearly to the learners.
2. The teacher should make it clear to the learners that the data will be kept confidential.
3. The teacher should remove doubts if any, regarding the manner of filling the questionnaire/inventory.
4. The teacher should take all other timely precautions for preparing a state of mind conducive to response.

Examples of Inventories

Guilford's Personal Inventory. It consists of 300 items, 30 items for each of the following traits:

G. General activity.
R. Restraint.
A. Ascendance.
S. Sociability.
E. Emotional Stability.
O. Objectivity.
F. Friendliness.
T. Thoughtfulness.
P. Personal Relations.
M. Masculinity.

Cleeton's Vocational Interest Inventory. This inventory contains separate forms for men and women. Its author claims that this is suitable for high school pupils and college students and for the youth who have left school. The form for men contains a total of 630 items to be checked and 40 questions to be answered in 'yes' or 'no'.

Advantages

Jane Warters writes, "Interest inventories are useful for helping a student to make a systematic approach to his problem of choice (choice of curricula, courses, vocations, recreational activities, and the like), for providing teachers and counsellors with information regarding the student's preferences and aversions, and for helping them to acquire a better understanding of the student's problems of choice and his need for further information and exploratory experiences." These inventories can be utilised as a means of widening and enriching the knowledge of the student. They may also be utilised for the purpose of developing an understanding and appreciation on the part of the students of different types of occupational life. They are very helpful for the employers also. They can use the test as an aid in selecting applicants for employment.

Limitations

1. It is very difficult to check the accuracy of the statements made by the individual who reports his interests.

2. Interests of high school students are not sufficiently permanent and as such they may fail to indicate occupational selection.
3. Interests of the Higher Secondary students are not varied and rich. The interests of the students are confined to those activities in which they have some experience. Therefore, these interests may not indicate the occupations the students should choose.
4. Interests are not necessarily closely related to abilities.
5. Differences in interest exist between children from different schools and classes suggesting influences by teachers.
6. Children's interests are the result of learning opportunities.
7. Boys and girls begin to show concern about possible vocational choices and goals when they reach adolescence.
8. Different occupations may involve the same or similar activities thus invalidating the efficacy of interests as a measure of selection of some occupation.

Recognised Type

A standardized test is one for which norms have been established. It means that the test has been given to a large number of students and scores have been given definite expectancy values or norms for given groups of pupils. A norm is an average or typical score which measures achievement (any trait or behaviour such as intelligence). So every standardised test has norms. It is prepared by a test specialist according to certain definite rules or standards of construction. It is intended for general use and covers a wider scope of material than is covered in an ordinary teacher-made test which is needed only to evaluate the achievement of students of a class.

Standardisation literally means 'brought to a level.'

Definition : According to Thomas: "A standardized test is one which has been given to so many people that the test makers have been able to determine fairly accurately how well a typical person of a particular age or grade-in school will succeed in it."

According to Newkirk and Greene, "A test is standardized (i) if it is composed of exercises that have been selected in the light of usual teaching practice and evaluated as to innate difficulty, and (ii) if it is accompanied by norms or, standards permitting the interpretation of results in levels of accomplishment. The Dictionary of CX Good explains a standardised test "a test for which content has been selected and checked empirically, for which norms have been established, for which uniform methods of administering and scoring have been developed and which may be scored with a relatively high degree of objectivity."

Lee J. Cronbach defines as " A standardized test is one in which the procedure, apparatus and scoring have fixed so that precisely the same test can be given at different times and places.." Important Characteristics of a Standardized Test

Ross has given the following characteristics of a standardised test:

(i) The content is standardized, i.e., item-selection has been done vigorously, after careful scrutiny and by competent judges.
(ii) Administration is standardized, i.e., directions, time-limit etc. are worked out carefully.
(iii) Scoring has been standardized, i.e., scoring keys are prepitred, definite rules for scoring have been formulated etc.
(iv) Interpretation has been standardized, i.e., norms for various groups are provided.

Importance and Uses

Standardized tests have assumed such an important role in the guidance programme that the two terms 'Guidance' and 'Tests' have become synonymous terms.

They are very useful for the following reasons:

1. They give us objective and impartial information about an individual.
2. Since they give us information in an objective manner, it becomes easier to convince the guardians of the assets and limitations of their wards.
3. They provide information in much less time than provided by any other device.
4. Since there is a definite way of expressing the results of these tests in the form of perceptiles or standard scores, it has the same significance for all the guidance workers and all of them have the same interpretations.

5. These tests measure those aspects of the behaviour which otherwise could not be obtained.
6. In subjective observation we may overlook shy children but these tests discover such cases also.

Classification

1. General intelligence or scholastic aptitude tests.
2. Special abilities or aptitude tests.
3. Achievement tests.
4. Interest tests or inventories.
5. Personality tests or personal adjustment tests.

Cultivation as Growth

Before finalisation, a test is tried out and administered on a number of subjects for the expressed purpose of refining its items by subjecting the performances of the 'standardization' sample to pertinent statistical analysis. The purpose is to ensure that items with adequate level of difficulty and which are capable of discriminating between the superior examinee and the inferior examinee have places in the test.

The validity and reliability of a standardized test are ensured right from the beginning of its construction.

A standardized test provides instructions and norms for the future users of the test. Such norms usually include pertinent details about the following.

(i) The age, gender and academic background etc. of the sample used to lay down the norms.
(ii) The mean score of the sample on the tests.
(iii) The standard duration and variance of the sample on the test.
(iv) The size of the sample.
(v) Conversion tables for interpreting raw scores.

A standardized test is constructed by test specialists or experts. A standardized test generally covers a broad or wide area of objectives and content common to the school system within a given geographical area. Test items of a standardized test cover a large segment of knowledge and skills than the teacher-made test.

In short following steps are followed for the standardization of a test/tool:

(1) Proper planning.
(2) Adequate preparation.
(3) Try-out of the test.
(4) Preparation of proper norms.
(5) Preparation of a manual containing instruction for administering a tool/test, scoring of totals and interpretation of data.

Teacher's Role

A number of the functions of a testing programme centre around the work of the classroom teacher. These relate to grouping for instruction, individualization of instruction, selection for special diagnostic and remedial services, and the assignment of marks.

Grouping Pupils for Instruction within a Class. One of the effective techniques teachers have developed for dealing with individual differences in pupils is to form within the class small groupings of pupils who have about the same level of skill. Pupils in these groupings may work on the same materials and at the same speed. Standardized tests are often called upon to aid in forming these within-class groups. They provide information quickly and objectively at the beginning of the school year and make it possible to short-circuit the slower and more subjective process of getting acquainted with each pupil's abilities and skills. Readiness tests serve this function in the first grade, and achievement tests at later levels.

Guiding the Planning of Activities for Specific Individual Pupils. Many teachers use test results to help in individualizing instruction. This is carrying the small-group procedure still further. Programmes of work in the skill subjects are adjusted to the present level of the individual pupil. The gifted child is encouraged to move ahead at his own speed, and enrichment activities are provided for him. The child of limited achievement is permitted to move more slowly toward more limited objectives. Both measures of scholastic aptitude and of educational achievement play a role in this type of planning.

Identifying Pupils who Need Special Diagnostic Study and Remedial Instruction. When a school system has resources for special diagnostic study of individual pupils and special teachers to provide remedial instruction, the testing programmes will usually provide important data to help in identifying the pupils most likely to profit from that instruction. If the classroom teacher wants to pick up pupils for such special services, he is likely to pick up the pupils whom he considers most below par in achievement. It is very difficult for him to distinguish between general low ability and specialized deficiency in a particular limited skill. A testing programme that appraises both achievement and aptitude is an aid in picking out those pupils who have a remediable defect.

Evaluating Discrepancies between Potentiality and Achievement. Picking pupils for special remedial coaching is a special case of the more general problem of identifying discrepancies between potential and actual achievement. Such discrepancies may serve to focus the efforts of the teacher upon particular pupils in his class, may help to orient and guide the teacher's discussions in a conference with parents, or may influence the statements or ratings in the periodic report to the home. This last situation is encountered in those school systems in which the report card attempts to evaluate the individual pupil's achievement in relation to his potentiality. Any attempt to evaluate achievement in relation to potentiality requires good measures of both potentiality and achievement. One function of a testing programme may be to help supply these.

Assigning Course Grades. A number of teachers, especially in the secondary school, use standardized test results as one consideration in assigning course grades. This may be appropriate in certain specific courses for which standardized tests exist whose content parallels closely the objectives of instruction in the course. However, the school-wide or city-wide programme of standardized testing ordinarily seems less well fitted to serve this purpose.

Important Features of a Teacher-made Tests. Some of the important features of teacher-made tests are:

(i) They attempt to assess comprehensively the extent and degree of student's progress with reference to specific classroom activities.
(ii) They permit the teacher to ascertain an individual pupil's strength and weaknesses and needs.
(iii) They provide immediate feedback for the teacher as to the effectiveness of his teaching methods and

accordingly can make necessary adjustments and improvements.

(iv) They motivate the students.

(v) They are simple to use.

(vi) They provide information which is the basis for a report on the progress of students.

Limitations

1. Tests are often ambiguous and unclear.
2. Tests are either too short or too lengthy.
3. Tests do not cover the entire content.
4. Tests are usually hurriedly conducted.
5. Tests serve a limited purpose.

Thorndike and Hagen point out the following distinction between the standardized tests (i.e. commercially distributed tests) and the teacher-made test for his own class.

1. The standardized test is based on the general content and objectives common to many schools the country over, whereas the teacher's own test can be adapted to content and objectives specific to his own class.
2. The standardized test deals with large segments of knowledge or skill, whereas a teacher-made test can be prepared in relation to any specific limited topic.
3. The standardized test is developed with the help of professional writers, reviewers, and editors of test items, whereas the teacher-made test must usually rely upon the skill of one or two teachers.
4. The standardized test provides norms for various groups that are broadly representative of performance throughout the country, whereas the teacher-made test has usually been given only to the pupils in a single class or school.

The distinctive features of the standardized test represent important advantages for some purpose and disadvantages for others. Basing the test upon a careful analysis of the common objectives expressed in textbooks, courses of study, and reports of committees of professional societies should guarantee that the thinking of many specialists has entered into the test plan. However, a published test is fixed for a period of years in terms of broad common objectives. It is not a flexible tool. It cannot be adapted to special current needs, to local emphasis, or to particular limited units of study.

The value of standardized tests lies particularly in situations in which comparisons must be made—comparisons of a school with other schools, comparison of achievement in different areas by a pupil or by a school group, or comparison of achievement with the potentiality for achievement indicated by an aptitude test. The norms provided with standardized tests make such comparisons readily possible. For a school, achievement may be compared with national norms. The standing of a single pupil, or of several pupils coming from different schools, may be determined by reference to the norms for the test. The age or grade equivalents, percentiles or standard scores of a pupil on tests in different subjects may be compared to establish his relative level of achievement, or these converted scores may be compared with a similar score from an aptitude test to see whether achievement is consistent with what we would expect from the pupils' aptitude.

The chief characteristics of standardized tests that differentiate them from teacher-made tests are:

(1) A standardized test is more objective.
(2) A standardized test is more reliable.
(3) A standardized test is more valid.
(4) A standardized test is easy to administer.
(5) A standardized test makes scoring easier.
(6) It is economical.
(7) It is comprehensive.

On the other hand a teacher-made test is more useful for specific issues that concern the daily teaching-learning situation faced by the teacher and the students. A teacher-made test is very helpful to the classroom teacher to modify the learning experiences according to the specific situations. Thus elements of 'individuality' and 'specificity' are more predominant in teacher-made tests.

In the light of these differences, we propose that chief reliance should be placed on teacher-made tests when we want to test in order to :

1. See how well students have mastered a limited unit of instruction.
2. Determine the extent to which distinctive local objectives have been achieved.
3. Provide a basis for assigning course marks.

Standardized tests should be used when we wish to test in order to :

1. Compare achievement with potentiality for an individual or a group.
2. Compare achievement of different skills or in different subject areas.
3. Evaluate the status of pupils from different schools or classes on a common basis.
4. Make comparisons between different classes and schools.
5. Study pupil growth over a period of time to see whether progress is more or less rapid than might be expected.

Resources at Disposal

1. Agra Psychological Research Cell, Tiwari Kothi, Belanganj, Agra-282004
   - (i) Jai Prakash: General Science Test
   - (ii) V.B. Patels: Study Habit Scale
   - (iii) I.N. Dubey: Radical Conservative Attitude Scale.
2. Bhargava Book House, Distributors and Suppliers, Labh Chand Market, Rajaki Mandi, Agra-282002
3. National Psychological Corporation,Publishers and Distributors of Psychological Tests and Books, Bhargava Bhavan, 4/230 Kacheri Ghat, Agra-282004
4. Mans Seva Sansthan 10, Luther Road, George Town, Allahabad.
   - (i) Baqer Mehdi: Verbal Test of Creative Thinking (Hindi)
   - (ii) Baqer Mehdi: Non-verbal Preference Record Thinking (Hindi)
   - (iii) L.N. Dubey: Hindi Achievement Test (8th Standard)
   - (iv) Sherry & Verma: Personal Value Questionnaire (Hindi)
   - (v) S.P. Kulshreshtha: Educational Interest Record (Hindi)
   - (vi) S.P. Kulshreshtha: Vocational Preference Record (Hindi)
   - (vii) L.N. Dubey: Mathematics Achievement Test (8th Standard)
   - (viii) K.K. Agarwal: Scientific Aptitude Test for High School Students

(ix) Singh & Sharma: Teaching Aptitude Test (Hindi)
(x) Shah & Bhargava: Levels of Aspiration Test

5. Centre for Psychological Aids, B-4, 80/2 Safdarjung Enclave, New Delhi- 110029.
6. Mansayan, S-524, School Block, Shakarpur, Main Vikas Marg, Delhi-110092
   (i) Prayag Mehta : Achievement Motivation Test and Inventory
   (ii) Bhagia: School Adjustment Inventory
   (iii) Udai Pareek: Picture Frustration Test
7. Psycho-Educational Testing Centre, C-2A/16/108, Janakpuri, New Delhi-110058
   (a) S.D. Kapoor: 16PF Personality Questionnaire
   (b) Jalota and Kapoor: Mandeley Personality Inventory (MPI)
   (c) Jai Prakash: Teaching Aptitude Test (TAT)
8. Psy-cum Services, B-4, 80/2, Safdarjung Enclave, New Delhi-110029
9. Smt. R.K. Sharma, 9, Shareshtha Vihar, Indraprastha Extension, Part II, New Delhi - 110092.
10. Dr. S.D. Kapoor, B-78, Amar Colony, Lajpat Nagar No. 4, New Delhi.
11. Indian Psychological Corporation, Lucknow-7
    (i) Nirmal Bhagia: Problem Check List
    (ii) S.P. Kulshreshtha: Introversion - Extroversion List
12. Anand Agencies, 1433(A), Shukrawar, Pune-411002
13. Varman D. Prohit & Sons, Manufacturers, Merchants and Engineers, 1206/27-B, Shivaji Nagar, Pune-411004
14. Rupa Psychological Corporation, 819/60-B Deoribar Bhelupura Varanasi-221010.
    (i) H.S. Asthana: Adjustment Inventory
    (ii) M.C. Joshi: Group Test of Mental Ability
    (iii) Joshi and Tripathi: Non-verbal Test of Intelligence Testing
    (iv) Kiran Sharma: Clerical Aptitude Test.

15

Teaching Motives

General Objectives

An instrumental objective may be defined as an intent communicated by a statement describing a proposed change in a learner statement of what the learner is to be like when he has successfully completed a learning experience. There are several objectives to be achieved through instruction and accordingly several learning experiences are provided. The statement of objectives of a teaching programme must denote 'measurable' attributes 'observable' in the learners. As Robert E. Mager has said, "An instructor will function in a fog of his own working until he knows just what he wants his students to be able to do at the end of the instruction."

An educational objective may be defined as a desired change in the behaviour of a person through education. An educational objective is a guide post or a platform which provides the basis for all educational efforts. It lays down fundamental guidelines.

Aims Fulfilled

According to Srivastava and Shouri (1989), the educational objectives serve the following functions:

1. Provide the desired directions to educational activities.
2. Determine the nature of educational activities.
3. Provide a basis for systematising or planning an educational programme.

4. Decide the points of emphasis in an educational activity.
5. Give unity and coherence to an educational programme.
6. Provide the basis for the measurement of growth and thus guarantee valid evaluation.
7. Help distinguish between various aspects of learning.
8. Help focus attention on proper attributes of teaching and evaluation.
9. Help grade learning experiences and also evaluation material.
10. Help maintain a balance between different aspects of an educational programme.
11. Help fix priorities in an educational programme.
12. Guide educational decisions in curricular and co-curricular areas.
13. Guide in the selection of relevant content.
14. Guide improvements in education.
15. Give meaning to and clarify the structure and content of curriculum.
16. Help make learning functional.
17. Help articulate learning in various fields.
18. Help discover or evolve proper learning situations.
19. Help define educational processes.
20. Help make the intangibles in education tangible.
21. Help identify weaknesses and strengths of pupils in learning.
22. Facilitate communication among educational workers.

The Need. Objectives give direction to classroom teachers. They indicate the way to follow. They help the teacher in instructional planning, and guiding students' learning. They also provide a criterion for evaluating the outcomes of the learning experiences. The evaluation of what has been achieved may be useful in determining what should be achieved. In other words refinement of objectives can be done on the basis of the achievement of objectives.

The Comparison

Educational Objectives	*Instructional Objectives*
1. Philosophy determines educational objectives.	1. Psychology is the basis of instructional objectives.
2. Educational objectives are very broad.	2. Instructional objectives are very specific.
3. Educational objectives are generalised outcomes.	3. Instructional objectives are specific.
4. All school subjects may have common educational objectives.	4. Each school subject has specific teaching or instructional objectives.
5. Examples of educational objectives are: development of character, emotional and national integration, democratic values, secularism etc.	5. Examples are: Behaviour patterns of a man of character-characteristics of man of character-how he conforms to a situation in honesty etc.
6. Educational objectives are to be realized over an extended period of time.	6. Instructional objectives have an immediate intent.
7. Educational objectives are normative in nature.	7. Instructional objectives are immediately related with the content.
8. Educational objectives are not always amenable to evaluation.	8. Instructional objectives are amenable to evaluation.
9. Educational objectives do not specify very sharply the learning outcomes.	9. Instructional objectives specify very sharply the learning outcomes.
10. Educational objectives include instructional objectives.	10. Instructional objective form a part of educational objectives.

The Central Board of Secondary Education (CBSE) has envisaged the following importance of learning outcomes in a brochure Improving Question Papers in Schools (1991).

1. Learning outcomes denote direction of change in the behaviour of students occurring as a result of teaching-learning.
2. Accomplishment of an outcome necessitates development of several specific skills or mental processes which have got to be perfected through a series of exposures at the teaching-learning stage.
3. The mental processes or specific skills acquired are more enduring than the subject matter and become part of human nature or the style of thinking.

4. The content/subject matter serves only as a means to accomplish these outcomes.
5. The learning outcomes and their related specific skills should be exploited both for purposes of teaching as well as testing.
6. The learning outcomes and the mental processes have to be related to small points of content to devise a teaching or testing situation.

Determining Sources

The work on determining levels of objectives may follow the following pattern:

Overall Objectives of Education

↓

Stagewise Objectives of Education

↓

(Primary, Secondary and University etc.)

↓

Subjectwise Objectives
(Social Studies, Hindi, Maths etc.)

↓

Classwise Objectives
(Classes I, VI, IX, XI etc.)

↓

Instructional Objectives
(Instructional objectives are also formed as learning outcomes.)

Theory of Taxonomy

The word taxonomy derived from a Greek word 'taxis' (taxaplural), means 'arrangement' or 'division', is a system of classifying animals and plants, typically by division, class, family germs and species. It is originally associated with biology. In education it is associated with B.S. Bloom, an educator of the U.S.A., who propounded this concept. He presented the taxonomy of educational objectives in the domain of cognition in 1956. Later on, his associate Krathwohl and Harrow presented the taxonomy in the affective and psychomotor domain respectively.

The taxonomy of educational objectives has a three dimensional division of learning experiences which are classified into the following domains as explained below:

Domain	*Learning*	*Symbolic Focus*
1. Cognitive	Knowing	Head
2. Affective	Feeling	Heart
3. Psychomotor	Doing	Hand

It can be depicted in the following manner.

Hierarchy

Knowledge (K) → Comprehension (C) → Application (A)

Analysis (AN) → Synthesis (S) → Evaluation (E)

Knowledge. It is defined as the remembering of previously learned material. It represents the lowest level of learning outcomes in the cognitive domain.

Comprehension. It is defined as the ability to grasp the meaning of material. The learning outcomes go one step beyond the simple understanding of material and represent the lowest level of understanding.

Application. It is the ability to use learned material in new and concrete situations. Learning outcomes in this area require a higher level of understanding than those under comprehension.

Analysis. It refers to the ability to breakdown material into its component parts so that its organisational structure may be understood. Learning outcomes here represent a higher intellectual level than comprehension and application because they require an understanding of both the content and the structural form of the material.

Synthesis. Synthesis refers to the ability to put parts together to form a new whole. Learning outcomes in the area stress creative behaviour, with major emphasis on the formulation of new patterns of structures.

Evaluation. Evaluation is concerned with the ability to judge the value of material (Statement, novel, poem, research report) for a given purpose. Judgements are to be based on definite criteria.

Objectives and Mental Process or Ability in Bloom's Taxonomy

	Objective	*Mental Process or Ability*
1.	Knowledge	1. Recall 2. Recognize
2.	Comprehension	1. See relationship 2. Cite example 3. Discriminate 4. Classify 5. Interest 6. Verify 7. Generalize
3.	Application	1. Reason 2. Formulate 3. Establish 4. Infer 5. Predict
4.	Analysis	Analyse
5.	Synthesis	Synthesize
6.	Evaluation	Evaluate

Taxonomy of Educational Objectives in the Affective Domain. "The affective domain includes those objectives which are concerned with changes in interests, attitudes and values and the development of appreciations and adjustment."

Condensed Version of the Effective Domain Taxonomy of Educational Objectives (Krathwohl et al. 1964)

Receiving (attending). This means that the learner should be sensitised to the existence of certain phenomena and stimuli. This includes awareness, willingness to receive and controlled or selected affection.

Responding. This is concerned with responses that go beyond merely attending to phenomena. A person is actively involved in attending to them.

This includes acquiescence in responding, willingness to respond and satisfaction in response.

Valuating. This includes acceptance of a value, preference for a value and commitment to or a conviction in regard to a certain point of view.

Organization. For situations where more than one value is relevant, the need arises for;

(a) the organization of the values into a system,
(b) the determination of the interrelationship among them, and
(c) the establishment of the dominant and pervasive value. It includes conceptualisation of a value and organisation of a value system.

Characterisation by a value or value complex. At this level, the already existing values are organized into some kind of an internally consistent system and control over the behaviour of an individual, who attains an integration of his beliefs and attitudes into a total philosophy.

If the objectives in the affective domain are attended to and are achieved, the evaluator will be in a position to predict the behaviour of an individual.

Specified Area

The psychomotor domain includes those objectives which are concerned with manual and motor skills.

Simpson (1966) and Kibler (1970) are the pioneers in the field of taxonomy of objectives in the psychomotor domain.

Dr. R.H. Dave of the NCERT has proposed a taxonomy in the psychomotor domain. The educational objectives proposed under this domain are:

(1) Imitation of an action, performance;
(2) Manipulation of an act. This includes differentiating among various movements and selecting the proper one;
(3) Precision in reproducing a given act. This includes accuracy, proportion and exactness in performance;

(4) Articulation among different acts. This includes coordination, sequence and harmony among acts.

(5) Naturalisation. Here a pupil's skill attains its highest level of proficiency in performing an act with the least expenditure of psychic energy. The act becomes so automatic that it is attended to unconsciously.

Significance and Utility

1. They can be useful in translating into practice the principle of comprehensiveness of evaluation by ensuring proper coverage of various aspects of pupil's growth : cognitive, affective and psychomotor.
2. The evaluation may prove useful in arriving at the meaningful synthesis of various dimensions of pupil's growth.
3. Identification of areas of inter-relationship among the three domains may be of particular significance in this regard.
4. The logical nature of classification may be helpful in identifying and grading teaching-learning situations which can be an important source of selecting appropriate testing situation too.
5. Curriculum development and preparation of instructional material can profit such a scheme of classification in several ways.
6. Preparation and analysis of textbooks based on well defined objectives may prove to be a great improvement.
7. They provide direction for the instructor.
8. They convey clearly instructional intent to others.
9. They provide a guide for selecting the subject-matter.
10. They provide a guide for selecting appropriate teaching methods.
11. They provide a guide for selecting suitable materials to be used during instruction.
12. They provide guide for constructing reliable tests and other instruments for evaluating student achievement.

13. Six categories in the taxonomy are arranged on the principle of graded complexity.
14. Taxonomy is very helpful in identifying the meaningful level at which the learner is working.
15. It becomes easier to select techniques and tools of evaluation.
16. It is helpful in ensuring proper coverage of various aspects of learner's growth—the main objective of education in terms of the many-sided development of the learner.
17. It is claimed by some educators that classification through its well-defined criteria "will provide a bridge for further communication among teachers, between teachers and evaluators, curriculum and research workers, psychologists and other behaviourist scientists."

The Limitations

Following arguments are usually given against the use of behavioural objectives:

(1) There is not always agreement on the appropriate classification for certain behaviours.

(2) In this classification, there is a tendency to overstress 'measurable behaviour' and to disregard the importance of those aspects of pupils work which are not 'measurable'.

(3) Evaluators are likely to ignore important goals other than pre-specified ones.

(4) Trivial objectives may be stressed at the expense of important ones.

(5) Pre-specifying objectives may prevent the teacher from capitalizing on the unexpected.

(6) Educational outcomes other than stated pupil behavioural changes lose significance.

(7) Measurability being mechanistic, it becomes dehumanizing.

(8) It is perhaps not realistic to expect teachers to state measurable goals.

(9) It is very difficult to identify measurable outcomes in certain subjects.

Criteria for Stating Objectives

1. Use such verbs in writing objectives that can describe the behaviour to be observed.
2. Specify conditions in which the learner performance occurs.
3. Specify the essential level of performance of the learner.
4. Cover objectives of all the three domains-cognitive, affective and eonative (psychomotor).
5. Cover objectives of different levels of learning outcomes.
6. Include both: (a) Kind of behaviour outcome expected, and (b) The content
7. Use functional objectives.
8. Group similar objectives together. Objectives should not overlap.
9. Conceive objectives that are developmental in nature.
10. Judge the worthwhileness of objectives from social accountability.
11. Formulate realistic objectives. They should be attainable.

The broader objectives should be broken down into specific ones to a limit where they stand fully clarified and delimited. This step is often known as specification of the objective or behaviour outcomes. For example: the statement of an objective in History would be 'to develop interest in the study of History'. The specification of this objective would be to demonstrate the achievement of the above objective, the student:

1. Collects coins and other types of historical material.
2. Prepares illustrative material aids, etc.
3. Participates in historical dramas and presentation of historical facts.
4. Visits places of historical interest, archaeological sites, museums and archives.
5. Reads historical documents, maps and charts.

The Precaution

While lauding the role of objectives in evaluation, Prof. C.L. Anand (1986) has struck a note of dismay in these words, "It is also sometimes felt that the terminology used in the statement of objectives especially of the type based on ' the Bloom's taxonomy is mostly a kind of educational jargon and many teachers refer to it simply because it is fashionable to do so. In fact they themselves may not be very clear about them and hence they become more of a hindrance than help to them. A good deal of work has by now been done in respect of the development of objectives of education by the NCERT, the SCERT and a host of professional bodies at various level. But unfortunately many of these curriculum objectives are referred to rather mechanically with little relation to the pupil behaviour or ability and the type of content involved. Therefore, despite this widespread attention to the statements of the objectives of education and even of the individual subjects for each class or grade, the impact of such statements on the curriculum or on what actually takes place in classroom is generally much less than what it otherwise ought to be."

A Particular Approach

In RCEM approach, there are four categories in place of six given by Bloom.

Objectives	*Mental Process*
1. Knowledge	1. Recognise
2. Understanding	2. Recall
	3. See relationships
	4. Cite example
	5. Discriminate
	6. Classify
	7. Interpret
	8. Verify
	9. Generalise
3. Application	10. Reason out
	11. Formulate hypothesis
	12. Establish hypothesis
	13. Infer
	14. Predict
4. Creativity	15. Analyse

Creativity replaces Bloom's three categories of analysis, synthesis and evaluation.

Merits

1. The approach being developed in Indian setting, it suits our schools.
2. It is applicable to cognitive, affective and psychomotor objectives of teaching and learning.
3. It lays stress on mental abilities or processes in writing objectives in behavioural terms. Therefore, it is capable of shifting focus from product to process in the writing of objectives.
4. It provides a list of 17 mental abilities or processes associated with instructional objectives. It is, therefore, definite.
5. Seventeen statements help us in writing objectives in school subjects.
6. This approach enables the teacher and the learner to seek their goals more easily and satisfactorily.
7. This approach makes the task of evaluation and test construction quite simpler and objective.

Limitations

1. The approach is based on the erroneous assumption that the human learning can be explained through seventeen mental abilities or processes.
2. It is a very challenging and tedious task to match the content element with the appropriate mental ability or process.
3. This approach is more suitable to cognitive objectives than the conative or affective objectives.
4. This approach does not make a clear-cut distinction among objectives belonging to the three domains of behaviour.
5. This approach is not very helpful in objectives concerning the development of skill, appreciation and interest in some of the subjects.

R.M. Gagne (1970) has classified learning into eight categories and accordingly he suggests evaluation criteria.

Types / Varieties / Conditions of Learning	*Brief Description*
1. Signal learning	The individual acquires a conditioned response to a given signal. The learning is involuntary.
2. Stimulus response	The individual makes a response to specific stimuli. The desired response is rewarded.
3. Chaining	This implies linking together of two or more previously learned stimulus response connections.
4. Verbal association	Chains that are verbal e.g. a child identifies an object and calls it by its proper name (e.g. 'the red ball') or he finds an English equivalent for a Hindi word.
5. Multiple discrimination	It means learning on the part of the learner to distinguish between motor and verbal chains he has already acquired.
6. Concept learning	It means a common response to a class of stimuli. In learning a concept the learner responds to stimuli by identifying its abstract characteristics like colour, shape etc.
7. Rule learning	In learning a rule, two or more concepts are related. For example, the water will boil at 100'C. Hence, temperature and boiling point are concepts.
8. Problem solving	This implies application of rules by the learner to achieve some goals. Problem-solving is the combined product of two or more lower-order rules.

Different Stages

1. Motivation 2. Apprehension 3. Acquisition 4. Retention 5. Recall 6. Generalisation 7. Performance 8. Feedback 9. Transfer of Learning.

Varieties of Learning or Categories of Human Capabilities as the Outcome of Learning. According to Gagne, there are five categories of varieties of human capabilities as the outcome of learning. They are: verbal information, intellectual skills, motor skills, and cognitive strategies. Each type of learning is acquired in different ways.

Action Verbs for Each Classification of Cognitive Domain

These are as under:

S.No.	*Classification*	*Action Verb*
1.	Knowledge	Recall, recognise
2.	Comprehension (understanding)	Cite
3.	Application	Formulate
4.	Analysis	Analyse
5.	Synthesis	Synthesize
6.	Evaluation (Judgement)	Evaluate

16

Identification Process

The Diagnosis

Just as medical diagnosis is concerned with the careful and extensive observation of a patient, likewise, educational diagnosis is concerned with careful and extensive observation of the learning and instructional difficulties of the ill earners. Purpose of both types of diagnosis is to locate the causes of the problems. The doctor as well as the teacher use some instruments for this purpose. The diagnosis in education is moving gradually and in some areas even rapidly in the direction of scientific accuracy and precision.

A teacher in educational diagnosis uses several analytical tools, diagnostic tests and statistical 'techniques in different subjects.

Two Type of Tests

Essence of Educational Diagnosis. The essence of good diagnosis is that one should get many distinct and relevant facts about the individual. One wants to have an appraisal of each of the component abilities into which the complex performance has been analyzed. At the same time, it is important that the separate appraisals have adequate reliability.

Diagnostic testing is important for two reasons. In the first place, in diagnostic work, we are in almost every instance interested in the individual. It is his personal strengths and weakness with which we are concerned. Group averages or group comparisons are of no particular interest to us in this context. We cannot fall back upon averages to balance out the chance errors in measuring a particular pupil. We need an accurate appraisal of the specific individual. This is made more acute by the fact that we are dealing with differences between the individual's performance in related tasks. We are interested in making such a statement as : "This pupil's ability to pick out the main idea in what he has read is poorer than his ability to answer questions on specific factual details."

Survey Achievement Testing and Diagnostic Testing. A survey achievement test undertakes to provide a general, over-all appraisal of status in some area of knowledge or skill. A diagnostic test undertakes to provide a detailed picture of strengths and weakness in an area. Furthermore, it is anticipated that this detailed analysis will suggest causes for deficiencies and provide a guide for remedial procedures. A survey reading test tells us that Sohan who is starting the fifth grade, performs on the test of reading paragraphs at a level typical of the usual child beginning the third grade. A series of diagnostic tests indicates that Sohan has a fair sight vocabulary of common words but no skills for working out unfamiliar words. He is unable to blend sounds to form words. He does not recognize the sounds that correspond to letter combinations, and that he makes frequent reversal errors. These findings, together with others, provide the basis for planning remedial teaching of word analysis and phonic skills that are specifically directed toward Sohan's deficiencies. Development of diagnostic tests involves two steps: (1) analysis of the complex performance – be it reading, multiplying fractions, or using a microscope-into its component sub-skills, and (2) developing tests for the component skills, free as far as possible from any other source of difficulty.

It has become fashionable in recent years to call many tests "diagnostic tests." In a sense, any test that yields more than a single overall score is diagnostic. Even if there are only two part scores, say, one for word knowledge and one for paragraph comprehension, the test makes it possible for us to say that Sohan showed better ability in word knowledge than he did in reading connected prose. This is certainly one diagnostic clue. Diagnosis is, after all, a matter of degree. We may probe and analyze with varying degrees of thoroughness and detail. We must ask concerning any test purporting to be diagnostic: How complete and how adequate are the diagnostic cues that this test provides? It is easy to overstate the value of the diagnostic information provided by a particular test.

A well prepared and trained teacher also employs devices and instruments for measuring oral activity and vision. Several types of instruments are used to locate causes of teacher's lack of progress in several areas of learning.

General survey achievement tests are used to local deficiencies of a general nature in the learners. Specific weaknesses are identified by the use of selected educational diagnostic test.

Analysis of the diagnostic test assumes significance for undertaking remedial work.

A Warning

Diagnostic test results must be interpreted with caution. The tests provide some rough and quite tentative hypotheses as to the individual's strengths and weaknesses. But these must be clearly recognized as tentative hypotheses and nothing more. The test profile suggests possible causes for the present difficulty and a jumping-off place for remedial work. If the remedial activities are successful, well and good. If not, the remedial teacher must stand ready to review his hypotheses and to explore other leads. Diagnostic test results are suggestions not commands.

Important Ways in Which Educational Diagnosis becomes Important. Following are the important ways which make educational diagnosis important:

(1) Educational diagnosis becomes the basis of 'remedial' work.
(2) Educational diagnosis assumes importance as being the basis of 'preventive' work.

The Utility

(i) Diagnostic tests serve as guides to the attainments of students.

(ii) Diagnostic tests serve as guides to locate difficulties of students.

(iii) Diagnostic tests help in isolating difficulties of students individually.

(iv) Diagnostic tests help in dividing students into groups for remedial teaching or special coaching.

Diagnostic Tests	*Achievement Tests*
1. Diagnostic tests are normally meant for the below average students.	1. Achievement tests are meant for the average students.
2. Diagnostic tests are used to identify difficulties and weaknesses of the students.	2. Achievement tests are used to evaluate the achievement level of the students.
3. Diagnostic tests lead to remedial teaching or special coaching.	3. Achievement tests are used to compare achievement of students and also for grading.
4. Diagnostic tests concentrate on difficult areas.	4. Achievement tests relate to the entire unit covered.
5. Diagnostic tests are not usually used to evaluate the efficiency of the teachers and the system.	5. Achievement tests at various occasions determine the effectiveness of the teacher in the teaching learning process.

Broad Areas Concerned with Diagnostic Testing. These are given below :

(a) Achievement in specific subjects.

(b) Achievement in specific areas of a subject or subjects.

(c) General educational achievement.

(d) Intelligence.

(e) Personality.

Tests Compared

Diagnostic evaluation is more comprehensive and detailed than formative and summative evaluation. Formative evaluation provides first-aid treatment for simple learning problems. On the other hand diagnostic evaluation involves the use of specially prepared diagnostic tests as well as several observational techniques. There are many learning difficulties that are likely to require the services of psychologists and specialists in some areas. Diagnostic testing aims at locating the causes of learner's problems and to formulate a plan of action.

Diagnostic evaluation is concerned with learner's persistent or recurring learning difficulties that have remained unresolved during the classroom teaching and formative evaluation. For instance, if a learner continues to experience failure in spelling, computation, science or other subjects, in spite of the use of alternative methods of instruction, then the need for a detailed diagnosis is indicated.

Results of summative evaluation are typically used for grading the learners. They are also used in judging the effectiveness of the teacher in the teaching-learning process and also sometimes evaluating the worthwhileness of the curriculum.

Formative evaluation provides feedback to the teacher and the learner regarding learner's progress.

Examples

Iowa Silent Reading Tests (Advanced Level). These include the following subjects, each supposed to represent a somewhat different aspect of reading skill.

Test 1.	Rate and Comprehension of connected prose.
Test 2.	Directed Reading of connected prose to locate answers to factual questions.
Test 3.	Poetry Comprehension, including mood, metaphor, etc.
Test 4.	Word Meaning in different content areas.
Test 5.	Sentence Meaning of brief sentences out of context.
Test 6.	Paragraph Comprehension, selecting central idea and comprehending essential details.
Test 7.	Location of Information, using an index, selecting key words.

Thorndike and Hagen explain these as under. How many of these are in fact both sufficiently reliable and sufficiently different to be usefully diagnostic is a real question. For example, the reliabilities of Test 5, Sentence Meaning, and Test 6, Paragraph Comprehension, are reported (probably somewhat optimistically, since the coefficients are based on odd versus even halves and the tests have quite short time limits) as .751 and .759. The correlation between the two tests is reported as .48. From these values, we may estimate the reliability of the difference score to be .53. Inferences from a datum having this level of reliability should be made very cautiously.

The use of sub-test scores such as those on the Iowa is probably most justifiable for a class or larger group. With a group average, chance errors tend to cancel out, and the low reliability of the scores becomes less important. If the group as a whole shows some marked weakness, as in the use of indices and library aids, for example, this may point out areas in which instruction has been neglected and suggest directions for instruction for the group as a whole.

Gray's Oral Reading Passages. Here the diagnostic study of reading is through standard oral reading passages. The test consists of a standard set of passages, ranging from easy and simple to quite difficult. The child who is being studied reads the passages aloud. The examiner uses a standard code to record on a copy of the passages all the errors and hesitations made by the pupil. Mispronounced words are underlined. Mispronounced vowels are shown by appropriate diacritical marks. Omissions are encircled. Substitutions and insertions are written in. Repetitions are indicated by a wavy line.

The record of the child's oral responses is valuable for the insight that it gives us into the actual process of reading. The usual objective written test shows us only the product of a child's efforts, the marks he makes on a test booklet or answer sheet. If he does poorly or makes mistakes, we are often at a loss to know why. In the oral test we can see the errors as they happen-each hesitation, each omission, each reversal. In this way we can identify more specifically the components that are giving the child trouble. They are not lost in the one final result, that the child is slow in reading the passage or does poorly on comprehension questions based on it.

Compass Diagnostic Arithmetic Tests. In these the authors undertake to break up each complex skill in arithmetic into its components-to-test the simplest components first, and then to add on additional elements until the full task has been tested. Thus, the diagnostic test concerned with division of whole numbers has subsections testing the child upon the following contributing skills and understandings: (1) the vocabulary of division, (2) fundamentals of short division, (3) short division with carrying, (4) the addition, subtraction, and multiplication used in later subtests, (5) estimating the first quotient figure, (6) fundamentals of long division and checking, and (7) finding errors in long division. A study of scores on these subsections may provide insight as to where the trouble really lies.

Test for Writing

Bisrampur Hindi Handwriting Scale. This scale includes various specimens of handwriting in gradation of quality. These scale helps in locating defects and their probable causes. For example, the defect may be too much slant, stroke in wrong direction, too stiff thumb etc.

Handwriting Scale developed by W.M. Ryburn in Urdu. W.C. Chatterjee's Handwriting Scale in Hindi.

Spelling Tests. Spelling tests and scales are valuable sources for diagnosing the spelling errors made by the students. They provide clues to the remedial procedure to be adopted in improving spelling.

Analysing Spelling Habits of the Students. Following factors are responsible for good/bad spelling among students:

(i) Articulation.
(ii) Hearing power.
(iii) Intelligence.
(iv) Emotional attitude.
(v) Personality characteristics like attentiveness, exactness.
(vi) Pronunciation.
(vii) Reading ability.
(viii) Study techniques.
(ix) Student's knowledge of phonics.
(x) Student's knowledge of meaning of words.
(xi) Vision.

Procedure for Diagnosing and Treating Problem Cases. Tidyman and Butterfield have suggested the following points for diagnosing and treating problem cases in spelling:

(1) Administer a standard spelling test to locate the amount of deficiency.

(2) Compare with attainment in other areas.
(3) Give an intelligence test to find out general mental capacity.
(4) Get hearing tested.
(5) Get vision tested.
(6) Give a reading test.
(7) Administer test of spelling consciousness to locate whether errors are on account of ignorance of the word or carelessness.
(8) Collect misspellings from spelling tests and written work.
(9) Classify types of spelling errors.
(10) Obtain as much information as possible regarding student's academic history, methods of beginning reading in particular, knowledge of meaning of words, knowledge of articulation, phonics and pronunciation etc.
(11) From above gather probable causes of difficulty in spelling.
(12) In the light of above, adopt appropriate measures such as the following:
    (a) Removal of physical defects like those connected with hearing or vision. Here take medical help.
    (b) Encourage each student to keep an individual list of such words as are often wrongly spelled.
    (c) Check written work carefully as regard spellings errors.
    (d) Use phonies drills.
    (e) Use drills upon particular types of spelling errors.
    (f) Develop confidence in the student for successful effort.
    (g) Develop systematic work study.
    (h) Use exercises in visualisation.

To conclude, it is very difficult to develop such spelling tests. They are very time consuming.

17

Various Devices

Tools play a significant role in the evaluation of curricular and co-curricular programme. They are important for evaluating the cognitive and non-cognitive development of the students. Without the tools, effectiveness of the educational programmes cannot be assured. It is, therefore, very essential that they should be as objective and perfect as possible.

Classification of Tools. There are a number of ways in which the tools are classified. Here only a few important classifications are given.

Classification of Tools - 1

Subjective Tools — Objective Tools

Classification of Tools - 2

Standardised Tools — Non-standardised Tools

Classification of Tools - 3

Verbal Tools — Non-verbal Tools

Classification of Tools - 4

Standardised Tools — Teacher made Tools

Classification of Tools - 5

Tests — Non-tests

Classification of Tools - 6

Prognostic Tools Non-prognostic Tools

Classification of Tools - 7

(1)	(2)	(3)	(4)	(5)	(6)	(7)	(8)
By kind of item are recorded.	By how observations	By conditions of adminis-tration	By emphasis on language	By time	By scoring scheme	By degree of standardi-sation	By the attribute to be measured

New Devices

Fairly exhaustive tools have been designed by educationists to evaluate the various aspects of child's growth. Following are the commonly used tools.

1. Achievement Tests.
2. Anecdotal Records.
3. Aptitude Tests.
4. Attitude and Behaviour Testing Tools.
5. Autobiographical Method.
6. Case History.
7. Intelligence Tests.
8. Interview.
9. Personality Tests.
10. Projective Tools.
11. Pupil's Dairy.
12. Questionnaires and Check Lists
13. Rating Scales.
14. Sociometric Tools.

Scoring Systems

By a rating is meant the judgment of one person by another. "Rating is, in essence, directed observation," writes Ruth Strang. A.S. Barr and others state, "Rating is a term applied to expression of opinion or judgment regarding some situation, object or character. Opinions are usually expressed on a scale or values. Rating techniques are devices by which such judgments may be quantified."

A rating scale is a method by which we systematize the expression of opinion concerning a trait. The ratings are done by parents, teachers, a board of interviewers and judges and by the self as well.

There are two characteristics of a rating scale. (1) Description of the characteristics to be rated, and (2) Some methods by which the quality, frequency or importance of each item to be rated may be given.

These rating scales give an idea of the personality of an individual.

Various Types

Descriptive Rating Scale. The rater puts a check in the blank before the characteristic or trait which is described in words or a phrase.

Example. Has this pupil initiative?

– Shows marked originality.
– Willing to take initiative.
– Quite inventive.
– On the whole unenterprising.
– Very dependent on others.

Numerical Scale. Here numbers are assigned to each trait. If it is a seven-point scale, the number 7 represents the maximum amount of that trait in the individual; 4 represents the average amount. Instead of 7 point-scale we can have 9 point or 5 point or 3 point scale. A nine point scale may be:

1. Most pleasant
2. Extremely pleasant
3. Moderately pleasant
4. Mildly pleasant
5. Indifferent
6. Mildly unpleasant
7. Moderately unpleasant
8. Extremely unpleasant
9. Most unpleasant

Graphic Scale. This is similar to the descriptive scale and the difference lies only in the way it is written. This is also called

"Behavioural Statement Scale." The following two examples may be noted:

(a) *Example.* Responsibility for completing work.

Very high	High	Average	Low	Very low

(b) *Example.* Social attitude.

Anti-social	Self-centred	Has no positive attitude	Usually considerate of others.	Strongly altruistic

Percentage of Group Scale. Here the rater is asked to give the percentage of the group that possesses the trait on which the individual is rated. For example-for rating the self-confidence of an individual, the rater may check one of the following:

Falls in the top 1 per cent.

Falls in the top 10 per cent, but not in the top one per cent.

In the top 25% but not in the top 10%.

In the top 50% but not in the top 25%.

In the lower half, but not in the bottom 25%.

In the bottom 25%, but not in the bottom 10%.

In the bottom 10%, but not in the bottom 1 per cent.

In the bottom 1 per cent.

Man to Man Scale. An individual is asked to rate the ratee by comparing him to the person mentioned on the Scale and assign the ratee his position. For example, A B C D E are the persons who have been already rated as very persistent, not easily stopped, works quite steadily, somewhat changeable, gives up easily.

Example, is he generally a persistence person?

A B D E

Because of subjectivity element, the use of this type is very limited.

Graphic Scale. In this scale a straight line is shown vertically or horizontically with various clues to help the rater. An example of such a scale is given below.

1	2	3	4	5
Very effective	Slightly effective	Average —	Slightly ineffective	Very ineffective

Rating by Cumulative Points. The weights of + I and -1 are assigned to every favourable and unfavourable attribute, characteristic or trait.

Standard Scale. This type of scale is used in evaluating the quality of handwriting on the basis of some pre-established scale values.

Advantages

1. Helpful in writing reports to parents.
2. Helpful in filling out admission blanks for colleges.
3. Helpful in finding out students needs.
4. Helpful in making recommendations to the employers.
5. Helpful in supplementing other sources of understanding about the child.
6. Rating scales especially are quite interesting to the raters, especially the graphic.

Limitations

1. Some characteristics are more difficult to rate.
2. Subjectivity element is present.
3. Lack of opportunities to rate students.
4. Raters tend to be generally generous.

The teachers or the counsellor may rate each individual on each quality on a three-point, four-point or five-point scale. In a five-point scale, the description of the qualities of an individual may be 'Outstanding', 'Very good', 'Good', 'Average' and 'Poor'.

1. The specific trait or mode of behaviour must be defined properly. For example, we want to rate a child's originality in performing a task. First of all we must formulate a definition of 'originality' and then try to rate it.
2. The scale should be clearly defined, i.e., we are rating at a three, four or five-point scale.
3. The trait to be treated should be readily observable.
4. Uniform standards of rating scale should be observed.
5. The rater should observe the rates in different situations involving the trait to be rated. This will bring reliability to the judgment of the rater.

6. The number of characteristics to be rated should be limited.
7. In the rating scale card, some space may be provided for the rater to write some supplementary material.
8. The directions of using the rating scales should be clear and comprehensive.
9. Several judges may be employed to increase the reliability of any rating scale.
10. Well-informed and experienced persons should be selected for rating.

The Mistakes

Generosity Error. Sometimes raters would not like to run down their own people by giving them low ratings. The result is that high rating is given in almost all cases. Such an error is known as 'generosity error'.

Stringency Error. The opposite of generosity error may be called stringency error. Some raters have a tendency to rate all individuals low.

The Halo Error. 'Halo' means a tendency to rate in terms of general impressions about the rates formed on the basis of some previous performance.

The Error of Central Tendency. There is a tendency in some observers to rate all or most of the raters near the mid-point of the scale. They would like to put most of the ratees as 'Average' etc.

The Logical Error. Such an error occurs when the characteristic or the trait to be rated is misunderstood.

Various Records

An Anecdotal Record is the observed behaviour of a child. It has been defined by Randall as a record of some significant item of conduct, a record of an episode in the life of the student; a word picture of the student in action... a word snapshot at the moment of the incident; any narration of events in which the student takes such a part as to reveal something which may be significant about his personality.

Raths Louis thinks that "an anecdotal record is a report of a significant episode in the life of a student."

According to Brown and Martin, "Anecdotes are descriptive accounts of episodes or occurrences in the daily life of the student."

Zhan, D. Willard regards an anecdotal record "as a simple statement of an incident deemed by the observer to be significant with respect to a given pupil."

Traxler thinks, "This records, as the name implies, involves setting down an anecdote concerning some aspect of pupil behaviour which seems significant to the observer."

Anecdotal record is a running cumulative description of actual examples of behaviour as observed by teachers and counsellor. The description of the behaviour is followed by a comment by the teacher. An example will make it clear:

Example

Place: English class.

Objective Description. I have been finding Ram day after day in the library reading magazines, yet he never has time to correct error or to work carefully on English assignments.

Comment. Ram does not like to write but likes to read. I have asked the librarian not to admit him during his free periods unless he hears from me that Ram has done his work.

The Guidelines

We cannot set any limit on the number of anecdotes to be recorded. It depends upon the time which is at the disposal of the teachers or guidance workers. The following points should be considered in connection with these records:

1. These supplement other records and should not be considered as substitutes.
2. The objective description of the behaviour should not be mixed up with the subjective comments.
3. Any significant behaviour, be it, in the classroom, in the school or outside the school, should be recorded.
4. Behaviour, whether it is favourable, unfavourable or neither favourable nor unfavourable to the child, should be recorded.
5. The facts presented in all the anecdotes must be shifted and arranged so that they may be studied in relation to one another.

6. The record should be regarded as confidential. It should not fall into irresponsible hands.

Values and Uses

1. They provide specific description of personality and minimise generalisations.
2. They are very helpful in understanding the child's behaviour in diverse situations.
3. They provide a continuous record.
4. They provide data for pupils to use in self-appraisal.
5. A summary of these records is valuable for forwarding with a pupil when he is transferred from one school to another.
6. The new members of the staff may use these records and acquaint themselves with the student body.
7. These records aid in clinical service.
8. They stimulate teachers to use the records.

The Characteristics

James M. Bradfield and H. Stewart Moredock have given the following characteristics of an anecdotal record.

1. What is written down is what was seen or heard. Inferences, guesses, assumptions are omitted unless they are clearly labelled as inferences, guesses or assumptions.
2. The observer has already determined what aspects of behaviours are related to the dimension being appraised. He observes these only and records them only.
3. If the record is to be cumulative, a plan of periodic observation and recording is established and adhered to.
4. Words and phrases are used whose meaning is clear, and so far as possible, unequivocal.
5. Words and phrases are employed that are definable in terms of things rather than other words. Concrete statements are preferred to abstract ones. For example, "He became pale and his hands trembled", not "He was disturbed."

6. Words and phrases that have strong emotional connotations are avoided, i.e., love, hate, insolvent, loyal, dishonest, etc.
7. Words and phrases which express the observer's judgment, or his opinion, and not his perception are avoided. Among the frequently encountered "judgmental terms" that should be avoided are the following:
   (a) Well-behaved.
   (b) Delinquent.
   (c) Aggressive.
   (d) Didn't try.
   (e) Industrious.
   (f) Nervous.
   (g) Happy.

Tests for Intellect

(a) Individual-administered to one examinee at a time.
(b) Group-administered like a school examinations, to many examinees at the same time.
(c) Performance-make little or no use of language, in contrast with the paper and pencil tests in (a) and (b).

Academic Achievement

(a) Survey-comprehensive examinations used to determine general academic standing.
(b) Subject-examination in specific fields, for example, English, Mathematics.
(c) Diagnostic-cover a wide range of academic skills on reading or arithmetic, for example) and are designed to reveal specific weaknesses and strengths.

Tests of Various Aspects of Personality

(a) Personal Adjustment Questionnaires-survey of worries, fear, social inadequacies.
(b) Attitude Surveys-upon social, economic and political questions.
(c) Interest Inventories-related to various occupations.

(d) Environmental Facts Related to Personality-questionnaire covering Socio-economic background and other variables.
(e) Projective Techniques - subtle and direct measures of dominant personality trends.

Intelligence Tests

A test of intelligence is that test which assesses the student's ability to perceive relationships, solve problems and apply knowledge in a variety of ways.

Classification of Intelligence Tests -I

Verbal	Non-verbal

Classification of Intelligence Tests- II

Paper-Pencil	Performance Test

Classification of Intelligence Tests - III

Speed Tests	Power Tests

Classification of Intelligence Tests - IV

Individual Tests	Group Tests

The Uses

Individual Tests. These tests are administered to one individual at a time. These cover age group from 2 years to 18 years. These are: (a) The Binet-Simon Tests, (b) Revised Tests by Terman, and (c) Mental and Scholastic Tests of Burt.

Group Tests. Group tests are administered to a group of people. Group tests had their birth in America-when the intelligence of the recruits who joined the army in the First World War was to be calculated. These are: (a) The Army Alpha and Beta Tests, (b) Terman's Group Tests, and (c) Otis Self-Administrative Tests.

Performance Tests. These tests are administered to the illiterate persons. These tests generally involve the construction of certain patterns or solving problems in terms of concrete material. Some of the famous tests are: (a) Koh's Block Design Test, (b) The Cube Construction Tests, and (c) The Pass Along Tests.

Verbal Test vs. Non-verbal Test. In a verbal test, the subject (student) responds to the items in the test by writing the replies or encircling or underlying or ticking the replies given in words while in a Non-verbal test, replies/responses are presented in designs or diagrams.

Speed vs. Power Test. Time limit is important in a speed test and this is not important in a power test. Subject (student) has a chance to attempt each item.

1. Selection of pupils for admission to various courses of study.
2. Classification of pupils.
3. Prediction of scholastic success.
4. Detection of superior and inferior intelligence among the pupils.
5. Selection of suitable occupations.
6. Awarding scholarships.
7. Judging Teacher's work.
8. Selection of students into educational institutions.
9. The discovery of unusual cases.
10. Prediction of success in college.
11. Diagnosis of backwardness.
12. Evaluation of methods and materials of instruction.

Though intelligence is defined in many different ways, the intelligence tests are based mainly on definitions in terms of ability to succeed scholastically.

Limitations of the Intelligence Tests. It would be a great mistake to think that these tests are all in all in measuring the various aspects of the personality of an individual. Intelligence is not the only factor which determines the equipment of a man for the journey of life.

The first limitation of such tests is that they seek to measure intelligence which in itself is not a clear conception to the psychologists and about which they differ among themselves.

Secondly, intelligence is not the only factor which plays a significant role in the success or failure of a man in a particular vocation. The intelligence tests fail to measure the depth, strength and qualities of a man pertaining to his emotional stability. They also fail to measure his ethical, social and aesthetic qualities which play a significant part in the life of an individual.

Thirdly, intelligence tests fail to take into account the environmental factors and the educational factors many a time and thus give misleading results. These tests may include material with which children of certain socio-economic groups have had more experience than those of other groups.

Fourthly, intelligence test scores among courses and vocations overlap.

Fifthly, intelligence tests do not measure intelligence with complete accuracy.

Sixthly, intelligence tests provide rough and general measures which need to be corroborated by results from other sources.

Seventhly, a proper use of the tests requires the development of local norms and the interpretation of individual scores against norms.

Eighthly, a good deal of care is needed on the part of the tester in the use of tests and interpretation of scores.

Ninthly, there are many things which the intelligence tests do not measure.

Lastly, intelligence tests are not pure measure of innate capacities of individuals.

To quote Prof Nunn, "You are for ever you, and I, I". It has been amply proved by the psychologists that all persons do not have the same amount of intelligence and all cannot work with the same speed and efficiency. The assumption that given the same opportunities all men will be equally successful is based upon faulty foundations. The intelligence tests are of a great use in the schools. To be a successful teacher, one must know one's pupils thoroughly and one must possess an instrument with which one can measure the intelligence of one's pupils and one must know the proper use of that instrument. The work of a teacher is the work of handling young growing minds and he must, therefore, know as much as possible of these minds. The Binet's rod of mental measurement is an instrument for the teacher to find out the exact calibre of the minds of his pupils. Intelligence Tests help to discover whether a child is backward or dull or intelligent. It is not possible to gauge the intelligence of children without the use of mental tests. The children's intelligence cannot be estimated from the marks obtained by them in their school-subjects. A child of 12 years and another of 14 years may be put on the same level if they obtain the same number of marks. But this is a defective method. Obviously, the child of 12 years is more intelligent than the child of 14 years in this illustration. Similarly, a child may be more industrious but comparatively dull and may score more marks than another child, who may in fact be more intelligent but less industrious. There are important spheres in which intelligence test can be employed.

The Categorisation

On the basis of I.Q., Terman gives the following classification on American testees:

Near genius or genius	above 140
Very superior intelligence	120-140
Superior intelligence	110-120
Normal or average intelligence	90-110
Dulness	80-90
Borderline cases	70-80

Definite feeble-mindedness which has been further classified as under:	below 70
Morons	50-70
Imbeciles	25-50
Idiots	below 25

Indian Procedure

The Bombay-Karnataka Revision Tests. Dr. V.V. Kamat revised Binet's scale to suit Indian conditions and administered intelligence tests to 1,074 children and adolescents of all ages from 2 to 20 of both sexes. The locality selected for the experiment was the town of Dharwar in the Bombay Presidency. The children selected were fairly representative of the general population of Indian children.

Dr. V.V. Kamat classifies Indian children as under:

Class	Range of I.Q.s
Near genius or genius	140 and above
Extraordinary	130-139.9
Very superior	120-129-9
Superior	110-119.9
Average or normal	99-109.9
Backward	80-98.9
Very backward	70-79.9
Borderline	60-69.9
Morons	40-59.9
Imbeciles	20-39.9
Idiots	Below 20

Another Process

Classification	Punjabi I.Q.
Genius	165 and above
Very superior	140-165
Superior	120-140
Average	85-120
Dull	70-85
Borderline	52-70
Feeble-minded	Below 55

Intelligence and Selection of Suitable Occupations. Burt draws up the following provisional scheme for occupational classification according to the degree of intelligence they require.

Higher Professional and Administrative Work (I. Q. 150)- Lawyer, physician, architect, teacher (University and Secondary).

Lower Professional Technical and Executive Work (I.Q. 130 to 150).

Clerical and Highly Skilled Work (I.Q. 115 to 130) - Shorthand typist, bank clerk, salesman, electrician, nurse.

Skilled Work (I.Q. 100 to 115) - Tailor, dressmaker, carpenter, cashier, printer.

Semi-skilled Repetition Work (I.Q. 85 to 100) - Barber, welder, minor, painter, baker.

Unskilled Repetition Work (I.Q. 70 to 85) - Manual labour, navy groom, packer.

Casual Labour (I.Q. 50 to 70) - Simplest routine work.

Institutional (I.Q. under 50) - Unemployable.

Selection of Courses. Different subjects require different degrees of intelligence. Some call for a higher order of intelligence and the others of a low. A nation-wide study conducted in the United States gave the following Median I.Q. of the High School boys in different courses.

Courses	Median I.Q.
Technical	114
Scientific	108
Academic	106
Commerce	104
Trade	92

Intelligence and Reading-Writing Abilities

Burt found the following correlation between:

Intelligence and composition	.63
Intelligence and reading	.56
Intelligence and arithmetic (Problems)	.85
Intelligence and spelling	.52
Intelligence and writing	.21
Intelligence and hand work	.18
Intelligence and drawing	.15

This means that children of high I.Q. are superior in the linguistic and abstract subject—composition, reading, arithmetic and spelling—than those of low I.Q.

Intelligence Tests Available in India

Group Test

1. A Group Test of General Intelligence by S. Chatterji
2. Group Test of General Mental Ability
3. Mixed Type Group Test of Intelligence (Verbal and Non-verbal) by P.N. Mehrotroa
4. Non-verbal Test of Intelligence by G.H. Nafde
5. Non-verbal Test of Intelligence (Adaptation of Jenkins Test), Central Institute of Education, Delhi

6. Non-verbal Group Test of Intelligence for Children (Hindi) by M.C. Joshi and R.B. Tripathi
7. Sadharam Mansik Yogyata Pariksha (Hindi) by S.S. Jalota and JB. Singh
8. Test of General Intelligence No. 1 (Hindi) by S.M. Mohsin
9. Verbal Intelligence Test (in Hindi) by R.K. Ojha and K. Roy Choudhary
10. Verbal Group Test of Intelligence (Hindi) Bureau of psychology, Allahabad (U.P.)
11. Verbal Group Test of Intelligence (Hindi) by S.M. Mohsin.

Individual Tests of Intelligence

1. Battery of Performance Test of Intelligence by C.M. Bhatia
2. Bicycle Drawing for Measuring Intelligence by T.R. Sharma
3. Draw-a-Man Test for Children by R Pathak
4. Draw-a-Man Test by A.N. Sharma
5. Indian Adaptation of Standard Binet Test 1960 (Hindi) by S.K. Kulshreshtha
6. Indian Adaptation of Weschler Adult Intelligence Scale by Ramlingaswamy

18

Perfect Devices

An evaluation tool may be defined as a sophisticated means of appraisal, intelligently and scientifically designed to evaluate/measure what is required to be evaluated or measured.

Two Fold Classification of a Good Tool

Practical	*Technical*
(1) Administrative ease	(1) Discrimination
(2) Acceptability	(2) Item analysis
(3) Cost effective	(3) Norms
(4) Face validity	(4) Objectivity
(5) Interpretation ease	(5) Reliability
(6) Meaningfulness	(6) Standardization
(7) Purposefulness	(7) Validity
(8) Scoring ease	
(9) Time saving	

The Qualities. Ebel (1965) suggested the following factors which should be kept in view while judging the quality of a test.

(i) Balance
(ii) Difficulty
(iii) Discrimination
(iv) Efficiency
(v) Fairness

(vi) Objectivity
(vii) Relevance
(viii) Reliability
(ix) Specificity
(x) Speed.

Features at Work

Administrative Case. A test which is simple to apply and have complete directions will always be a good test.

Acceptability. A good test must be acceptable to all the persons and in all the circumstances and situations, e.g., the Binet Simon Intelligence Test. This is a test which is acceptable to all the individuals of any grade in all the situations.

Cost Effective. As far as possible, a good test should be economical not only from money point of view, but from the point of time and effort required by the testing procedure.

Face Validity. It implies how worthwhile a test will appear to testee, who takes it and to other layman who will see the results. For example, the medicine prescribed by a doctor will not be so effective, if the patient has less of faith in prescription. Similarly, testee will be resentful and distressful, if the test does not appear to be worthwhile to him.

Interpretation Ease. A good test is one, which could easily be interpreted by the class teacher and the tester himself.

Meaningfulness of Test Scores. A test must provide clues to the objectives for which it is administered.

Purposefulness. One must search for a test that fits the decisions to be made. It is unrealistic to evaluate a test in abstract. The test manual should be approached with a definite measurement problem in mind, e.g., selecting students for a course in humanities or sciences or a special branch in these fields.

Scoring Ease. Scoring would be easy if items have been objectively constructed and the scoring procedure adopted is also objective. In the test itself, separate space should be provided for scoring. Scoring may be done by hand as well as by machines. So stencil-scoring, punch-card scoring or any other method may be used.

Time Saving. The time available for testing is usually very short, as tests requiring longer time are not easily accepted. It is, therefore, better to prefer shorter tests other things being equal. The reliability and validity of a test, does not always depend on its length. Shortening tests to a very few items will destroy their value but not much is gained by lengthening tests beyond 100 items. Hence, this fact should be kept in mind while considering the time factor.

Scientific Features

Reliability. A test is said to be reliable if it gives the same results whenever it is repeated. If there is no variation in a pupil's score obtained in a test today and obtained after a sufficient long time, the test is said to be reliable. The test should also give the same result, if it is applied by different persons who follow the set instructions. There are two methods which are usually employed to determine the validity of test: (1) The test-re-test method. (2) The split-half method. According to the first method, the same test is applied after some months to the individuals and the scores of two administrations of the test are compared and correlation of co-efficient is calculated. The test is said to be fairly reliable if the correlation is 90. In the second method, test is arbitrarily split up into two equal halves, the scores on odd and even items are counted separately and correlation co-efficient is calculated.

Validity of a Test. A test is said to be valid if it succeeds in measuring what it aims at measuring. The validity of a test can be judged in more than one way (1) A test is said to be valid if its results correspond to the judgment of competent judges. The scores of an individual on the test may be compared with a list prepared by the class teacher and the correlation can be found. (2) By comparing the scores obtained through new test with the scores compared through the Simon-Binet Test. (3) By correlating the results of a group test with those of an individual test given to the same group of students.

Objectivity. Objectivity refers to the extent the opinion or judgement of the scorer is eliminated from the scoring process. Objectivity is high in most of the standardized tests of achievement, aptitude, creativity and intelligence, etc. The test items are of objective type-fill in the blanks, multiple choice, true-false, etc. Objectivity is usually attained by:

(i) stating the items precisely and specifically.
(ii) requiring short and specific answers.
(iii) scoring the test by the use of a previously determined scoring key or providing specific guidelines for scoring.

Predictability. The test should be such as can give a forecast of the possibilities of the future achievement of the students.

Symbolic Focus
Head
Heart
Hand

Accepted Relevance

Before understanding the meaning of the validity of a test, we may mention a few definitions of validity.

In the words of Thorndike, "A measurement procedure is valid in so far as it correlates with some measurement of success in the job which it is being used as a predictor."

Leo J. Cronbach says "Validity is the extent to which a test measures what it purports to measure."

Gates defines validity of a test as, "A test is valid when it measures truly and accurately the ability or quality one wants to appraise."

Boring and others believe, "The degree to which the test actually succeeds in measuring what it sets one to measure is called validity."

Gronlund states," Validity refers to the extent to which the results of an evaluation procedure serve the particular uses for which they are intended."

Stanley and Hopkins have observed, "The validity of a measure is how well it fulfils the function for which it is being used-the degree to which it is capable of achieving certain aims." Validity is chiefly a concern for the 'basic honesty' of the test or the tool in the sense of doing what one promises to do. To be precise validity implies how well a tool measures what it intends to measure.

Nature of Validity. Following points regarding the nature of validity may be noted:

(i) Validity is a matter of degree. It is best considered in terms of categories that specify degree such as higher validity, moderate validity and low validity.

(ii) The validity pertains to the results of a test or evaluation instrument and not to the instrument itself. We sometimes speak of the validity of a test for the sake of convenience but it is more appropriate to speak of the validity of the test results or more specifically of the validity of the interpretation to be made from the results.

(iii) No test can be said to have 'high' or 'low' validity in the abstract. Its validity must be determined with reference to the particular use for which the test is being considered.

(iv) The validity of a test cannot be reported in general terms.

Types of Validity

(1)	(2)	(3)	(4)	(5)
Content validity	Criterion related validity (a) Concurrent (b) Predictive	Construct validity	Face validity	Factorial validity

Content Validity. Content validity is the most important criterion for the usefulness of a test/tool. It is especially important in the case of an achievement test. Content validity relates to the process of matching the test items with the instructional objectives. The content validity relates to the degree to which a test samples the content area which is to be measured. All major aspects of the content area must be adequately covered by the test items and they must be in the correct proportions.

Criterion-related Validity. Criterion-related validity implies the extent to which a tool performance is related to some other valued measure of performance.

(i) *Concurrent Validity.* It means correlating the test scores with another set of criterion scores.

(ii) *Predictive Validity.* It refers to the extent to which a test can predict the future performance of the students/ learners. This type of validity is important for those tests which are used for classification and selection purposes. The degree to which a test can predict the future performance of the individuals depends upon the degree of relationships between the two variables- the test and the criterion. The higher the relationship between these variables, the greater will be the predictive validity of a test. The most important and difficult task in this method is to determine the criterion which is the index of future performance. Predictive value is reported through a coefficient of correlation obtained when predictor and the criterion data are correlated.

Construct Validity. Construct validity refers to the extent to which a test reflects constructs presumed to underline the test performance and also the extent to which it is based on the theories regarding these constructs.

Face Validity. Face validity refers not to what the test measures but what the test 'appears to measure'.

Factorial Validity. According to Guliford, the factorial validity is the clearest description of what an evaluation/ measurement tool measures. The relationship of the different factors with the whole test is called factorial validity.

Various Types

(i) An admission test to B.Ed. course to select suitable candidates - Criteria related (Predictive).

(ii) A test given at the end of the academic year of +2 course to measure how much the learners have achieved of the course Content Validity.

(iii) A test designed to be comparably similar in structure and content to another test. - Criteria related (concurrent).

(iv) A test designed to measure intelligence among a group corresponding to the variation in age.—Construct Validity.

Different Attitudes

There are mainly two approaches to find out the validity of a test- (1) Logical Validity, and (2) Empirical Validity.

Logical Validity. When one attempts to judge precisely as to what the test measures, one makes logical analysis. Logic is based on consistency of thought. There are two methods of finding logical validity:

Deductive Validity. Deduction is from general judgment to particular judgment. When trying to find out deductive validity of a test, one tries to see as to whether the test corresponds to the definition of the trait intended to be measured. The traits should be objectively defined, e.g., in a test of vocabulary knowledge for 8th grade, the word knowledge and vocabulary must be well defined, as:

Knowledge = ability to give definition

Vocabulary = words commonly used in 8th grade textbook.

Inductive Validity. When one proceeds from particular to general, one adopts an inductive method. In this method we assign the name to the trait on the basis of the test and find the validity and instead of seeing whether a test measures a particular trait, we see what it measures.

Factors at Work

Proficiency in Certain Areas of Knowledge. There are some tests in which irrelevant factors are included, which influence the test scores.

Cultural Factors. The logical validity is affected by cultural factors.

Response Set. Mental set is a state which causes one to obtain different scores at different times if the same test is presented in different ways, i.e., change in order of items in battery of a multiple choice items, eg., Seashore test.

Representativeness of the Topic. A test should include items relative to the topic.

Empirical Validity (Statistical Validity). When the validity of a test is determined by correlating it with criterion, the validity is known to be statistical validity. The extent of the correlation indicates how well the test predicts the criterion against which it is tested.

Reliability of a Test

The second most important characteristics of a good evaluation test or tool is reliability.

In the words of Anatsai "The reliability of a test refers to the consistency of score obtained by the same individual on different occasions or with different sets of equivalent items."

According to Frank S. Freeman, "The term reliability refers to the extent to which it gives consistent result on testing and retesting."

L.J. Cronback regards reliability as "consistency throughout a series of measurements."

To Ross, "Reliability means consistency." Ross has further observed, "The ideal test tells the truth consistently."

Nature of Reliability. Gronland is of the view that while considering reliability, following points may be taken note of:

(1) Reliability pertains to the results obtained with an evaluation tool and not to the tool itself.

(2) An estimate of reliability always relates to a particular type of consistency.

(3) Reliability is a necessary condition but not a sufficient condition for validity.

(4) Reliability is basically statistical in nature.

Factors Influencing the Reliability of an Evaluation Tool/ Test

Intrinsic Factors	*Extrinsic Factors*
Factors which lie within the test itself.	Factors which are outside the test itself.
(i) Length of the test.	(a) Group variability.
(ii) Homogeneity of items of the test.	(b) Guessing and chance errors.
(iii) Difficulty value of items.	(c) Environmental factors.
(iv) Discriminative items.	(d) Momentary changes.
(v) Scores reliability.	

Length of the Test. In some tests, total test as well as sub-test scores are given. The reliability of the whole test is generally higher in comparison with that of the sub-tests. This is because the whole test has more items, i.e., it is longer. Spearynan Brown formula may be used to calculate reliability after increasing test length.

Variability of the Group. If the range of the sample group is wide, the realiability coefficients obtained would also be high. A homogeneous range would provide low coefficients.

Ability Level of Students. Reliability is related to the ability level of students. Some tests have high reliability for older students and low reliability for younger ones, because older students have better understanding level.

Scoring Technique. There is higher possibility of mistakes if scoring is done by hand. These mistakes may be in checking answers, as well as totalling. If tests are machine-scored, there would be less number of mistakes and reliability would be higher.

Guessing. There are great individual differences in guessing capacity of student and therefore, it leads to some unreliability in test scores. A larger number of true false items results in more guessing and so it increases unreliability.

Method of Test Construction. The nature and form of test items, their difficulty, extent of dependence of one item on another, objectivity of scoring, sampling, nature of the group on which the test has been standardized influence test reliability. An increase in the number of alternate-responses would increase reliability.

Testing Conditions. Results obtained from the administration of the test in a quiet place, say testing room/classroom would not be same as obtained at an open place or in the hall. Likewise the attitude of the examiner as well as of the students also influences reliability of the test. Cheating or the absence of it is also likely to influence results.

Chance Fluctuations or Momentary Distractions. Sudden stomache or headache, broken pen or pencil, concern about family may also affect reliability.

The Procedures

Following are the methods for determining the reliability of a test.

1. Test-retest
2. Equivalent Form
3. Split-half
4. Inter-item Consistency

Test-retest Method. For establishing reliability through this method, the same test is administered twice to the same group of students/learners/subjects with a given time intervals between the two administrations of the test. With the help of these two sets of scores, correlation is computed. This correlation coefficient provides a measure of reliability It indicates how stable the test results are over the given period of time. Thus this correlation coefficient can also be referred to as a correlation of stability.

There are certain assumptions made when we compute a coefficient of stability.

First, the characteristics being measured by the test is stable over time.

Second, practice or forgetting does not affect significantly the trait being measured by the test.

Third, no differential learning should occur between the two administrations.

Equivalent Form Method. Determination of reliability by means of equivalent form method involves the use of two different but equivalent forms of the test. These forms are also called alternative or parallel forms. Equivalent forms cover the same content, use same types of items, instructions, time limits and formats of equal difficulty. The two forms of the test are administered to the same group of students/learners/subjects in close succession or with minimum time lag. The correlation coefficient is computed from the two sets of scores. This correlation coefficient provides a measure of equivalence. It indicates the degree to which both forms of the test measure the same aspects of behaviour. Inconsistencies in scores in this method can be attributed to difference in content sampling or item sampling. Long intervals between the two administrations will lower the reliability.

Split-half Method. For determination of reliability by means of the split-half method, the test is to be administered once to a group of selected students. The test is split in nearly comparable halves. There are several ways of dividing a test. In most cases the first half and the second half of a test would not be comparable on account of difference in nature and difficulty level of items as well as in the cumulative effects of warming up, practice, fatigue and any other factor varying progressively from the beginning to the end of the test. If the items are arranged in an approximate order of difficulty, then the test can be split into two halves by using odd-numbered items in one half and even-numbered items in the second half. Then this method would provide two comparable halves. Once the two comparable halves are obtained, the two half-scores can be obtained for each student of the group. From these two sets of scores, the correlation can be computed by following the usual method of correlation.

Split-half formula is as under.

$$\text{Reliability on full test} = \frac{2 \text{ x reliability on first } \tfrac{1}{2} \text{ test}}{1+\text{reliability on second } \tfrac{1}{2} \text{ test}}$$

Inter-item Consistency Method. (Homogeneity-Kuder Richardson Reliability Method). For determining reliability through this method, the test is to be administered once and is based on the consistency of students' responses to all items in the test. The inter-items consistency is influenced by two sources of error variance-40 Content sampling (ii) Heterogeneity of the behaviour domain sampled. The more homogeneous the domain, the higher the inter-item consistency. For example, if one test includes only subtraction items, another test includes addition, division and multiplication items, the former test will most probably show greater inter-item consistency than the latter. In the latter test which is more heterogeneous, one student may perform better in addition than in any of the other arithmetic operations, another student may score reliably higher on the division items but low on addition and multiplication and so on. Thus, in the latter test there might be little or no relationship between a student's performance on the different types of items. Therefore, the inter-item consistency means that every item in the test has high correlation with every other item of the test.

Interpretation of a Reliability Coefficient. There are three considerations which must be kept in mind while interpreting reliability. First, the reliability of a test as estimated by one technique in one situation and with one example will not be the same as an estimate obtained with a different technique, in a different situation, or with a different sample.

Second, a reliability co-efficient situation is only an estimate of the magnitude of inconsistency in test scores and it does not indicate the causes of the inconsistency.

Third, reliability is not the be-all and end-all of a measuring tool. It is not an end in itself rather a step on a way to that goal.

Relevance and Application

Reliability is a pre-requisite of validity. Reliability is a matter of stability of test scores whereas validity is the correlation of the test with certain outside independent criteria.

Factors which can decrease the Reliability of a Test

(i) Homogeneous grouping of students.
(ii) Guessing.
(iii) Poor testing environment.
(iv) Items having high difficult value.
(v) Items having low discriminating power.

Assessment of Items

Item analysis is a technique of determining whether an item is too easy or too difficult and to what extent it is able to discriminate between high and low achievers. The reliability and validity of any test depends on the reliability and validity of its items.

The item analysis is done both qualitatively and quantitatively.

Facility Value and Discriminating Index of an Item of a Test. Facility value and discriminating index are the two aspects of item analysis. The facility value refers to the number of students who can respond to the item with facility or rightly. Discriminating index indicates test's ability to discriminate between the high and the low achievements.

19

General Practice

Commonly Used Tests may be categorised in two categories:

(i) Diagnostic Tests.

(ii) Achievement Tests.

Difference between Diagnostic Tests and Achievement Test. Diagnostic tests are used in identifying weaknesses of the students and not for finding out the proficiency level of the students.

Meaning of a Diagnostic Test. A diagnostic test is used to find out the difficulties faced by the students in understanding and learning certain concepts and principles. Teaching-learning becomes effective only when the learning difficulties of the students are identified and appropriate steps are taken thereafter to remove them. Generally, we find that difficulties vary from individual to individual, subject to subject and group to group. A diagnostic test pinpoints the types of errors that a student has made.

Common Tests

Following points may be kept in view while selecting and using diagnostic tests:

(1) While selecting a test, specific type of information needed may be kept in view.

(2) A diagnostic test is used to identify the weaknesses in learning, of the students and not their level of proficiency.

(3) A diagnostic test simply indicates the typical errors a students makes. It does not indicate the causes of the

errors. The causes of the errors are inferred from the types of errors made.

(4) Information provided by the diagnostic errors may be supplemented by other tools and techniques of evaluation and measurement.

(5) Diagnostic tests do not have a high validity. Therefore, other tests need to be made use of for having a comprehensive knowledge about the weaknesses of the students.

Age-old System

First Voice against the System. A Calcutta Principal in 1871 said that because of the examinations, "Education is cramming of a large amount of ill digested knowledge" and the students were reduced to "Mere machines of memory".

Hunter Commission and the Calcutta University Commission. These Commissions in very unambiguous terms denounced the system and pointed out its shortcomings.

Sri S.N. Mukherji, Chairman, Examination Section, All India Educational Conference, 1944, observed: "The conclusion is irresistible that education in India dominated by external control and tutelage in the form of fragmentary and unscientific examination has resulted in the perpetuation of mediocrity and retardation of genius, facts which are necessary concomitants, if not inevitable consequences, of the prevailing system."

University Education Commission, presided over by Dr. Radhakrishnan wrote, "For nearly half a century, the examination has been recognised as one of the worst features of Indian Education."

Secondary Education Commission, summarizing the glaring shortcomings of our examination very aptly and emphatically stated, "External examinations are exercising a restricting influence over the entire field of education to such an extent as almost to nullify its real purpose."

WH. Ryburn strongly criticises them when he writes, "It goes without saying that examinations are the enemies of creative work, at least as they are usually conducted."

Significance of Examinations

1. An enemy of true education.
2. An incubus.
3. A blood sucker.
4. A bane of educational system.
5. A necessary evil.
6. A glorification of memory.
7. A begetter of rivalry and strife.
8. A dead hand of education.
9. A growing tyranny.
10. A presumptuous attempt to gauge the depth of human ignorance.
11. An obstacle to learning.

The main defects of examinations are as under:

Examinations Lack Definite Aim. Our examinations are not geared to the realization of specific objectives. The same test serves different purposes like passing a course, admission to the next course, passport to employment, discovering individual capacities, securing scholarship etc., with the result that it becomes invalid for any purpose.

Sultan Mohiyuddin writes, ""Business firms wanting employees look at the results of the examination, the high schools base their admission on it, and government accepts it as a passport to all departments of service; there are no specific, mental or moral traits, and disabilities that the ordinary examination seeks to discover and measures and there is, therefore, no definite guidance it can offer to the professions, business houses and higher educational institutions."

Element of Chance. Element of chance plays an important role and decides the fate of large number of students. It is often found that some students prepare a few selected questions and leave everything to chance. If perchance, the same questions are set in the examination, they pass with credit. The question themes, have they actually attained the requisite standards? Now take the case of another student who has been regular in his work throughout the year. He might not secure as good marks its the one mentioned above. Should we conclude that former is more intelligent than the latter?

Lowering of Educational Standard. According to the Secondary Education Commission, the examination determines not only the content of education but also the methods of teaching, in fact, the entire approach to education. The efficiency of a teacher is judged by the pass percentages of his results. The teachers adopt the trick of the trade to improve their results. 'Idea of exam', the sole aim and 'Cram' the only method, dominates the entire educational system. The students do not feel interested in a subject unless it is included in the examination scheme. They are more interested in notes and guides rather than in text-books with the result that they ignore habits of independent study. Stress is laid on spoon-feeding and pupils are encouraged to memorise facts and vomit them out in the examination.

To quote the Secondary Education Commission, "The present system of examination does not test anything except memory and a certain kind of verbal felicity."

Thomson called them, "a presumptuous attempt to gauge the depth of human ignorance."

Valentine rightly observed, "There is a grave danger of certain studies being crammed and spoilt by the prospect of an examination ahead."

P.C. Wren quotes Sir Oliver Lodge, "External examinations which have to be prepared specially are hampering to the teacher. They tend to keep his attention directed to some artificial and rather than to the immediate object of his work - namely the drawing out and development of the minds committed to his care."

Lowering of Moral Standard. Examinations teach the students different ways of becoming dishonest. Books are smuggled in the examination centres and attempts are made on the life of the supervisors who try to catch the students using unfair means.

Ignoring Qualities of Character. They fail to provide any measure to test the originality, initiative, truthfulness, honesty, sociability of an individual and thus they fail to test real education. Sultan Mohiyuddin writes, "Training in originality and independence of thought, correctness of judgement or reasoning, responsiveness to noble ideas and sentiments and enjoyment of beautiful things - these cease to be the aims of teacher's effort for they are not judged by the traditional examination. Examination is the sole aim and cram the sole method.

Subjectivity. Subjective attitude of examiners influence the marks of individuals and leads to a great variability in marking. Vernon points out, "The same script might receive a different mark if read after instead of before dinner."

Dr. R.K. Singh says, "Our examinations are subjectively weighed and subjectively scored and are not, therefore, dependable indices of pupils' achievements." The Harvard University Commission in England says, "Where the panel of readers (examiners) is large, where thousands of books are being rated, where physical conditions of weather and health are not always under control, and where practically all judgments are subjective, it would be indeed strange if discrepancies in ratings are not numerous; if mistakes are not frequent and costly."

Heavy Mental Strain. Most of the students are in the habit of working strenuously just near the annual examination and this severely tells upon their health, leads to mental dyspepsia and discourages the formation of healthy mental habits.

Develop Frustration. Failures in examinations lead to frustration and even to suicides in some cases.

As a matter of fact, the examinations have met with heavy criticism from all quarters. This criticism is due to the excessive domination of the examination system and a large number of students subjected to it. Candidates complain against the examination system because of its harmful influence on school work; the parents denounce it because of its mental strain; the teachers against the examination because of its injurious effect on the physical and mental health of the children; the practical psychologists speak ill of it because of its unreliability and invalidity and the educational theorists attack it because of its lack of definiteness in aim and purpose.

Measures for Improvement

Introduction of New Types of Tests. Attempts should be made to minimise the subjective element. Essay type of questions should be reduced and supplemented by new-type of objective.

Thought-provoking Questions. Questions should be thought-provoking and evenly distributed over the entire course. Question should be such as to discourage cramming.

Class Work. Due consideration should be given to the regularity of the students in class work.

Appointment of Examiners. The paper-setters and examiners for external examinations should be drawn from the teachers who actually teach subjects in schools.

Viva Voce Tests. External examinations may be supplemented by viva voce tests, if possible.

Standard of Marking. Standard of marking should be prescribed so as to minimise the variability in marking.

Balanced Questions. Difficult as well as easy questions should find a place in the question papers. These should not be either too difficult or too easy.

Monthly Tests. Instead of terminal examinations, a system of monthly tests should exist. However, a recapitulatory test may be held at the end of the year.

Faith in the Teacher. The teacher should be trusted. He should be given a fair opportunity to know and study closely the students he teaches.

Cumulative Records. These should be maintained in respect of all the students.

Grades. In place of numerical marking, the system of symbolic marking be adopted. Five-point scale seems to be the best type of symbolic marking scale i.e., 'A' stands for excellent, 'B' for good, 'C' for fair and average, 'D' for poor and 'E' for very poor.

Examination as Means. Examinations should be regarded as means and not ends. These should be conducted in such a manner that they become effective instruments of education. They should serve as stimulus to learn new facts, gain new experiences, discover weak points and estimate progress.

Oral Examinations. Oral examinations should be held in addition to the written ones. Some qualities like candidate's alertness, intelligence, special interests, mental outlook, his personal qualities of mind and character and his mastery of acquired knowledge can be better tested by viva voce tests than by written examinations.

Variety of Evaluation Techniques. A well-conducted examination should test both the actual attainment and capacity for future achievement. A combination of the traditional examination and carefully constructed intelligence test, therefore, supplies a more reliable means of selecting candidates for higher courses of study than the traditional examination alone.

Demerits and Limitations of the Traditional Question Paper

The traditional question paper is associated with the essay type questions. A question paper of this type suffers from the following limitations:-

(i) It consists of a very limited number of questions from 6 to 10 questions.

(ii) Questions do not cover the major portion of the syllabus.

(iii) Chance element predominates.

(iv) Questions mostly encourage memorisation and cramming.

(v) Options are very often provided. Students are asked to attempt any five or six questions out of ten questions (usually this is the number).

(vi) Directional words like 'State', 'Describe', 'Explain', 'What do you know' and 'Interpret' make the question paper vague. Answers vary to a considerate extent.

(vii) Students depend upon 'guess work'.

(viii) Marking becomes very subjective.

(ix) Standardization of marking becomes very difficult.

Syllabus Covered

The following points may be kept in view while framing right kind of essay form questions:

1. Sufficient time must be devoted by the teacher on the framing of questions. The question should be worded in such a way that content of the answer will be according to the expectations of the teacher in the case of all students.
2. The questions should not be too general and vague. They should define the task for the candidate and indicate clearly the scope of the answer.

3. A large number of short and more specific questions requiring short or limited answers should find a prominent place in the paper and be preferred to a few long and general questions.
4. The time allowed for the examinations should be carefully considered in relation to the amount of writing required on the part of the students. The examination should be so timed that the students are usefully engaged for the whole duration.
5. The questions may be arranged in order of difficulty, i.e., from the easier to the more difficult.
6. Clear instructions to the students regarding the number of questions to be attempted, marks given to each question, or part thereof, and marks reserved for any special purpose, such as diagrams, neatness, etc., may be given in the beginning of the question paper.
7. As far as possible, equal marks may be allotted to each question.
8. Choice may not be provided in a question paper. However, if provided, it should be within a section, in which case one of the alternatives provided in the question has to be attempted and the pupil cannot leave out the question altogether.
9. Question paper may be reviewed before it is handed over to the person concerned. Quite a few points may strike the paper setter on this second reading. A paper setter should safeguard his reputation as a setter by taking all the care that is possible at the beginning.
10. Questions should be framed in such a way that they test different abilities of a student.
11. A key and marking scheme should be provided.

Purposes of Essay Questions. Following purposes are usually envisaged:

(i) Power of selective recall of information.
(ii) Capacity of comparison and contrast.
(iii) Ability of establishing relationships.
(iv) Power of interpretation and application.
(v) Ability of creative thinking.
(vi) Ability of problem solving.

Types of Essay Questions. Some of the commonly used types of essay questions are given below.

1. Selective recall.
   e.g. What was the religious policy of Ashoka?
2. Evaluative recall.
   e.g. Why did the Marathas fail against the English?
3. Comparison of two things.
   e.g. Compare the contributions made by Kanishka and Harsha to Buddhism.
4. Comparison of two things.
   e.g. Compare Early Vedic Age with the Later Vedic Age.
5. Decision-for or against.
   e.g. Which type of questions do you think are more reliable—Essay or objective. Why?
6. Causes or effects.
   e.g. Discuss the effects of population explosion on India.
7. Summary of some unit of the text or of some article.
   Summarise the main events of the reign of Harsha.
8. Analysis.
   e.g. What was the role played by Subhas Chandra Bose in India's freedom struggle?
9. Statement of relationship.
   What is the relationship between demand and supply of a commodity?
10. Illustration of principles in science, language, etc.
    e.g. Illustrate the principle of demand and supply.
11. Application of rules or principles in given situations.
    When does the Law of Diminishing Return operate?
12. Discussion.
    Discuss the essentials of the success of democracy. Why did Chanakya write 'Arthashastra'?
13. Statement of author's aim.
14. Criticism - Give a critical analysis of Ala-ud-Din's economic policy.
15. Outline the steps followed by Akbar in his religious policy.
16. Describe the main events of the reign of Muhammad Tughlaq?

Criterion of a Good Essay Type Question Paper

Following are the characteristics of a good essay type question paper:

1. Does it give appropriate weightage to instructional objectives?
2. Does it provide balanced weightage to the content units?
3. Does it accord due weightage to all types of questions?
4. Does it include internal options in place of external options?
5. Does it show large variations in the difficult levels of questions?
6. Is the language of question easy, simple and understandable?
7. Are all questions in the question paper well worded ?
8. Does it contain questions relevant to content?
9. Is its arrangements of questions suitable?
10. Is its format proper ?
11. Is there a complete comparability between English and Hindi and regional language versions of the question paper?
12. Does it contain clear general instructions to students?
13. Does it indicate the scope and credit for each question.?
14. Does it contain 20% easy, 60% average and 20% difficult questions.

Main Characteristics of a Good Question (All Forms of Questions)

1. It should measure a single specific objective or a learning outcome.
2. It should sample a significant content area.
3. It should state the subject matter in a correct and accurate way.
4. It should be within the scope of the syllabus or textbook.
5. Its form should be suitable.
6. It should be set at the desired level of difficulty.
7. It should be well within the comprehension of the pupils.

8. It can be attempted within a reasonable length of time.
9. It should provide an appropriate testing situation.
10. It should set the task of pinpointing almost a definite.
11. It should be worded in a clear, precise, simple and unambiguous language.
12. It should exclude very difficult and unfamiliar word or term.
13. It should be concise enough and avoid unnecessary reading load.
14. It should be free from superfluous words or terms.
15. It should communicate the intent of the item written effectively.
16. It should use the most appropriate directional word (e.g. classify, enumerate, list etc.).
17. It should be translated into regional languages without distorting sentence structure and its import.

Specimen of a Good Question Paper

Coverage of the Course. It should be set in such a way that it covers nearly 75 percent of the syllabus.

Learning Objectives. It should include questions relating to various instructional objectives/learning outcomes as shown below:

S. No.	*Objectives*	*Marks*	*% of Marks*
1.	Knowledge	30	30%
2.	Understanding	45	45%
3.	Understanding	15	15%
4.	Skill	10	10%

Weightage to Form of Questions. It should be shown below :

S. No.	*Form of Question*	*Marks for each Question*	*% of Marks*
1.	Essay type or long answer	8	32
2.	Short answer	8	40
3.	Objective type or very short answer	9	18
4.	Map	1 or 2 as the case be	10
			100

Expected Length of Each Question. It is shown below:

- Long Answer Upto 200 words each
- Short Answer Upto 100 words each
- Objective or very short answer upto 30 words each.

(Note: Slight changes may be made according to the requirement of a particular subject.

Weightage to Difficulty Level of Questions. It is given below:

(a) Easy	15%
(b) Average	70%
(c) Difficult	15%

Sample of a Good Question Paper

Class X

SOCIAL SCIENCE

Time Allowed: 3 hours Maximum Marks: 100

General Instructions

1. The question paper is divided into 4 sections namely :

Section A-History	35 marks
Section B-Civics	20 marks
Section C-Geography	35 marks
Section D-Economics	10 marks

2. All questions are compulsory.
3. All questions of each section must be attempted together at one place.
4. Write the same question number as given in the question paper while answering a question in your answer book.
5. (i) Answer to questions of 1 mark should not exceed 20 words each.
   (ii) Answer to questions of 2 marks should not exceed 30 words each.
   (iii) Answer to questions of 3 marks should not exceed 60 words each.
   (iv) Answer to questions of 4 marks should not exceed 80 words each.

(v) Answer to questions of 5/6 marks should not exceed 100/120 words each.

6. Stencils or templates for drawing outline maps may be used wherever necessary.
7. Attach the maps provided within the answer book.

SECTION A - HISTORY

1. What is meant by cutting of 'Chinese melon'? 2
2. What was the condition of the non-Russian minorities in Russia before the Russian revolution. 2
3. Which were the countries that signed the Anti-Comintern Pact? Why was this Pact signed? 2
4. In the eighteenth century, in India, social and religious reform movements were linked with each other. What were the reasons for the same? 2
5. Mention the reasons for conflict in the Balkan region. 4

   Or

   Mention the reasons behind U.S.A.'s entry into the First World War.
6. Trace in brief the nationalist movement in Turkey between the two World Wars. 4

   Or

   After the Second World War, why did the newly independent countries of Asia and Africa choose to remain non-aligned?
7. Explain the contribution of Swami Vivekananda to the Indian reform movement. 4

   Or

   Explain the ills of the Indian society in the eighteenth century.
8. Trace the many changes of historical importance that have taken place in the Soviet Union in recent years. 6

   Or

   Trace the main changes that have taken place in Germany after the Second World War.

9. Evaluate the influence of socialistic ideas on the Indian national movement. 6

Or

Assess the importance of the Civil Disobedience Movement in the Indian freedom struggle.

10. On the given outline map of India, mark the following: 3
    (i) The place where the Prarthana Samaj was founded.
    (ii) The headquarters of the Theosophical Society.
    (iii) The place where the Mohammedan Anglo-Oriental College was established.

Or

On the given outline map of the world, mark any three countries that were responsible for starting the Non-Aligned Movement.

Note. The following questions are for BLIND CANDIDATES only in lieu of Q. No. 10.
(i) Where was the Prarthana Samaj founded?
(ii) Where is the headquarters of the Theosophical Society?
(iii) Where was the Mohammedan Anglo-Oriental College established?

Or

Name any three countries which were responsible for starting the Non-Aligned Movement.

SECTION B - CIVICS

11. Giving two examples of minorities, mention why minorities should be protected in a democracy. 2
12. Mention any two features of a nation. 2
13. Suggest any three measures to remove economic inequality in India. 3
14. Explain the importance of electronic mass media today. 3
15. Analyse India's relations with U.S.A. 4
16. Explain a Money Bill. How is it passed in the Indian Parliament?

Or

Why is the Prime Minister called 'First among equals'? What are his/her functions?

SECTION C - GEOGRAPHY

17. In the given outline map of India, locate the following carefully with appropriate symbols and write the name of each item near its location: 5x1=5
18. One area under canal irrigation in delta regions.
19. Study the data given below carefully and answer the following questions: 2x1=2

Temperature and Rainfall Data (BANGALORE)
Temperature: Mean Monthly in Celsius Degrees
Rainfall: Average Rain in Milimetres

Months	Jan.	Feb.	Mar.	Apr.	May	June	July	Aug.	Sept.	Oct.	Nov.	Dec.	Annual
Tempe.	20.5	22.7	25.2	27.1	26.7	24.2	23.0	23.0	23.1	22.9	18.9	20.2	
Rainfall	7	9	11	45	107	71	111	137	164	153	61	13	889

(19.1) Name the raniest and driest months.

(19.2) Find out annual range of temperature. Show calculations also.

20. Explain three measures to increase marine fish catch in India. 3x1=3
21. Name major vegetation regions to which Date-palm and Mahogany trees belong. Name two projects which were established to protect endangered species of wild life. Give two characteristics of Laterite Soils. 1+1+1=3
22. Name the longest irrigation canal of the world built in north west India. How is it a boon to the people of that region? Give one point. Northern plains are densely populated. Write one reason for it. 1+1+1=3
23. Explain the role of handloom, power loom, composite textile mills and spinning mills in Indian Cotton Textile Industry. Write one point of each. 4x1=4
24. Explain four measures to reduce growing pressure on Indian Railways. 4x1=4
25. In which hemisphere does India lie with reference to Prime Meridian? Mention the value of the standard Meridian of India. How did northern plains come to existence? Write three points briefly. 1/2+1/2+3 = 4

26. Describe in detail 'coal' under following heads: 3+1+1=5
    (a) Distribution of coal (excluding lignite) in India.
    (b) Demerits of Indian coal (any two).
    (c) Need of conservation of coal (two points).

SECTION D-ECONOMICS

27. Explain how important are 'non-factory manufacturing units', 'FERA Companies', 'MRTP Companies' and 'Private enter-prises' in India's present industrial structure. Give four points. 4x1=4
28. Scarcity of essential goods, so far as market supply is concerned, arises from three sources in our economy. Write about these three sources briefly. 3x1=3
29. How far land tenure system is responsible for the backwardness of Indian agriculture? Write three points. 3x1=3
    (Based on the pattern of CBSE, Delhi)

Achievement Test Available in India and Abroad

1. Academic Achievement Motivation Test (Hindi) by T.R. Sharma
2. Achievement Motivation Test (Hindi) by V.P. Bhargava
3. An Achievement Test in Hindi for Class VIII, Central Institute of Education, Delhi
4. Achievement Values and Anxiety Inventory (English/Hindi) by Prayag Mehta
5. Adult Education Achievement Test by VV. Malaya
6. Coimbatore Achievement Test (Social Studies) by R.K. Mission
7. Coimbatore Standard Test in English by A. Aram and R. Rangaswamy
8. English Test Part I and II (Spelling Test), B.H. College, Agra
9. General Classroom Achievement Test by A.K. Singh and A. Sen Gupta

10. General Science Achievement Test by J.S. Gupta
11. Hindi Achievement Test by L.N. Dubey
12. Mathematics Test (Arithmetic, Algebra and Geometry), B.R. College, Agra
13. Mohsin's Scholastic Attainment Test in General Science for Class VII (Hindi), Educational and Vocational Guidance Bureau, Patna, Bihar
14. Mother Tongue Test (Hindi) by B.K. Srivastava
15. Statistics Achievement Test (Hindi) by R.C. Deva
16. Vigyan Pariksha (General Science Test) for Class VIII by S.L. Saxena

General Achievement Tests (Foreign)

General achievement test batteries may broadly be classified as under:

Achievement Batteries intended to measure achievement in many scholastic areas such as languages, mathematics and social sciences etc.

Achievement Batteries to measure achievement in basic skills such as reading and spelling etc.

Stanford Achievement Test Battery. This battery was first published in 1923 and revised in 1929. It is meant for grades seven and consists of 9 tests and takes 227 minutes. Norms have been provided in age and percentiles. The 9 tests relate to (i) Paragraph meaning (ii) Word meaning (iii) Spelling (iv) Language (v) Arithmetic computation (vi) Arithmetic reasoning (vii) social studies (viii) Science (ix) Study skills.

Every-pupil Tests of Basic Skills. This battery measures basic skills like reading, comprehension, vocabulary, map reading, use of dictionary, index and references, reading of charts, graphs and tables, punctuation, spellings and vocabulary. It is meant for grades 5 to 9. It takes 268 minutes. Pupil-norms and percentile grade norms are available.

1. California Achievement Test.
2. Iowa High School Content Examination Battery.
3. Cooperation Achievement Tests.

4. Willing Scale for Measurement Written Language.
5. Iowa Grammar Information Test.
6. Iowa Language Abilities Test.
7. Los Angeles Diagnostic Test in Language.
8. Iowa Silent Reading Tests.
9. California Reading Tests.
10. Michigan Speed of Reading Test.
11. The Brown-Carlsen Listening Comprehension Test.
12. Iowa Spelling Test.
13. American Handwriting Scale, prepared by P.V. West in 1929.
14. Thorndike Handwriting Scale for Children.
15. Seattle Algebra Test.
16. Seattle Plan Geometry Test.
17. Nelson Biology Test.
18. Cooperative History Test.

Bank for Questions

The question bank is a planned library containing questions, tests or other assessment material to be used by students, teachers and evaluators of the teaching-earning process. Material to be banked in the question bank. Following types of material is banked in the question bank.

(i) Objective type question.
(ii) Short answer and structured questions.
(iii) Essay type questions in some cases.
(iv) Tests of different types.
(v) Practical tests.
(vi) Assignments.
(vii) Projects.
(viii) Exercises.
(ix) Marking schemes.

The Advantages

(1) Questions can be used at all stages of the teaching-learning process i.e. introduction, development and assignments (including home assignments).

(2) Preparing question papers for weekly, monthly and terminal tests etc.
(3) Preparing question papers for summative evaluation.
(4) Framing a unit or topic test for formative evaluation.
(5) Diagnosing learners difficulties.
(6) Saving energy, time and thinking that are used into setting good question papers.
(7) Undertaking statistical analysis of evaluation, and assessing its worthwhileness.
(8) Ensuring the comparability of academic standards from year to year. It is possible to compare the performance of two groups of learners on questions which they both attempted.

Preparation of Questions. Questions for the question banks, as far as possible should be prepared by practicing teachers in workshops conducted by experts. Enrichment of question banks by updating, discarding, replacing, modifying and adding new questions should be a continuous process.

Progress in Question Banks. The CBSE, Delhi has taken the initiative in publishing question banks for the secondary and senior secondary examinations.

For the higher education stage, the Association of Indian Universities, New Delhi, has published several Question Banks in about 30 subjects. Private publishers have flooded the market for question banks of all sorts at the school level.

Unwritten Examination

Oral examinations have been in existence since time immemorial, The oral examinations date back to the beginning of human language. Oral examinations were in vogue during the Vedic period in India. An oral examination implies face to face question-answer activity between the evaluator and the learner. The evaluator asks questions and the learner attempts to answer them.

Forms of Oral Examinations

These are : (i) Group discussion (ii) Intervi^w (iii) Debate (iv) Quiz contest (v) Viva-voice. (vi) Asking spellings etc.

The Purposes

(i) To evaluate learner's mannerism.

(ii) To evaluate learner's spontaneity.

(iii) To evaluate learners insight that directs and focuses his skill in critically analysing a problem.

(iv) To evaluate the spoken power of the learner.

(v) To evaluate the soundness of the knowledge acquired by the learner, through various forms of questions.

(vi) To diagnose learner's limitations and weaknesses and to take remedial measures.

(vii) To supplement the information obtained through other evaluation techniques.

(viii) To evaluate learner's cognitive, affective and psychomotor abilities.

Limitations

(1) They are time consuming.

(2) They tend to be subjective.

(3) It is very difficult to maintain uniformity in evaluation.

(4) Oral examinations provide lot of scope for favouratism.

(5) They are very expensive.

(6) An examiner is likely to be put under great pressure from different sources.

(7) Several influences may lower the validity of the oral examinations.

(8) Oral examinations may work to the advantage of the highly articulate learners.

(9) Gradually the sampling of the learner's knowledge and understanding becomes very narrow.

Written Response Test

A written response test is somewhere between the traditional examination (oral-response) and the written examination. In this type of test, the questions are presented by the evaluator by the use of the spoken word and are answered in writing by the learner. Dictation in languages may be considered as a form of written response test. Oral questions can be asked in almost all subjects and the students asked to write the answers.

Merits

(i) It is a handy technique for the classroom teacher.

(ii) It can be used to evaluate several learners simultaneously.

(iii) Spelling skills of the learners can be measured by the teacher pronouncing the words and the students writing them on a sheet of paper.

(iv) It is very convenient in the ordinary situation when there is paucity of resources.

(v) It is very helpful to evaluate the auditory comprehension of the learner.

Limitations

(1) Skill of the learner in writing tends to vitiate evaluation.

(2) It is not purposeful in the case of handicapped students.

(3) It is of little use in evaluating communicating skills.

The Practicals

A practical test measures the development of the practical skills of the learner in the teaching of science subjects, vocational courses like carpentry, tailoring, typing etc. It plays a significant role in professional courses like engineering, medicine and teaching.

Need for Prac..cal Tests. Following are the factors which necessitate the use of practical tests in evaluation.

(1) Without practical skills, proficiency in certain subjects like sciences, professional, technical and vocational courses cannot be achieved. In fact without practical work, some subjects have little utility.

(2) Theoretical aspects of some subjects can be explained and comprehended through practical work only.

(3) Practical work involves the application of knowledge.

(4) Practical work introduces, develops and reinforces theoretical concepts.

Measures to Improve the Reliability and Validity

(1) Listing clearly the objectives of practical work in terms of process of performance and product of performance.

(2) Ensuring coverage of various content areas of the prescribed syllabus.
(3) Assigning adequate weightage to processes.
(4) Ensuring uniformity of testing conditions for conducting the practicals.
(5) Issuing uniform instruction to examiners.
(6) Ensuring comparability of question papers.

Concluding Observations. In spite of improvement in practical evaluation, its objectivity still remains questionable. There are numerous cases when there is no correlation between the theoretical and practical performance of the learners. Several influences are at work to vitiate the results of practical evaluation.

20

Conclusion

Education is considered as an investment in human beings in terms of development of human resources, skills, motivation, knowledge and the like. Evaluation of both the processes and products of education becomes imperative not only to convince as to what business is going on in the whole education enterprise, but also and more seriously, to know as to what extent the goals of education have been achieved. In short, it helps build an educational programme, assess its achievements and improve upon its effectiveness. It serves as an in-built monitor within the programme to review, from time to time, the progress in learning. It also provides valuable feedback on the design and the implementation of the programme.

Thus, the role that evaluation plays in any educational programme is significant. With this brief introduction we shall now look into concept and role of educational evaluation.

The evaluation process ascertains the work-ability of learning experiences and change of behaviour of the students. The term evaluation conveys several meanings in education and psychology. The evaluation is both qualitative as well as quantitative process. The term evaluation has been defined in the following manner:

According to Bradfield and Moredock, "Evaluation is an assignment of symbols to a phenomenon in order to characterise the worth of value of a phenomenon usually with reference to some social, cultural or scientific standard."

According to Hanna, "Evaluation is the process of gathering and interpreting evidence on changes in the behaviour of all students as they progress through school."

Writingstone states in the Encyclopaedia of Educational Research that, "Evaluation is a relatively new technical term introduced to designate a more comprehensive concept of measurement that is implied in conventional tests and examinations."

It is evident from the above definitions that evaluation in educational context implies broad programme than the examination in which achievements, attitudes, interests, personality traits and skills factors are taken into consideration. Thus, cognitive, affective and psychomotor learning outcome are measured in the evaluation process. The success and failure of teaching depends upon teaching strategies, tactics and aids. Thus, evaluation approach improves the instructional procedure. Glaser's basic model of teaching refers to this step as a feedback function. This step provides an empirical basis to modify and improve the teaching-learning situations. There are three main functions of this step

(1) Evaluation of the learning system.
(2) Measuring learning and
(3) Managing by learning objectives.

A teacher can turn his unsuccessful teaching into successful with the knowledge and application of these functions. There are two distinct situations where the 'Evaluation' is being used in relation to education. This is to avoid any likely confusion that you may have regarding the concept of evaluation that we are concerned with in this. The two distinct situations are

(i) Evaluation in an Educational Programme (EIEP), and
(ii) Evaluation of an Educational Programme (EOEP).

The EIEP is concerned with the product of education, i.e.. the question of the extent or the quality of education achieved. But the concern of EOEP is more with the process and product relationship in education, i.e., with the question of how effective a process of education is in achieving a desired product. As such EOEP is more a concern of educational planners rather than of the people at the lower range of an educational system. To make it simple, EOEP is not a part of the daily affair of a teacher or a learner; it is the job of educational planners, administrators and researchers. It is not part of any educational programme as EIEP is. The EOEP stays outside a programme and observes the working of the Programme and its components (including EIEP). With its observations, EOEP helps in shaping, revising and replacing educational programmes to achieve better results.

A well-planned and well-executed EIEP, while serving its purposes, can serve the purposes of EOEP also. It can provide a sound basis for an overall evaluation of the efficacy of an educational programme. But when the purpose is to assess the worth of specific constituents of an educational programme, such as the relevance of objectives, the usefulness of instructional materials, the effectiveness of the techniques of presentation etc., EOEP has to resort to tools and criteria different from those of EIEP. Considering the immediacy of our needs in this system, we have, by and large, restricted ourselves to EIEP, which is almost a daily concern of teachers.

Besides the contexts of use of the term 'evaluation', there is another source which is likely to cause confusion. It is the use of the terms 'evaluation', 'measurement' and 'test'. Do these different terms mean one and the same ? Very often they are assumed to do so and are used as though they are synonymous and mutually interchangeable. But the fact is that they carry different functional meaning and as such one cannot replace another without causing considerable damage to the sense conveyed. What do the terms 'measurement' and 'test' mean ?

Measurement is a part of the process of Evaluation. When we assign a score on a given task performed by a learner, we are doing an act of measurement. When we compare this score with those of other learners and judge whether it is good/bad/average or satisfactory/unsatisfactory, we are doing the act of Evaluation. Thus evaluation is a wider and more inclusive term than measurement.

Here is an illustration. To say "Suresh clocked -100 meters in 112 seconds" is a report of measurement. But to say "Suresh took a lesser time than everyone else" is an evaluation.

Test is a device to obtain measurement in education. It is one among the several devices like holding interviews, competitions and group- discussions or assigning projects, assignments etc. that can be used to measure a given characteristic with an individual. But it is of greater practical utility than most others and therefore the most commonly used form of measurement in education. A test usually presents a uniform set of tasks to all members of a given group at a scheduled time with a due prior notice. Sometimes unannounced tests are possible and useful in classroom situations.

We should also mention that the term 'Assessment' is used more or less in the same sense as evaluation.

The term 'Evaluation', is used in Education for two purpose. The evaluation term is used for measuring the learning system and learning objectives at the end of a course. The evaluation is also used as an Approach of Education which is advocated by B.S. Bloom, it is known as tripolar process-educational objectives, learning experiences and change of behaviour or evaluation procedure. It refers that teaching and learning should be objective centered. In the teacher-education programme, the design of lesson plan is based on the concept of evaluation approach.

The modern concept of evaluation assigns it a wider and more vital scope of use. Its treats evaluation is one of the three major components of an educational programme, the other two being the educational objectives and the learning experiences. Each of these components play the dual role of the beneficiary and the benefactor with the other two of the components. In other words, each of the components gains its sustenance from the other, while at the same time each contributes to the strength of the other two components.

The effectiveness of the programme depends on how effectively the dual-role between the components is materialised. . Put in this perspective, evaluation procedures serve as a tool not to measure the extent of achievement of the educational objectives but also to develop, review and modify suitably the educational objectives and the learning experiences in an on-going process. Of course, the evaluation procedures too get developed, reviewed, and modified by the educational objectives and the learning experiences.

The evaluation procedures in this scheme of inter-related network, then may take the initial, intermediary and terminal position in the course of activities of a given educational programme. In an ideal programme evaluation will take all the three positions. But at each position its purpose and function will be different. At the initial position it may be to identify the learner's ability at the course-entry level so that learning experiences to be given to the course entrant may be designed in appropriate qualitative and quantitative chunks. At the intermediary position it may help the teacher to check the effectiveness of the course, the achievement of the learner, and his pace of learning; thereby it may help both the teacher and the learner to monitor the progress of learning towards the set objectives. At the terminal level it may help to ascertain the achievement of the set goals and also to grade learners on their attainment.

This may give you a broad suggestion as to the purpose and function of educational evaluation. If you work out this suggestion further in the practical situations of education, you may identify a number of specific purposes and functions related to them. We have given below the most common purposes and the related functions for which evaluation is used within educational systems.

The evaluation process produces the data for cognitive, affective and psychomotor objectives. The traditional examinations confine to cognitive objectives only. In this way, the evaluation is more broad process. The various types of techniques are used in it.

(a) The oral, written, essay type, objective type, practical examination and observation techniques are used for evaluation of the cognitive objectives.

(b) The interest inventory, attitude scale, values test and observation techniques are employed for appraising the affective objectives.

(c) The performance test, practical examination and observation techniques are employed for assessing the psychomotor objectives.

The criterion test is used rather than achievement test, because criterion test concerns with objectives of teaching and instruction whereas achievement test concerns with content coverage. There are three major characteristics of a criterion test or techniques of evaluation.

The Criterion test must cover the terminal behaviour of teaching or instruction. Each item of the criterion should assess a specific objective. The criterion behaviour should represent the total terminal behaviours.

Additional Reading

Bhaskara Rao, Digumarti (1994). *Scientific Aptitude*, New Delhi: Ashish Publishing House. ISBN 81-7024-658-X.

Bhaskara Rao, Digumarti (1995). *Animal Kingdom*. New Delhi: Discovery Publishing House. ISBN 81-7141-274-2.

Bhaskara Rao, Digumarti (1995). *Batracology*. New Delhi: Discovery Publishing House. ISBN 81-7141-279-3.

Bhaskara Rao, Digumarti (1997), *Scientific Attitude*. New Delhi: Discovery Publishing House. ISBN 81-7141-308-0.

Bhaskara Rao, Digumarti (1996). *Scientific Attitude vis-à-vis Scientific Aptitude*. New Delhi: Discovery Publishing House. ISBN 81-7141-308-0.

Bhaskara Rao, Digumarti, Editor (1996). *Encyclopaedia of Education for All*, 5 Volumes. New Delhi: APH Publishing Corporation. ISBN 81-7024-759-4 (set).

Vol. I *Education for All: The World Conference*. ISBN 81-7024-760-8.

Vol. II *Education for All: The EPA-9 Summit*. ISBN 81-7024-761-6.

Vol. III *Education for All: Quality Education for All*. ISBN 81-7024-762-6.

Vol. IV *Education for All: Planning and Monitoring*. ISBN 81-7024-763-4.

Vol. V *Education for All: The Indian Scenario*. ISBN 81-7024-764-0.

Bhaskara Rao, Digumarti, Editor (1996). *Global Perceptions on Peace Education*, 3 Volumes. New Delhi: Discovery Publishing House. ISBN 81-7141-319-6.

Bhaskara Rao, Digumarti, Editor (1996). *National Policy on Education*. 2 Volumes. New Delhi: Anmol Publications Pvt. Ltd. ISBN 81-7488-323-1.

Bhaskara Rao, Digumarti, Editor (1997). *Care the Child*, 2 Volumes. New Delhi: Discovery Publishing House. ISBN 81-7141-394-3.

Bhaskara Rao, Digumarti, Editor (1997). *Education for the 21st Century*. New Delhi: Discovery Publishing House. ISBN 81-7141-389-7.

Bhaskara Rao, Digumarti, Editor (1997). *Reflections on Scientific Attitude*. New Delhi: Discovery Publishing House, ISBN 81-7141-319-6.

Bhaskara Rao, Digumarti, Editor (1997). *Success Story of a Primary Education Project*. New Delhi: APH Publishing Corporation. ISBN 81-7024-850-7.

Bhaskara Rao, Digumarti, Editor (1997). *World Food Summit*. New Delhi: Discovery Publishing House. ISBN 81-7141-386-2.

Bhaskara Rao, Digumarti, Editor (1998). *Adolescence Education*. New Delhi: Discovery Publishing House. ISBN 81-7141-432-X.

Bhaskara Rao, Digumarti, Editor (1998). *Community and School Nutrition Education*. New Delhi: Discovery Publishing House. ISBN 81-7141-435-4.

Bhaskara Rao, Digumarti, Editor (1998). *District Primary Education Programme*. New Delhi: Discovery Publishing House. ISBN 81-7141-396-X.

Bhaskara Rao, Digumarti, Editor (1998). *Earth Summit*, 2 Volumes. New Delhi: Discovery Publishing House. ISBN 81-7141-435-4.

Bhaskara Rao, Digumarti, Editor (1998). *National Policy on Education: Towards an Enlightened and Humane Society*, New Delhi: Discovery Publishing House. ISBN 81-7141-426-5.

Bhaskara Rao, Digumarti, Editor (1998). *Reforming School Education*. New Delhi: Discovery Publishing House. ISBN 81-7141-403-6.

Bhaskara Rao, Digumarti, Editor (1998). *Teacher Education in India*. New Delhi: Discovery Publishing House. ISBN 81-7141-406-0.

Bhaskara Rao, Digumarti, Editor (1998). *World Summit for Social Development*. New Delhi: Discovery Publishing House. ISBN 81-7141-420-6.

Bhaskara Rao, Digumarti, Editor (2000). *Education for All: Achieving the Goal*, 3 Volumes, New Delhi: APH Publishing Corporation. ISBN 81-7648-152-1.

Vol. I *The Global Consensus*. ISBN 81-7648-155-6.

Vol. II *Mid-Decade Review Reports of Regional Seminars*. ISBN 81-7648-154-8.

Vol. III *Issues and Trends*. ISBN 81-7648-155-6.

Bhaskara Rao, Digumarti, Editor (2000), *International Encyclopaedia of AIDS*, 11 Volumes in 13 Parts. New Delhi: Discovery Publishing House. ISBN 81-7141-6 (Set).

Vol. 1 *Introduction to HIV/AIDS*. ISBN 81-7141-523-7.

Vol. 2 *HIV/AIDS—Issues and Challenges*, 2 Parts. ISBN 81-7141-524-5.

Vol. 3 *HIV/AIDS—Socio Economic Realities*. ISBN 81-7141-524-3.

Vol. 4 *HIV/AIDS—Law Ethics and Human Rights*, 2 Parts. ISBN 81-7141-526-1.

Vol. 5 *AIDS and NGOs*. ISBN 81-7141-527-X.

Vol. 6 *AIDS and Home Care*. ISBN 81-7141-528-8.

Vol. 7 *STD Case Management*. ISBN 81-7141-529-6.

Vol. 8 *HIV/AIDS Prevention and Care—Teaching Modules for Nurses and Midwives*. ISBN 81-7141-530-X.

Vol. 9 *HIV Prevention Education for Education for Educational Institutions*. ISBN 81-7141-531-8.

Vol. 10 *Instructional Modules for AIDS Education*. ISBN 81-7141-532-6.

Vol. 11 *School Health Education to Prevent AIDS and STD—A Package for Curriculum Planners*. ISBN 81-7141-5338-4.

Bhaskara Rao, Digumarti, Editor (2000). *International Encyclopaedia of Science and Technology Education*, 11 Volumes. New Delhi: Discovery Publishing House. ISBN 81-7141-548-2 (Set).

Vol. 1 *Science and Technology Education*. ISBN 81-7141-568-7.

Vol. 2 *Science Education in Developing Countries*. ISBN 81-7141-570-9.

Vol. 3 *Organisational Structure of Science*. ISBN 81-7141-570-9.

Vol. 4 *Science Education in Asia and the Pacific*. ISBN 81-7141-571-7.

Vol. 5 *Science and Technology Education for All*. ISBN 81-7141-572-5.

Vol. 6 *Values, Ethics, Talent and Girls in Science and Technology Education*. ISBN 81-7141-573-3.

Vol. 7 *Popularization of Science and Technology Education*. ISBN 81-7141-574-1.

Vol. 8 *Science, Power and Society*. ISBN 81-7141-575-X.

Vol. 9 *Information Technology*. ISBN 81-7141-576-8.

Vol. 10 *Teacher Training in Science and Technology Education*. ISBN 81-7141-577-6.

Vol. 11 *Teacher Training in Science and Technology: A Curriculum Framework*. ISBN 81-7141-578-4.

Bhaskara Rao, Digumarti, Editor (2001). *Distance Education in Different Countries*. New Delhi: APH Publishing Corporation. ISBN 81-7648-229-3.

Bhaskara Rao, Digumarti, Editor (2001). *Decentralised Management of Education (Management of Education in Panchayati Raj and Municipal Bodies)*. New Delhi: Discovery Publishing House. ISBN 81-7141-617-9.

Bhaskara Rao, Digumarti, Editor (2001). *Electrochemistry for Environmental Protection*. New Delhi: Discovery Publishing House. ISBN 81-7141-619-5.

Bhaskara Rao, Digumarti, Editor (2001). *Global Educational Studies*. New Delhi: Discovery Publishing House. ISBN 81-7141-616-0.

Bhaskara Rao, Digumarti, Editor (2001). *Global Synthesis of Educational Assessment*. New Delhi: Discovery Publishing House. ISBN 81-7141-613-6.

Bhaskara Rao, Digumarti, Editor (2000). *International Encyclopaedia of Human Rights*. 7 Volumes in 13 Parts. New Delhi: Discovery Publishing House. (Royal Size). ISBN 81-7141-567-9 (Set).

Vol. 1 *International Instruments of Human Rights*, 2 Parts. ISBN 81-7141-595-4.

Vol. 2 *Regional Instruments of Human Rights*. ISBN 81-7141-604-7.

Vol. 3 *Human Rights and the United Nations*, 2 Parts. ISBN 81-7141-605-5.

Vol. 4 *Fact Files of Human Rights*, 3 Parts. ISBN 81-7141-605-3.

Vol. 5 *Study Stories of Human Rights*, 3 Parts. ISBN 81-7141-607-3.

Vol. 6 *International Meetings on Human Rights*, 2 Parts. ISBN 81-7141-608-X.

Vol. 7 *Professional Training in Human Rights*. ISBN 81-7141-609-8.

Bhaskara Rao, Digumarti, Editor (2001). *Jomtein Decade of Education*. New Delhi: Discovery Publishing House. ISBN 81-7141-618-7.

Bhaskara Rao, Digumarti, Editor (2001). *Nuclear Materials: Issues and Concerns*, 2 Volumes. New Delhi: Discovery Publishing House. ISBN 81-7141-611-X.

Bhaskara Rao, Digumarti, Editor (2001). *World Conference on Education for All*. New Delhi: APH Publishing Corporation. ISBN 81-7141-274-9.

Bhaskara Rao, Digumarti, Editor (2001). *World Conference on Higher Education*, New Delhi: Discovery Publishing House. ISBN 81-7141-610-1.

Bhaskara Rao, Digumarti, Editor (2001). *World Conference on Science*. New Delhi: Discovery Publishing House. ISBN 81-7141-612-8.

Bhaskara Rao, Digumarti, Editor (2003). *Inspiring Experience in Teacher Education*. New Delhi: Discovery Publishing House. ISBN 81-7141-656-X.

Bhaskara Rao, Digumarti, Editor (2003). *International Studies in Education*, 3 Volumes, New Delhi: Discovery Publishing House. ISBN 81-7141-647-0.

Bhaskara Rao, Digumarti, Editor (2003). *Military Conversion: Impact on Science and Technology*, New Delhi: Discovery Publishing House. ISBN 81-7141-578-4.

Bhaskara Rao, Digumarti, Editor (2003). *United Nations Millennium Summit*. New Delhi: Discovery Publishing House. ISBN 81-7141-632-2.

Bhaskara Rao, Digumarti, Editor (2003). *World Assembly on Aging*. New Delhi: Discovery Publishing House. ISBN 81-7141-637-3.

Bhaskara Rao, Digumarti, Editor (2004). *World Conference on Human Rights*. New Delhi: Discovery Publishing House. ISBN 81-7141-661-6.

Bhaskara Rao, Digumarti, Editor (2003). *World Education Forum*. New Delhi: Discovery Publishing House. ISBN 81-7141-639-X.

Bhaskara Rao, Digumarti, Editor (2004). *Education Employment and Human Resource Development*. New Delhi: Discovery Publishing House. ISBN 81-7141-681-0.

Bhaskara Rao, Digumarti, Editor (2004). *Successfully Schooling*. New Delhi: Discovery Publishing House. ISBN 81-7141-677-2.

Bhaskara Rao, Digumarti, Editor (2004). *European Education and Teachers*. New Delhi: Discovery Publishing House. ISBN 81-7141-702-7.

Bhaskara Rao, Digumarti, Editor (2004). *Teachers in a Changing World*. New Delhi: Discovery Publishing House. ISBN 81-7141-694-2.

Bhaskara Rao, Digumarti, Editor (2004). *Learning to Live Together*, 4 Volumes. New Delhi: Discovery Publishing House.

Vol. 1 *International Conference on Learning to Live Together.*

Vol. 2 *Globalisation and Living Together.*

Vol. 3 *Curriculum for Learning to Live Together.*

Vol. 4 *Science Education for the Contemporary Society.*

Bhaskara Rao, Digumarti (2004). *International Guidelines on Open and Distance Education*, New Delhi: Discovery Publishing House.

Bhaskara Rao, Digumarti, Editor (2004). *Adult Learning in the 21st Century*. New Delhi: Discovery Publishing House.

Bhaskara Rao, Digumarti, Editor (2004). *Educational Practices: Research and Recommendations*. New Delhi: Discovery Publishing House.

Bhaskara Rao, Digumarti, Editor (2004). *Chernobyl: Never Again*. New Delhi: APH Publishing Corporation.

Bhaskara Rao, Digumarti, Editor (2004). *Virology and Immunology*. New Delhi: APH Publishing Corporation.

Bhaskara Rao, Digumarti, C.A.P. Swami and B.S.V. Dutt (1997). *Self-Evaluation in Student Teaching*. New Delhi: Discovery Publishing House. ISBN 81-7141-374-9.

Bhaskara Rao, Digumarti and B.S.V. Dutt, Editors (2003). *Education: Programmes and Policies*. New Delhi: APH Publishing Corporation. ISBN 81-7648-470-9.

Bhaskara Rao, Digumarti and D. Naresh Kumar (2004). *School Teacher Effectiveness*. New Delhi: Discovery Publishing House.

Bhaskara Rao, Digumarti and D. Sridhar (2002). *Job Satisfaction of School Teachers*. New Delhi: Discovery Publishing House. ISBN 81-7141-652-7.

Bhaskara Rao, Digumarti and Digumarti Pushpa Latha (1994). *Achievement in Biology*. New Delhi: Discovery Publishing House. ISBN 81-7141-264-5.

Bhaskara Rao, Digumarti, C. Sridevi and K. Vijaya (1995). *Achievement in Social Studies*. New Delhi: Discovery Publishing House. ISBN 81-7141-281-5.

Bhaskara Rao, Digumarti and Digumarti Pushpa Latha (1995). *Achievement in English*. New Delhi: Discovery Publishing House. ISBN 81-7141-283-1.

Bhaskara Rao, Digumarti and Digumarti Pushpa Latha (1994). *Achievement in Science*. New Delhi: Discovery Publishing House. ISBN 81-7141-280-70.

Bhaskara Rao, Digumarti and Digumarti Pushpa Latha (1995). *Achievement in Mathematics*. New Delhi: Discovery Publishing House. ISBN 81-7141-278-5.

Bhaskara Rao, Digumarti and Digumarti Pushpa Latha, Editors (1998). *International Encyclopaedia of Women*. 5 Volumes. New Delhi: Discovery Publishing House. ISBN 81-7141-410-9.

Vol. 1 *Status of World's Women*. ISBN 81-7141-494-X.

Vol. 2 *Women, Education and Empowerment*. ISBN 81-7141-498-1.

Vol. 3 *Women Challenges and Advancement*. ISBN 81-7141-497-4.

Vol. 4 *Women and Family Health*. ISBN 81-7141-497-4.

Vol. 5 *Women and International Action*. ISBN 81-7141-498-2.

Bhaskara Rao, Digumarti, Digumarti Pushpa Latha and Digumarti Harshitha, Editors (2001). *Biological Warfare*. New Delhi: Discovery Publishing House. ISBN 81-7141-597-0.

Bhaskara Rao, Digumarti, Digumarti Pushpa Latha and Digumarti Harshitha, Editors (2001). *Women as Educators*. New Delhi: Discovery Publishing House. ISBN 81-7141-602-0.

Bhaskara Rao, Digumarti and Digumarti Harshitha, Editors (2001). *Education in India*. New Delhi: APH Publishing Corporation. ISBN 81-7141-207-2.

Bhaskara Rao, Digumarti, Digumarti Pushpa Latha and Digumarti Harshitha, Editors (2001). *Assessing Learning Achievement*. New Delhi: Discovery Publishing House. ISBN 81-7141-601-2.

Bhaskara Rao, Digumarti, Digumarti Pushpa Latha and Digumarti Harshitha, Editors (2001). *Energy Security*. New Delhi: Discovery Publishing House. ISBN 81-7141-598-9.

Bhaskara Rao, Digumarti, Digumarti Harshitha and K.R.S.S. Rao, Editors (1999). *Advanced Biotechnology*. New Delhi: Discovery Publishing House. ISBN 81-7141-516-4.

Bhaskara Rao, Digumarti and K.R.S. Sambhasiva Rao, Editors (1996). *Current Trends in Indian Education*. New Delhi: Discovery Publishing House. ISBN 81-7141-311-0.

Bhaskara Rao, Digumarti and K. Vijaya (1995). *A Text Book of Evaluation*. Ambala Cantt: The Associated Publishers.

Bhaskara Rao, Digumarti and N.V.M. Mohana Rao (2002). *Problems of Mentally Handicapped Children*. New Delhi: Discovery Publishing House. ISBN 81-7141-645-4.

Bhaskara Rao, Digumarti and S. Chandra Mohan (2002). *Sports Management*. New Delhi: APH Publishing Corporation. ISBN 81-7648-467-9.

Bhaskara Rao, Digumarti and Sk. Johni Basha (2004). *Teachers' Population Education Awareness*. New Delhi: APH Publishing Corporation.

Bhaskara Rao, Digumarti, V.V. Rao, V.V. Lakshmi and V.V. Krishna, Editors (1999). *Status and Advancement of Women*. New Delhi: APH Publishing Corporation. ISBN 81-7648-169-6.

Babu, P.C., Author and Digumarti Bhaskara Rao, Editor (2004). *Flowers of Wisdom*. New Delhi: Discovery Publishing House. ISBN 81-7141-695-0.

Bhagya Lakshmi, Lingineni, Author and Digumarti Bhaskara Rao, Editor (2000). *Reading and Comprehension*. New Delhi: Discovery Publishing House. ISBN 81-7141-543-1.

Bhuvaneswara Lakshmi, Gadde, Author and Digumarti Bhaskara Rao, Editor (2000). *Attitude Towards Science*. New Delhi: Discovery Publishing House. ISBN 81-7141-541-6.

Devraj, T.A.S., Author and Digumarti Bhaskara Rao, Editor (1997). *Trace Analysis of Uranium and Thorium*. New Delhi: Discovery Publishing House. ISBN 81-7141-375-7.

Durga Rani, K., Author and Digumarti Bhaskara Rao, Editor (2000). *Educational Aspirations and Scientific Attitudes*. New Delhi: Discovery Publishing House. ISBN 81-7141-555-55.

Dutt, B.S.V. and Digumarti Bhaskara Rao (2001). *Empowering Primary Teachers*. New Delhi: Discovery Publishing House. ISBN 81-7141-615.2.

Ediger, Marlow and Digumarti Bhaskara Rao (1996). *Science Curriculum*. New Delhi: Discovery Publishing House. ISBN 81-7141-321-8.

Ediger, Marlow and Digumarti Bhaskara Rao (2000). *Teaching Mathematics Successfully*. New Delhi: Discovery Publishing House. ISBN 81-7141-552-0.

Ediger, Marlow and Digumarti Bhaskara Rao (2001). *Teaching Science Successfully*. New Delhi: Discovery Publishing House. ISBN 81-7141-600-4.

Ediger, Marlow and Digumarti Bhaskara Rao (2001). *Teaching Social Studies Successfully*. New Delhi: Discovery Publishing House. ISBN 81-7141-596-2.

Ediger, Marlow and Digumarti Bhaskara Rao (2002). *Philosophy and Curriculum*. New Delhi: Discovery Publishing House. ISBN 81-7141-631-4.

Ediger, Marlow and Digumarti Bhaskara Rao (2002). *Improving School Administration*. New Delhi: Discovery Publishing House. ISBN 81-7141-633-0.

Ediger, Marlow and Digumarti Bhaskara Rao (2002). *Elementary Curriculum*. New Delhi: Discovery Publishing House. ISBN 81-7141-658-6.

Ediger, Marlow and Digumarti Bhaskara Rao (2003). *Language Arts Curriculum*. New Delhi: Discovery Publishing House. ISBN 81-7141-657-8.

Ediger, Marlow and Digumarti Bhaskara Rao (2004). *Teaching Language Arts Successfully*. New Delhi: Discovery Publishing House. ISBN 81-7141-678-0.

Ediger, Marlow and Digumarti Bhaskara Rao (2004). *Teaching Mathematics in Elementary Schools*. New Delhi: Discovery Publishing House. ISBN 81-7141-687-X.

Ediger, Marlow and Digumarti Bhaskara Rao (2004). *Teaching Science in Elementary Schools*. New Delhi: Discovery Publishing House. ISBN 81-7141-709-4.

Ediger, Marlow and Digumarti Bhaskara Rao (2004). *School Curriculum and Administration*. New Delhi: Discovery Publishing House. ISBN 81-7141-709-4.

Ediger, Marlow and Digumarti Bhaskara Rao (2004). *Modern Elementary School*. New Delhi: Discovery Publishing House.

Ediger, Marlow and Digumarti Bhaskara Rao (2004): *Relevancy in Elementary Curriculum*. New Delhi: Discovery Publishing House. ISBN 81-7141-751-5.

Ediger, Marlow and Digumarti Bhaskara Rao, (2004). *Teaching Social Studies in Elementary Schools*. New Delhi: Discovery Publishing House.

Ediger Marlow, B.S.V. Dutt and Digumarti Bhaskara Rao (2004). *Teaching English Successfully*. New Delhi: Discovery Publishing House. ISBN 81-7141-707-8.

Harshitha, Digumarti and Digumarti Bhaskara Rao, Editors (2004). *Educational Innovations*. New Delhi: Discovery Publishing House.

Indira Devi, Author and J. Prasanth Kumar and Digumarti Bhaskara Rao, Editors (2004). *Values in Language Text Books*. New Delhi: Discovery Publishing House.

Jayasree, Kandi, Author and Digumarti Bhaskara Rao, Editor (1999). *Correlates of Socialisation*. New Delhi: Discovery Publishing House. ISBN 81-7141-517-2.

John Babu, Chikati, Author and T.J.R. Prasad, G.M. Madhukar and Digumarti Bhaskara Rao, Editors (1996). *Problem Solving in Mathematics*. New Delhi: APH Publishing Corporation. ISBN 81-7648-273-0.

Lalitha, T., Author and K.S. Prabhakaram, D.S.N. Sastry and Digumarti Bhaskara Rao, Editors (2004). *Educational Philosophic Beliefs*. New Delhi: Discovery Publishing House. ISBN 81-7141-765-5.

Madhu Bala, Jampala, Author and Digumarti Bhaskara Rao, Editor (2004). *Adjustment Problems of Hearing Impaired*. New Delhi: Discovery Publishing House.

Marja, Talvi and Digumarti Bhaskara Rao, Editors (1996). *Educational Leadership and Social Changes*. New Delhi: Discovery Publishing House. ISBN 81-7141-320-X.

Nirmala Jyothi, M., Author and Digumarti Bhaskara Rao, Editor (2003). *Non-detention Systems in School Education*. New Delhi: Discovery Publishing House. ISBN 81-7141-654-3.

Prabhakaram, K.S., Author and Digumarti Bhaskara Rao, Editor (1998). *Concept Attainment Model in Mathematics Teaching*. New Delhi: Discovery Publishing House. ISBN 81-7141-424-9.

Prasanth Kumar, J., Author and Digumarti Bhaskara Rao, Editor (1998). *Effectiveness of Distance Education System*. New Delhi: Discovery Publishing House. ISBN 81-7141-437-0.

Prasanth Kumar, J., Author and G. Sundara Rao and Digumarti Bhaskara Rao, Editors (2000). *Open University Student Support Services*. New Delhi: Discovery Publishing House. ISBN 81-7141-550-4.

Ramatulasamma, K., Author and Digumarti Bhaskara Rao, Editor (2002). *Job Satisfaction of Teacher Educators*, New Delhi: Discovery Publishing House. ISBN 81-7141-655-1.

Rama Krishnaiah, D., Author and Digumarti Bhaskara Rao, Editor (1998). *Job Satisfaction of College Teachers*, New Delhi: Discovery Publishing House. ISBN 81-7141-438-9.

Rama Kumar Ratnam, M., Author and Digumarti Bhaskara Rao, Editor (1998). *Dukka: Suffering in Early Buddhism*. New Delhi: Discovery Publishing House. ISBN 81-7141-653-5.

Rathaiah, Lavu and Digumarti Bhaskara Rao, Editors (1996). *International Innovations in Education*. New Delhi: Discovery Publishing House. ISBN 81-7141-359-5.

Ramesh, Ganta and Digumarti Bhaskara Rao, Editors (1998). *Environmental Education: Problems and Prospects*. New Delhi: Discovery Publishing House. ISBN 81-7141-423-0.

Rathaiah, Lavu and Digumarti Bhaskara Rao (1997). *Achievement Correlates*. New Delhi: Discovery Publishing House. ISBN 81-7141-385-4.

Reddy, Sudhakar Y., Author, and Digumarti Bhaskara Rao, Editor (2003). *Creativity in Adolescents*. New Delhi: Discovery Publishing House. ISBN 81-7141-659-4.

Reddy, M.S., Author and Digumarti Bhaskara Rao, Editor (2004). *Creativity in College Students*. New Delhi: Discovery Publishing House. ISBN 81-7141-697-7.

Radramamba, B., Author and Digumarti Bhaskara Rao, Editor (2003). *Problems of Teaching*. New Delhi: APH Publishing Corporation. ISBN 81-7648-462-8.

Sanjeeva Rao, P.C., Author and Digumarti Bhaskara Rao, Editor (1996). *A Text Book of Geology*. New Delhi: Discovery Publishing House. ISBN 81-7141-313-7.

Satya Narayana V., Author and Digumarti Bhaskara Rao, Editor (2001). *Physical Education, Social Attitudes and Leadership Qualities*. New Delhi: Discovery Publishing House. ISBN 81-7141-593-8.

Srinivasulu Reddy, M., and K.R.S. Sambasiva Rao, Authors and Digumarti Bhaskara Rao, Editor (1999). *A Text Book of Aquaculture*. New Delhi: Discovery Publishing House. ISBN 81-7141-482-6.

Srinivasa Rao, Mandalapu, Author and Digumarti Bhaskara Rao, Editor (2004). *Achievement Motivation and Achievement in Mathematics*. New Delhi: Discovery Publishing House. ISBN 81-7141-674-8.

Vanaja, M. Author and Digumarti Bhaskara Rao, Editor (1999). *Inquiry Training Model*. New Delhi: Discovery Publishing House. ISBN 81-7141-515-6.

Vanaja. M. and N. Sneha Latha, Authors and Digumarti Bhaskara Rao, Editor (2004). *Student Shyness*. New Delhi: APH Publishing Corporation.

Valeri V. Koustiouk, Author and Digumarti Bhaskara Rao, Editor (2002). *A Text Book of Cryogenics*. New Delhi: Discovery Publishing House. ISBN 81-7141-642-X.

Valeri V. Koustiouk, Author and Digumarti Bhaskara Rao, Editor (2004). *Refrigeration and Environment*. New Delhi: APH Publishing Corporation.

Veena Kumari, Balusu and Digumarti Bhaskara Rao (1996). *Operation Black Board*. New Delhi: Ashish Publishing Corporation. ISBN 81-7024-711-X.

Veena Kumari, Balusu, Author and Digumarti Bhaskara Rao, Editor (2000). *Psycho-Social Correlates of Achievement*, New Delhi: Discovery Publishing House. ISBN 81-7141-547-4.

Vanaja, M., Author and Digumarti Bhaskara Rao, Editor (1999). *Inquiry Training Model*. New Delhi: Discovery Publishing House. ISBN 81-7141-515-6.

Venkata Rao, P. and Digumarti Bhaskara Rao (1989). *A Text Book of Zoology—Junior Intermediate*. Guntur: Vignan Publishers.

Venkata Rao, P. and Digumarti Bhaskara Rao (1989). *A Text Book of Zoology—Senior Intermediate*. Guntur: Vignan Publishers.

Venugopala Rao, K., Author and Digumarti Bhaskara Rao, Editor (2000). *Teacher Morale in Secondary Schools*. New Delhi: Discovery Publishing House. ISBN 81-7141-551-2.

Vidya, C., Author and Digumarti Bhaskara Rao. Editor (1996). *A Text Book of Nutrition*. New Delhi: Discovery Publishing House. ISBN 81-7141-309-9.

Vidya Bharathi, D., Author and Digumarti Bhaskara Rao, Editor (2000). *Educational Philosophies of Swami Vivekananda and John Dewey*. New Delhi: APH Publishing Corporation. ISBN 81-7648-309-9.

Books in Telugu Language

Bhaskara Rao, Digumarti (1986). *Dhrushya Sravana Bodhanapakaranalu* (Audio Visual Teaching Aids). Guntur: Nagarjuna Publishers.

Bhaskara Rao, Digumarti (1993). *Jeevasashtra Bodhana* (Teaching of Biology). Guntur: Nagarjuna Publishers.

Bhaskara Rao, Digumarti (1995). *Vignanasasthra Bodhana* (Teaching of Science) Guntur: Nagarjuna Publishers.

Bhaskara Rao, Digumarti (1997). *Vidya Manovignana Seshtram* (Educational Psychology). Guntur: Creative Press.

Bhaskara Rao, Digumarti (1998). *DSC Study Material*. Guntur: Nagarjuna Publishers.

Bhaskara Rao, Digumarti (1998). *Upadhyayudu Vidya*. (Teacher and Education). Guntur: Nagarjuna Publishers.

Bhaskara Rao, Digumarti (1998). *Vidya Drukpadalu* (Prespectives of Education). Guntur: Nagarjuna Publishers.

Bhaskara Rao, Digumarti (1999). *EdCET Teaching Aptitude*. Guntur: Nagarjuna Publishers.

Bhaskara Rao, Digumarti (2001). *Bharata Samajamulo Upadyayudu Vidya* (Teacher and Education in Emerging Indian Society). Guntur: Nagarjuna Publishers.

Bhaskara Rao, Digumarti (2001). *Bhoutika Sastra Bodhana Paddathulu* (Methods of Teaching Physical Science). Guntur: Nagarjuna Publishers.

Bhaskara Rao, Digumarti (2001). *Jeeva Sastra Bodhana Padhathulu* (Methods of Teaching Biology). Guntur: Nagarjuna Publishers.

Bhaskara Rao, Digumarti (2001). *Vidya Manovignana Sastram* (Educational Psychology). Guntur: Nagarjuna Publishers.

Bhaskara Rao, Digumarti (2003). *Patsala Yajamanyam/Paripalana* (School Management and Administration). Guntur: Nagarjuna Publishers.

Bhaskara Rao, Digumarti (2004). *Vidya Sanketika Sastram mariyu Computer Vidya* (Educational Technology and Computer Education). Guntur: Nagarjuna Publishers.